Fundamentals of Research in the Behavioral Sciences: Principles and Practice

Fundamentals of Research in the Behavioral Sciences: Principles and Practice

Franklin C. Shontz, Ph.D.

Greater Kansas City Mental Health Foundation
and
University of Kansas
Lawrence, Kansas

1400 K Street, N.W.
Washington, DC 20005

Cover design by Joe Kolb
Text design by Richard E. Farkas
Typeset by Harper Graphics, Inc.
Printed by Arcata Graphics/Fairfield

Library of Congress Cataloging in Publication Data

Shontz, Franklin C.
  Fundamentals of research in the behavioral sciences.

  Includes bibliographies and index.
  1. Psychology—Research—Methodology. 2. Medicine—
Research—Methodology. I. Title. [DNLM: 1. Behavioral
Sciences—methods. 2. Research—methods. 3. Statistics.
BF 76.5 S559f]
BF76.5.S48   1986   150'.72   86-1242
ISBN 0-88048-215-X

—*Contents*—

Figures xi
Tables xii
Appendixes xiv
Preface xv

Chapter 1   Overview   1

Numbers, Mathematics, and Computers 2
What Is Research? 4
  Library Research 4
  Field Research 4
  Survey Research 5
  Laboratory Research 6
  Tests 7
    Reliability 8
    Validity 10
    Norms 12
  Predictive Studies 13
  Control of Conditions and Experimentation 14
    Practical considerations 16
  Experiments as Ideals 17
Appropriate Measurement 17
  Names and Numbers 19
  Numbers and Meanings 20
  Uses of Statistics 22
Forms and Qualities 22
  Discrimination 23
"Researchable" Issues 24

Chapter 2   Carrying Out Research   27

General Principles 27
  Designing Research 27
  Interpreting Outcomes 28
  Nonstatistical Inferences 29
  Statistical Inferences 30
    The concept of randomness 30
    The null hypothesis 32

Two kinds of error 33
Example 34
Testing Theories 35
Definitions 36
Correlation and Causation 38
Pragmatics 40
Practical Considerations 42
Feelings About Research 42
Economics 43
A Fly in the Ointment: Technical Difficulties 43
Control groups 44
"Waiting-list" controls 44
Informed consent 45
Anonymity and confidentiality 45
Another Fly in the Ointment: Changing Established Procedures 46
Case studies 48
Surveys 48
Predictive studies 48
Monitoring 49
The Value of Appreciation and Understanding 50
The Place of Criticism 51

Chapter 3   Reading and Writing Research Reports   53

Communication in Science 53
The Research Report 55
Title 55
Author Identification 56
Abstract 57
Introduction 57
Method 58
Results 61
Graphic presentations of data 62
Simple line graphs 62
Scattergrams 64
Bar graphs 65
Pie charts 68
Discussion and Conclusions 69
References 70

Chapter 4   Qualitative and Quantitative Aspects of Research   71

Qualitative Data 71
Identifying Types 72
Qualitative Data and Research Variables 73
Converting Qualitative to Quantitative Data 74
Coding 75

Counting 76
Comparing Counts by Inspection 77
   Cross-classification 78
   Group equivalence 79
Quantitative Data and Qualitative Classes 79
   Redundancy and Meaning 83
The Development of Theories 84
   Similarities Within Classes 84
   Relations Among Classes or Types 85
   Analyses and Theories 86
   Processes 87
Integration 89

Chapter 5   Estimating Probabilities   91

Logical and Empirical Bases 91
   Frequency Distributions 95
   Outcomes 97
   Binomial Expansion 97
      Permutations and combinations 99
   Variability 101
   The Mean as an Average Deviation from Zero 101
Central Tendency 102
   Mean 102
   Median and Mode 103
Spread or Dispersion 104
Normal Curve 106
   Standard Deviation 111
      Degrees of freedom 113
   Standard Scores 114
      Limitations 115
      Calculating a standard score 116
   Standard Errors 118
      Confidence intervals 119

Chapter 6   Analyses of Frequency Counts: Chi Square   121

Frequency Data 121
   Precision 122
Chi Square 124
   Rationally Determined Expectancies 124
      Calculations 126
      Significance 126
   Degrees of Freedom 127
   Another Possible Research Design 127
      Estimating expected frequencies 129
   Correction for Discontinuity 132

The *Phi* Coefficient 132
The Contingency Coefficient 135
Change Scores 135
    How many tails? 137
Final Example 139
  A Disadvantage 140
Random Assignment 141

Chapter 7   Analyses of Ranks   145

Properties of Ranks 145
  Problems in Discrimination 146
Ranking Procedures 148
Testing the Difference Between Two Groups 151
  The *U* Test 153
More Than Two Groups 156
One Group, Repeated Measures 157
    Wilcoxon test 158
  More Than One Set of Differences 159
    Coefficient of concordance 161
Rank Order Correlation 161
  Statistical Significance 165
  Reliability and Validity of Agreements 166

Chapter 8   Continuous Data   171

Continuous and Interval Scales 171
  Interval Scales in Psychosocial Research 173
The *F*-Test for Two Groups 174
  Between-Groups Sum of Squares 176
  Within-Groups Sum of Squares 177
  Summary Table and *F*-Test 178
  Total Sum of Squares 179
  Partitioning 179
  Mean Squares 180
    The value of *F* 181
    Significance of *F* 181
The *t*-Test 182
  Significance of *t* 182
  Another Formula for *t* 182
    Too many *t*-tests 183
The *F*-Test for Repeated Measures 184
  Calculations 186
  Interpretation 188
The *t*-Test for Repeated Measures in One Sample 188
One-Way Analysis of Variance for More Than Two Independent
  Groups, No Repeated Measures 190
  Interpretation 192

More Than Two Measurement Periods 193
  Repeated Assessments of the Same Group 193
  Assessing Different Groups at Each Period 194

Chapter 9   More Complicated Analyses   199

Preliminaries: Statistical Analysis and Research Design 199
  One Extreme 199
  The Other Extreme 200
  The Purpose of Analysis of Variance: A Quick Review 201
  One-Way Analysis of Variance 201
    Comparing variances within groups 201
Examples of More Complicated Designs 203
  A 2×2 Factorial Design 204
    Variations in this design 205
    Main effects 205
    Interaction 206
    Summary table 208
    Unequal ns 209
    More about degrees of freedom 209
  A Three-Factor Factorial Design 210
    Main effects 211
    Extensions of the design 214
  Mixed Designs 215
  Further Complexities 219
Analysis of Variance as Information Processing 220

Chapter 10   Product-Moment Correlation   223

Variation, Covariation, and Differences: A Summary 223
  Not-So-Obvious Examples 226
Product-Moment Correlation Coefficient 227
  Limitations 228
Regression 230
  Another Scattergram 231
    Variations on the theme 233
Calculations 234
  Numerator 234
  Denominator 237
  Ratio 237
  Raw Score Formula 238
  One More Example 239
    First method 239
    Second method 240
  Statistical Significance 241
Prediction 241
  Adjusting for Unit Sizes 241
  Fixing Two Points 244

Common Variance 245
   Error 246
Multiple Correlation 247

Chapter 11   Correlation: A Fundamental Idea   251

The General Concept of Association 251
   Strength of Association 252
     Degrees of freedom 252
Frequency Data: Chi Square and the *Phi* (Fourfold-Point)
   Coefficient 253
   Test of Significance 254
   Phi and *r* 256
   Phi and the Contingency Coefficient 257
   A Family of Statistics 258
Nonparametric Statistics 258
   Central Limit Theorem 259
     Spearman's *rho* 260
     Significance of *rho* 262
Product-Moment Correlation and the *t*-Test 262
   Common Variance 265
     Product-moment correlation and the *F*-test 267
   More Than Two Groups 268
A General Principle 268
   Intraclass Correlation 269
   Components of Variance 269

Chapter 12   Critical Reviews of Two Research Reports   271

The First Article 272
   Title 272
   Abstract 273
   Introduction 273
   Method 274
   Results 275
   Discussion and Conclusions 277
   References 280
The Second Article 281
   Construct Validity 281
   Effects of Group Differences on Correlation Values 282
   Results: Reading a Table 284
   Investigators' Conclusions 285
Some Final Notes 285

References   307

Index   311

—Figures—

Figure 3.1. A simple line graph. 63

Figure 3.2. Scattergrams of 10 pairs of scores. 64

Figure 3.3. Two ways of showing expected frequencies of combinations of heads and tails in 160 throws of five coins each 66

Figure 3.4. Hypothetical comparison of admission rates of older and younger patients to three wards. 67

Figure 3.5. A deceptive pie-chart. The director's salary has been extended beyond the circumference. 69

Figure 4.1. A possible model of some factors predicting school grades. 88

Figure 5.1. Probability distribution for a series of tosses of six coins per toss. 96

Figure 5.2. A normal curve divided at $\pm$ 3.00 standard deviation units. 107

Figure 5.3. Raw scores, z scores, and T scores of a hypothetical attitude scale. 116

Figure 9.1. Interaction of treatment effects and age of subjects...... 207

Figure 9.2. Three-dimensional representation of a $2 \times 2 \times 2$ factorial research design. 212

Figure 10.1 Two possible types of bivariate relationships. 230

Figure 10.2. A scattergram of 15 data points. 232

Figure 10.3. A plot of mean Y values for each value of X in Figure 10.2 (solid line) and of the least square regression line (broken line). 242

—Tables—

Table 2.1. Types of Errors and Correct Inferences About the Null Hypothesis 33

Table 4.1. Data from a Hypothetical Study of Ethnic Origins of Families of Complainers 78

Table 5.1. Deviation Scores Derived from Raw Scores on Six-Item Test 112

Table 5.2. Calculation of Standard Deviation 112

Table 6.1. Hypothetical Data from a Study of a Staff Member's Ability to Recognize Schizophrenic Patients 126

Table 6.2. Hypothetical Data from the Alternative Research Design 128

Table 6.3. Observed and Expected Frequencies for Data in Table 6.2 130

Table 6.4. Components of Chi Square for Data in Tables 6.2 and 6.3 131

Table 6.5. Data for *Phi*-Coefficient Example 133

Table 6.6. The Wrong Way to Arrange Data from a Study of Improvement 136

Table 6.7. The Right Way to Arrange Data from a Study of Improvement 137

Table 6.8. Hypothetical Data for a Study of Three Treatment Conditions 139

Table 6.9. A Collapsed Table of Chi Square Data 140

Table 7.1. Hypothetical Rankings of Candidates for Employment 147

Table 7.2. Combining Ranks When Certain of Differences Between Subgroups 148

Table 7.3. Illustrating Tied Ranks 149

Table 7.4. Hypothetical Ranks of Children's Drawings 152

Table 7.5. Rearranged Ranks of Children's Drawings 152

Table 7.6. Reversed Ranks of Children's Drawings 153

Table 7.7. Example of Use of Ranks in Repeated-Measures Study 158

Table 7.8. Examples of Two Levels of Agreement Among Raters 160

Table 7.9. Matrix of *Tau* Values Among Three Judges 165

Table 8.1. Hypothetical Scores in a Research Study on the Effect of Altering the Institutional Environment 175

Table 8.2. Summary of Analysis of Variance (ANOVA) 179

Table 8.3. Results of a Hypothetical Study of a Smoking Reduction Program 184

Table 8.4. Summary of Analysis of Variance 186

Table 8.5. An Expansion of the Research on Environment Modification 191

Table 8.6. Summary Table of One-Way ANOVA for Four Groups ... 192

Table 9.1. A 2 × 2 Factorial Design, with Independent Groups ... 204

Table 9.2. Data for a 2 × 2 Factorial Design, with Independent Groups 206

Table 9.3. Summary Table of Analysis of Variance for 2 × 2 Design 208

Table 9.4. Numbers of Subjects Assigned to Cells of a 3 × 4 Design, with Unequal n's 210

Table 9.5. Degrees of Freedom for Main Effect and Interactions in a 2 × 2 × 2 Factorial ANOVA 213

Table 9.6. Degrees of Freedom for Main Effects and Interactions in a 2 × 3 × 4 × 2 Factorial ANOVA with 3 Subjects Per Cell ... 215

Table 9.7. Hypothetical Data for a Mixed-Model ANOVA Design .. 217

Table 9.8. Analysis of Variance of 3 × 3 Mixed Model Study 218

Table 10.1. A Matrix of Correlation Coefficients for Eight Variables 225

Table 10.2. Data for Calculating a Product-Moment Correlation Coefficient 235

Table 10.3. Deviation Scores and Cross-Products of Data in Table 10.2 235

Table 10.4. Raw Scores Shown in Figure 10.2 and Their Cross-Products 240

Table 11.1 Hypothetical Results of a Study of Preassignment to Treatment 254

Table 11.2. Hypothetical Scores, Ranks, Differences, and Cross-Products in a Study of Benefit from Care 260

Table 11.3. A Hypothetical Study of Side Effects 263

Table 11.4. Summary Table of Analysis of Variance 264

Table 11.5. Use of a Dummy Variable in a Two-Group Study 266

—Appendixes—

Appendix 5.A. Partial List of Normal Curve Properties (See also Figure 5.2) 120

Appendix 6.A. Selected Critical Values of Chi Square 143

Appendix 6.B. Some Random Digits 143

Appendix 7.A. Abbreviated Table of the Mann-Whitney U Statistic, for Directional (One-Tailed) and Nondirectional Test at the .05 Level 168

Appendix 7.B. Abbreviated Table of Critical Values in the Wilcoxon Matched-Pairs, Signed-Ranks Test at the .05 Level 168

Appendix 7.C. Partial Table of Directional Probabilities for Values of S in Kendall's *tau* 169

Appendix 8.A. Abbreviated Table of Critical Values of F at the 5% and 1% Levels for use in ANOVA (1% Level Underlined) 196

Appendix 8.B. Some Critical Values of t for Two-Tailed Tests 197

Appendix 10.A. Critical Values of Product-Moment Correlation Coefficients 249

Appendix 12.A. Drugs and Personality: Extraversion-Introversion 287

Appendix 12.B. Correlates of Sensation Seeking by Heavy, Chronic Drug Users 295

—*Preface*—

This book was written to meet a need that is not being satisfied by textbooks currently used in courses on elementary statistics. The need for a book like this arises, in part, because textbooks on statistics unavoidably contain a great deal of mathematics, and that causes many people trouble. Students for whom mathematics is particularly difficult or distasteful, those who have never had an appropriate course in mathematics, or those who have not had one in many years are likely to find that the contents of even the most clearly organized textbook on statistics and research methodology are inaccessible to their understanding. Such persons certainly exist in quantity at the undergraduate level, but a good many have also been spotted in graduate schools, where people in the behavioral sciences are being educated, and even on internships and post-doctoral residencies or fellowships.

The need for this book has also arisen because many of those who are required to take courses in statistics do not expect to be carrying out actual research or data analysis as part of their professional activity. They appreciate the advantage of knowing how to read, understand, and criticize the scientific literature intelligently, but they do not require a high level of proficiency in actually designing and carrying out experiments or running statistical tests. Many such persons who take courses in statistics may fail to grasp the broader, more basic principles of the scientific approach because they are obliged to devote too much of their time and attention to calculations.

I have also met certain advanced students who are quite sophisticated about the technical details of statistics but who welcome the opportunity to go back over the fundamentals they feel they have forgotten or never fully learned. I suspect, too, that a large number of practicing professionals would like to know more than they do about statistics and research methods. But they are too busy to take another course and are intimidated by the prospect of having to try learning it on their own from a text that is filled with numbers and equations.

This book was written to help all such persons who want to learn or review basic principles, and it is meant to cover just what the title says: the *fundamentals* of research. The level of difficulty, particularly of its first half, was established on the basis of my experience teaching undergraduates in psychology as well as psychiatric residents about research methods and statistics. Throughout this book, numerical examples are brief, and all are worked out step by step. No serious mathematics is introduced until Chapter 5, and even that is kept as simple as possible.

Because fundamental principles are emphasized, rather than techniques or computational procedures, exercises and homework-type problems are not included. To learn the basics, it is less important to memorize formulas or solve problems mechanically than to understand what one is doing. Therefore, the reader will benefit most by thinking about and working through numerical examples along with the text, perhaps using a hand calculator and following each set of calculations as they develop.

Someone who is in an advanced stage of training and wishes mainly to review fundamentals should find this book to be virtually self-teaching. It could therefore be used as a background text for journal clubs or seminars for professionals in which research literature is read and evaluated. It may be used as a text in courses that provide supervised research in the behavioral sciences, or by students who plan to take more traditional courses in statistics later on. It may also serve as a supplement in regularly taught undergraduate courses in statistics or methodology and in content courses that concentrate on critically evaluating the research literature. Although the text has not been tried out in high schools, parts of it, if not the whole, may be suitable as an introduction for advanced students who have an interest in careers in the behavioral sciences or health professions.

With regard to the writing and preparation of this book, I owe special debts of gratitude to several people. To James V. Spotts, a close friend and valued colleague for many years, who encouraged and supported the writing of this book in innumerable ways. To Charles B. Wilkinson, whose efforts are largely responsible for stimulating the expansion of the book from a set of lecture notes into an organized text. To Connie R. Morgan, who diligently typed several early versions of the manuscript. Finally, to all the students whose difficulties in learning statistics and research methods made me feel the book was worth writing and, at the same time, suggested how future readers' needs might best be met.

—1—

OVERVIEW

This book was written to help people in the behavioral sciences and health professions gain an appreciation and understanding of some basic principles, methods, and techniques of research. Although some sections of the book contain a few numbers and describe how investigators use mathematics, this book is not primarily a text on statistics. Far from it. Statistics is only one of many tools an investigator may use when carrying out research.

Also this book contains discussions of certain basic principles of research design, but it is not about how to do experiments, as such. The classical experiment is a powerful form of research, but many other useful forms deserve mention as well, from informal studies to carefully planned laboratory procedures. Laboratory research is often not possible in clinical or other institutional settings. In some instances, laboratory research may not even be the best way to answer the types of questions that are likely to arise in such settings. These often concern matters of practice rather than theory, such as the effectiveness of agency management, client responses to changes in care, and effects of policy decisions. Therefore, somewhat more attention is paid here to research on practical matters than to research that tests theories; that is, this book often pays more attention to what can be done in the course of the everyday operations of an agency than to what should be done in a laboratory, where all conditions can be fully controlled. Furthermore, this book deals with

1

fundamentals rather than technical details. It is based on the assumption that technical details are more easily acquired if basic principles are clearly understood first.

Numbers, Mathematics, and Computers

The foundation of all science is controlled observation, and the most systematic way to handle observations is to organize them into groups or classes. After being separated into groups or classes, observations in each group or class can be counted. Counts can be scaled by placing them in order, from most to least, along some dimension. The result is a set of numbers, or quantities, and the operations that are performed to change observations into numbers are called *measurement.* Because numbers can always be treated mathematically, some believe that the main requirement of science is that it be mathematical, or quantitative. Some years ago, an authority said that everything that exists must exist in some quantity. The conclusion seems to follow that everything that is to deserve the name science must be expressible as numbers, and that research on human action or traits must be mathematical, too.

Modern students, preparing to become professionals in the fields of mental or physical health, are increasingly being required to take courses in research that demand a rather high level of mathematical skill and knowledge. The modern student must not only learn about such statistical standbys as *chi square, t-test,* and correlation coefficients, but must be prepared to encounter multivariate analysis of variance, discriminant function analysis, and multiple regression as well.

The advent of computer technology has been helpful because computers eliminate much of the boredom of hand calculation and reduce error rates greatly. Nevertheless, it has had several side effects that may make life difficult for the student, if not for the advanced investigator. One is that computer technology promotes an extremely rapid evolution of new quantitative techniques. Often it seems that by the time one has mastered current procedures, they have become obsolete. Keeping up seems impossible. Another side effect is that students are now required to learn not only mathematics but how to operate computers as well.

A serious problem may arise because irresponsible or careless use of computers can lead to false conclusions about research findings. These machines have no way of knowing whether the data put into them were well or poorly gathered, reliable or unreliable, valid or invalid. Computers cannot tell whether a program selected for the analysis of data is appropriate or inappropriate. Computers simply do what they are told, even if what they are told to do is foolish. Random data will sometimes yield computer outputs that look meaningful, although they really are not. The value of what comes out of a computer can be no better than the quality of what goes in. The popular expression *GIGO,* which means "garbage in, garbage out," describes the problem concisely.

Because of the rapid growth of technical possibilities and complexities, people who wish to become investigators can no longer be taught all they need to know in one or two courses. However, those who do not plan to pursue careers in research may still benefit from learning at least the fundamental ideas of scientific strategy. This knowledge will be useful to them in several ways. For one thing, these students will find that they can gain a personal appreciation of what research can and cannot do. For another, they will be able to read published reports of research with a higher level of understanding, even though they lack the technical skills to carry out complex investigations themselves.

An additional important benefit is that a basic understanding of research strategy will enable a psychiatrist, behavior therapist, counselor, or other health professional to carry out useful projects that will answer important questions. To be useful, not all research need be highly technical nor even quantitative; neither must it yield a final, conclusive answer to a specific question. For example, a well-planned tracking of patients' lengths of hospital stay over a period of time can be made to qualify as research and can be useful to an administrator who wishes to be sensitive to trends or changes. To be sure, complicated mathematical procedures, called *time series analyses,* are available and can be used on such data. Well-trained professionals should know that these exist and roughly what they can be expected to do. They need not know how to carry them out, but they will find it helpful to be able to recognize when someone else should be called in to do so.

Last but not least, an appreciation of basic principles can be especially useful to those who plan to enter careers in research. Many students who concentrate upon acquiring technical skills in statistics or research design neglect to consider why these skills are useful and when it is desirable (or undesirable) to apply them. That should not happen to those who study carefully the material presented here.

What Is Research?

Conceived most broadly, research means collecting, analyzing, and interpreting information, or *data* (singular *datum*), in an attempt to answer questions. Research usually combines observation and reasoning. Its observational component is often referred to by the word *empirical*. If you look up this word in a dictionary, you will find that it has several meanings. The one that applies here is *based on sensory experience or observation.*

Attempts to answer questions by appealing to reason, common sense, or intuition alone do not qualify as empirical research. Appeals to reason, memory, or mental processes play their part in stimulating new ideas, developing research designs and procedures, and interpreting outcomes. These may be called the subjective component of research, while observation, measurement, and the control of conditions may be called its objective component. Science requires investigators to use both. Many kinds of research can be carried out, although the various types, some of which are discussed in the following sections, are not entirely distinct.

Library Research

Library research, often carried out by historians, might require traveling about the world to examine books, newspapers, letters, and material in libraries and covering events that occurred during a certain period of time at a certain place. A scientist also performs library research when tracing the history of investigation on a topic of research interest. So does the administrator of an agency who searches published material to find out what other agencies have tried in their attempts to solve a certain problem and how successful they have been. So does the psychiatrist or clinical psychologist who hears of a new form of psychotherapy and examines all available published reports to learn how it is applied and the success others have had with it.

Field Research

Field research is conducted by going to a place where something interesting is happening and observing what occurs. Usually field researchers prefer to carry out their work without interfering with or influencing events any more than is absolutely necessary. An anthropologist conducts field research by living for some time with a group of people (perhaps a far-off tribe, patients in a mental institution, prisoners in jail, or bag people on the streets) and observing their actions. A local politician working within a mayor-council system of government might conduct informal field research by visiting another community that uses a council-city-manager form of government and in this way find out by direct observation how that form of civic structure works. A health professional who wants to learn how to organize a community mental health center, a hospice, sheltered workshop, or newly developed type of school for the retarded might visit several such agencies and gather information from them. This, too, would be field research, although it might not be as well organized as an expedition by a fully equipped anthropological team.

Field research is sometimes advocated because it is typically *naturalistic*; it describes events that take place in "real life," nonlaboratory environments. As indicated above, the investigator often strives not to interfere with or even participate directly in the processes of interest. That may raise questions because a scientist cannot be certain that people who know they are being filmed or videotaped are behaving just as they would if the taping were not being done. On the other hand, an investigator must be concerned about violations of privacy that may occur if people do not know their actions are being recorded.

Field research is sometimes considered preliminary and inconclusive. It may be called descriptive, informal, exploratory, or hypothesis-generating, as opposed to analytical, causal, or hypothesis-testing, terms that are reserved to describe research patterned upon formal laboratory experiments.

Sometimes field research is not purely observational but attempts to alter the state of affairs in a nonlaboratory environment. An example is the carrying out of field trials (clinical trials) of a drug or therapeutic procedure in actual treatment settings. As will be shown, this type of investigation is sometimes called a *quasi-experiment* (Campbell and Stanley 1963). It is treated in a later section of this chapter as a variation of classical experimental methods.

Survey Research

Survey Research is a special form of field research that is systematically designed to make conditions of observation uniform and to make data analysis as straightforward as possible. Usually observations are collected and recorded in such a way that they are easily converted into numbers. One classical tool of the survey is the questionnaire. Another is the structured interview, which is really a questionnaire that is administered orally in a face-to-face situation.

The board of a social agency may want to know how patients or staff feel about a new policy or practice. Agency staff may arrange to carry out a survey to learn whether patients approve or disapprove of it. Large-scale epidemiological studies to determine morbidity rates or rates of incidence of various types of physical illnesses or behavior disorders are essentially descriptive surveys. In a political unit, club, or other organization, the voting process, by which people are elected to office or other decisions are made, is a type of survey research. Voting is special, however, because specific actions follow automatically once the data are quantified (once the votes are counted), whereas most research surveys are mainly descriptive in intent.

Survey methods are less naturalistic than other methods of field research, which seem more likely to catch people as they "really" are. For example, in a formal survey, patients or clients may say they approve of a new agency policy, but they may express this approval only because they feel pressured by the staff to do so. They may believe they will receive poorer care if they disagree, or they may simply wish to be cooperative or to please the investigator. Observed informally, under more "natural" conditions in the waiting room, on the ward, or in the cafeteria, the same patients might be heard complaining that they do not like the policy.

Survey research is favored by many investigators over informal observation because it is efficient and relatively precise. The use of certain techniques of data analysis (one of which is called *causal modeling*) even seems to suggest that survey research can achieve the same level of certainty about cause-effect relations as experimentation. Such is not the case, of course. Nonetheless, a carefully planned descriptive survey can usually be designed to overcome most objections that may be raised against it.

Laboratory Research

Least naturalistic is research that is conducted in laboratories. Although laboratories are often complicated places, they are all constructed with the same purpose: to enable an investigator to control conditions that might cause the event of research interest to occur.

People often think of laboratories only as places where experiments are conducted. Not all laboratory research is experimental, however, and not all experiments are carried out in laboratories.

The most important thing about an *experiment*, as that word is used here, is that the investigator deliberately changes at least one condition (the *independent variable*) to observe the effects that the change has on at least one other set of conditions (the *dependent variable*).

If an investigator brings people into a laboratory and hooks them up to sensitive recorders of a variety of physiological functions (for example, *alpha* waves in the brain) and does no more than measure these functions while the subjects are resting, no experiment is being conducted. The investigator may be trying to find out only how great the differences are between people on the functions measured, or what the average values of these functions are for people in general. In short, the investigator may be administering a *test*.

Tests

A test is a way of taking measurements so that conditions are held as constant, or kept as similar as possible, every time a measurement is taken. In testing, no deliberate experimental changes in conditions are allowed. In a sense, every systematic observation is a test, or part of a test. All empirical research therefore includes some testing, if only as a way of measuring outcomes.

In a psychological test, differences in obtained scores must be due only to differences in persons on the variable measured, not to changes in the conditions under which people were tested. Defining the conditions under which measures are taken and specifying how scores are to be derived and interpreted is called *standardizing* the test. Standardization helps ensure comparability of results.

An example of a standardized psychological test is the well-known *Wechsler Adult Intelligence Scale-Revised* (WAIS-R). This test must be individually administered by a trained examiner who has been taught the proper ways to give and score each of the 11 subscales of the instrument. Training of examiners ensures that whenever the test is given, it is administered and scored by the same set of rules. Equally well-known tests, similar to the WAIS-R, have been developed for evaluating children (the *Wechsler Intelligence Scale for Children-Revised* [WISC-R]) and preschoolers (the *Wechsler Pre-Primary Scales of Intelligence* [WPPSI]).

Two important features that must be considered when judging whether a test is useful are its *reliability* and *validity*. In general, evidence concerning reliability indicates how dependable, objective, or sensitive a test is. As suggested earlier, standardizing administration conditions is one way of increasing a test's reliability. A test's validity depends on how accurate it is or how well it does what it was designed to do.

Reliability. The term reliability appears often in research reports, especially in psychology. It has several specific meanings and can therefore be confusing to someone who is not familiar with the variety of ways in which it is used. Most research-related meanings of reliability refer either to the consistency or the precision of sets of numerical data.

Consistency may mean consistency of a set of scores over time; consistency between sets of scores obtained from different groups of items on the same test; or consistency between sets of judgments, obtained from different sources, such as raters or judges.

Suppose a vocational counselor administers a test of aptitude for nursing to a group of 100 persons. Then, six weeks later, the counselor readministers the same test to the same people. If the test is reliable, in the sense of giving constant scores over time, then persons who had high scores on the first testing will have high scores on the second testing, too. Similarly, persons who had low scores on the first testing will have low scores on the second testing. A statistic, called the *product-moment correlation coefficient* (described in Chapter 10), may be calculated to measure the stability of scores over time. The number that results from the calculations is used as an indicator of *test-retest* reliability.

One problem with this approach to determining reliability is that the conditions under which the test is administered will probably change in uncontrolled ways between testings. Another is that people's standings on the variable of interest may also change in uncontrolled ways between test periods. Also a retest with the same instrument may be more a test of practice or of memory than of the trait or ability that is being assessed.

The problem of remembering test items or answers may be avoided by using two equally good, but different, versions of the same test, called *equivalent forms, parallel forms,* or *alternate forms.* They eliminate the need to repeat exactly the same test. Another advantage of equivalent forms is that they can be administered either as part of a test-retest procedure or on a single occasion.

The main difficulty with alternate-forms reliability is that it is easier to talk about designing equivalent forms than it is to actually construct them. One of the more well-known attempts in psychology to develop alternate forms is the *Sixteen Personality Factors Questionnaire*, which has five forms (A through E) for adults.

As yet another alternative, the counselor in our example may decide not to examine test-retest or equivalent-forms reliability, but to determine the test's *internal consistency*. This requires examining the agreement among scores, calculated from different sets of items on a single test, when the test is administered only once. One way to do this is to pull out half the items of the test (perhaps every other item) and pretend that these make up one of two equivalent forms of the instrument, the other form being made up of the rest of the items. Correlating scores on the two halves, and applying a special adjustment to make up for the reduction in test length that results from dividing the test in two, produces a *split-half* reliability coefficient.

A difficulty with this approach is that there are many ways to split a test into halves, and each way will give a different reliability value. Which one is right? If a test is made up of items that are scored dichotomously (in only one of two possible ways, such as right or wrong, plus or minus, yes or no), then the consistency of all items with the total score can be determined by a special formula, called the *Kuder-Richardson-20*. Under most conditions, this formula will give the average of all the split-half coefficients that could be calculated from the data.

When scores on every item are not dichotomous, as would be the case if the test consisted of a series of ratings, each on a scale of 1 to 5, a coefficient called *alpha*, sometimes called Cronbach's alpha, or the coefficient of generalizability (Cronbach 1970), may be computed. It is similar to the Kuder-Richardson value, but, as will be noted later, it is more general in its applicability.

A special problem of reliability arises when judges are asked to make decisions that involve classifying members of a group of people. Suppose two judges must independently assign each person who enters a clinic for care to one of five possible diagnostic categories. Interjudge reliability is a matter of how closely these judges agree in their assignments. It would seem that all one needs to do is count up the number of times the judges agree. If desired, that figure can then be stated as a proportion or percentage.

The problem here is that simple counts do not make allowance for the fact that a certain percentage of agreement would be found even if the judges performed their tasks randomly. Adjustments must be made for this, and a special statistic, called *kappa*, has been devised that accomplishes that objective (Cohen 1960). *Kappa* can also be calculated for more than two judges or groups. Interjudge reliability is discussed further in Chapter 4, which shows how it is used for dealing with descriptive data, such as interview materials.

The concept of precision as a way of thinking about reliability is related to that of consistency, especially internal consistency. An approach to reliability that is finding increasing favor is based on the division of a series of scores into two parts or components. One part represents "true" scores (or the best estimates that can be obtained of them). The other represents errors of measurement. The logic is that if all scores contained no error whatever, they would be as precise as they can be. This ideal state of affairs might be indicated by the number 1.00.

If scores were completely inconsistent (over time, across items, between parallel forms, or between any other sets of supposedly comparable estimates), the data would contain no "true" values and be completely imprecise. This opposite state of affairs might be indicated by the number 0.00.

One version of the formula that produces such numbers is

$$\text{rel.} = \frac{\delta t^2}{\delta t^2 + \delta e^2}$$

where δt^2 represents true values and δe^2 represents errors. If δt^2 is zero, then rel. equals 0.00. But if δe^2 is zero, rel. equals 1.00. The lower δe^2 is, the higher rel. becomes.

The reasoning behind the formula is the basis for an important statistic, the *intraclass correlation coefficient*, explained more fully in Chapter 11. Subsequent chapters explain why the terms in this formula are squared and why they are labeled as they are. The important things to remember now are that reliability may be assessed in many ways and that no single way of determining it is right for all situations.

Validity. The validity of a test depends on what it is intended to measure or accomplish. Although validity is usually thought of as belonging to the test itself, it actually is determined greatly by the particular use to which the test is being put. The American Psychological Association (1974) recognizes three principal ways of establishing validity.

Establishing *content validity* requires demonstrating that the items of a test sample the proper domain or universe. Obviously, a test of reading skill should not be made up of problems in arithmetic. But, on the other hand, a test of reading skill does not necessarily have content validity just because it contains material to be read. The material must be at an appropriate level of difficulty for the persons being tested; it should cover suitable subject matter; and it should probably include some measure of comprehension of what is read as well as of mere ability to reproduce words.

Establishing the second type of validity, *criterion-related validity*, requires demonstrating that scores on the test correlate with other independent measures that are called criteria (singular, criterion). A *concurrent criterion* is made up of data collected at nearly the same time that the test is administered. For example, the concurrent validity of a new test designed to measure depression might be estimated by correlating scores on the new test with psychiatric diagnoses or with scores on another, already well-established test of depression.

A *predictive criterion* is a state or event that can be observed only in the future. The predictive validity of a test measuring potential to benefit from treatment can be established only by relating scores on the test, obtained at one time, to measures of treatment outcome, obtained later.

Establishing the third form of validity, *construct validity*, is necessary when the test is intended to measure a theoretical construct or a trait that cannot be related in a simple or obvious way to other measures or to a specific future state of affairs. Examples of such constructs or traits are anxiety, ego strength, conflict, and desire to achieve success.

Construct validity is established by showing that hypotheses derived from theory are confirmed when tested by empirical research. All kinds of research can be used, from purely naturalistic, observational studies to carefully controlled laboratory experiments. For example, to provide construct validation for a new test of extraversion, a research study may be set up in which subjects choose either to work with a group while solving a problem or to attempt to solve it by themselves. Theory leads the investigator to expect that people who score as extraverts on the test will choose to work in groups and introverts will prefer to work alone. If that actually happens, the research demonstrates the construct validity of the test. The same study could be designed to include data on concurrent validity by administering to subjects another, well-established test of extraversion.

Construct validity can even be approached by a procedure that is called *item-analysis*, which in turn is similar to some techniques for determining internal consistency, a form of reliability. The investigator may include in the new test several items that theory says have nothing whatever to do with extraversion. By correlating responses on all items with each other, or with the total score, the investigator may test several predictions. One is that responses to items measuring extraversion will be highly correlated with each other (*convergent validation*). Another is that responses to the theoretically irrelevant items will be unrelated to responses to items measuring extraversion (*discriminant* or *divergent validation*).

There is no single way in which to establish that test scores are valid, any more than there is a single way to establish that test scores are reliable. Therefore it is all the more important for the reader of research reports to be aware of where and how these judgments are made and what effects they may have on procedures and outcomes.

Norms. Establishing that a test gives reliable and reasonably valid data does not tell what particular test scores mean. The usual standards for interpretation of an individual's psychological test scores are established by examining the performances of others. Data collected on a test from a large number of people examined under standard conditions tell what to expect from other people in the future. These expectations are called *norms*. Obviously, the persons for whom norms are established should be as much like the persons who will be evaluated later as possible. The normative group must accurately represent the *population* from which later testees will come.

The procedure by which normative populations are selected from larger groups is called *sampling*, and sampling methods is a topic of considerable importance, especially in fields such as sociology, where investigators wish to describe large populations accurately. Problems related to sampling occur in survey research, and it is reasonable to think of the process of setting up norms for a test as a type of survey research. There is, however, this difference: data from surveys are not usually applied to individuals but are used to measure group trends or averages. Once a test has been standardized and normed and its reliability and validity established, it may be used to evaluate persons one at a time.

Predictive Studies

One of the most important uses of tests and surveys is to aid in forecasting or predicting events or behavior. Surveys taken over a period of time can show trends that may be projected as a way of making guesses about the future. Aptitude test data from a particular person may lead a vocational counselor to "predict" that this individual will do better in one type of job than another. In a psychiatric hospital, research might be conducted to discover whether certain types of psychological tests or data from other sources can be used to predict which patients are likely to respond quickly to treatment or which patients are likely to become management problems on the wards. Such research might be designed according to a plan that develops from theory or from clinical experience. When research has a theoretical basis, it may be used as a way of testing *hypotheses* or hunches about the factors that determine treatment outcomes or the development of problems.

As an alternative, predictive research may be *actuarial*. In this case, the investigator collects all possible information on every patient who enters the institution, regardless of whether the information seems related to the outcomes that are of interest (the criteria). Later the investigator examines this mass of data to discover whether any of the information seems to relate systematically to treatment success or to the occurrence of behavior problems. Data that relate systematically to particular results become potential predictors that are worth studying further.

All predictors that are turned up in this way should be retested later because of the possibility that they capitalized on chance, that is, took advantage of unstable or accidental relationships that may appear in the data only once and never again. This possibility will be discussed later.

One way to reduce the likelihood that unreliable relationships will appear is to use selective judgment when deciding which data are to be collected and used. For example, an investigation that relates everything to everything might show a one-time correlation between treatment outcome and patients' telephone numbers, but few people would take such a correlation seriously. Indeed, it would be surprising if this type of data were included in the analysis in the first place. Even actuarial research is never 100 percent statistical; it is always guided by some judgmental processes. Judgment is used in deciding which data will be collected and which will be correlated with the criteria. After analysis is complete, judgment is used to make sense of the outcome.

Another way to eliminate unstable relationships in a predictive study is to *cross-validate*, that is, to repeat the study using as predictors in the second study only those indicators that appeared to be successful the first time. A predictor that holds up under the test of cross-validation is much more likely to bear a stable relationship to criteria than one that does not.

An important test in psychology, the *Minnesota Multiphasic Personality Inventory* (MMPI), was originally devised as an actuarial instrument. It was constructed with the idea that scores on various subscales could be used to establish patients' psychiatric diagnoses. Test construction was essentially a matter of attempting to develop predictors by examining responses, given by selected groups of persons, to each of 550 personality-type questionnaire items. Each group was made up of patients who had already been assigned specific diagnoses, such as hypochondriasis, hysteria, and schizophrenia. Those items that were answered in a distinctive way by members of a diagnostic group were combined into a single scale.

To oversimplify slightly, the test makers reasoned that a person who answered many items on a scale in the same way as members of a particular diagnostic group had answered them would probably be assigned the label appropriate to that group if examined by a psychiatrist. If that reasoning proved to be correct, the test would accurately "predict" psychiatric diagnoses. Psychiatrists would no longer need to perform diagnostic tasks, because the test could be used to carry them out more quickly and objectively.

When actually put to use, the MMPI did not prove successful for this purpose. However, it did find acceptance in clinical practice as a general test of personality, and it is still employed as such in many settings (Greene 1980).

Whether used descriptively or predictively, neither testing nor survey methods are experimental, strictly speaking, because both examine persons under conditions that are held as nearly constant as possible. As has already been noted, this text treats a research study as an experiment only if some conditions are deliberately changed by the investigator so that the effects of the change can be observed or measured.

Control of Conditions and Experimentation

In behavior and health-related research, experiments are often conducted on species other than human beings: mice, rats, monkeys, and pigeons, for example. The main reason for this is that such animals can be inbred to produce nearly pure genetic strains which can then be raised under virtually identical conditions. These practices reduce the differences among organisms within a species on a variety of factors and are part of the scientist's effort to hold constant conditions other than those—the independent variables—that are to be manipulated systematically.

In some instances, use of genetically pure strains of subjects has an additional advantage: strains can be selected or bred for specific characteristics that make them particularly useful. For example, a strain of mice that is very likely to develop a certain type of cancer may be especially valuable in research to identify substances that produce this particular form of the disease. The *power* of the experiment is thereby increased; that is, it becomes more sensitive to changes due to the manipulation of conditions.

Consider an additional example. The chances of demonstrating that reinforcement is effective in controlling behavior are good when the subject is a rat in a so-called Skinner box. A Skinner box is a simple affair: a cage containing a lever that the rat can push and a chute to deliver a pellet of food—reinforcement—whenever the investigator chooses. Clearly, the chances of demonstrating reinforcement effects are not as good when the subject is a person you have just met and are talking with at a cocktail party and the reinforcement is a smile or a nod of approval every time the person does a specific thing, such as eat a cracker. Under these circumstances, so many conditions are uncontrolled that relationships between reinforcement and rate of appearance of the target behavior are not likely to show up clearly.

In general, the likelihood that any experiment will yield a clearly evident and interpretable result is increased by procedures that hold irrelevant conditions constant and that increase the sensitivity of subjects to the effects of changes in manipulated conditions.

Few experiments on aspects of human behavior that are of interest to professionals who work in service-delivery settings can be conducted under laboratory conditions. Nevertheless, many questions that professionals want to answer seem to call for the use of experimental methods. What factors are responsible for a recent increase in aggressive outbursts on Ward 3B? Would a new admissions procedure significantly improve treatment outcomes, reduce treatment time, or decrease recidivism (the tendency of certain clients to relapse or return to poor adjustment patterns)? Would a change in counseling methods improve patient responses to surgery or to other uncomfortable medical procedures?

Questions like these cannot be answered experimentally with certainty unless an investigator has the power to hold all irrelevant conditions constant and to change only the relevant ones. For example, there might be reason to believe that the aggressive outbursts on Ward 3B are due to the actions of a new nurse or attendant. To obtain a rigorous (that is, a precise, strict, or exact) test of this belief, or hypothesis, an investigator must have the power to transfer staff and patients from ward to ward. Furthermore, the wards included in the experiment must be equivalent, because the suspected staff member may arouse aggression from only one type of patient or only in the presence of one particular ward physician.

As if this were not difficult enough, the investigator must somehow deal with what psychological investigators call *subject reactivity*. People are not passive in response to changes in their situations. Staff members will probably react strongly to being moved about from ward to ward without apparent reason. Patients will react to sudden and arbitrary changes as well. Certainly the staff member who is thought to be the cause of the disturbances will be affected by any hint that he or she is being investigated.

All such effects produce either bias or unwanted interferences (error) in research conditions. The curious may want to read the important texts by Chassan (1979), Colton (1974), and Kazdin (1980; Chapter 3) that provide additional detailed discussions of threats to the validity of this type of clinical research in psychiatry, general medicine, and clinical psychology.

Practical considerations. Of course, this elaborate discussion of how an agency busily engaged in providing services to clients might conduct an experient is purely academic. No administration would permit such research to be carried out, even if the problems in the research design itself could be solved. The study is far too expensive; it would interrupt ongoing routines, thereby reducing the overall effectiveness of service delivery.

Furthermore, the outcome hardly seems worth the trouble the study would cause. What if the suspected person were not found to be the cause of the increase in aggressive outbursts? Would another equally complicated experiment then be carried out to test another hypothesis? What if the suspected person were found to be the cause? Should that person be dismissed, transferred, disciplined, or counseled? What guarantee does the investigator have that hiring a new person will not cause even worse behavior to occur? The research itself would yield no answers to such questions.

Experiments as Ideals

Scientific investigators recognize that the conditions necessary for the conduct of "true" experiments cannot often be met in the so-called "real" world. Nevertheless, they like to hold up the laboratory experiment as the ideal that all research should approximate as closely as possible. As noted earlier, research that involves the observation of the effects of changes that are brought about outside the laboratory is sometimes called *quasi-experimental research*. Thus, for example, if a community introduces an educational program designed to prevent smoking into one school but not into another, an investigator might consider the children in the first school to be an *experimental,* or *treatment, group* and the children in the second school to be a *control group*, for whom conditions are not changed. The outcome measure (or dependent variable) might consist of students' responses to a questionnaire that asks how often they smoke.

This is not a rigorous experiment for it leaves many conditions uncontrolled, such as possible differences between the backgrounds of the children who attend the two schools. It also has other problems, such as the questionable accuracy (validity) of students' reports as an indicator of actual level of smoking activity. Nevertheless, because the investigation is designed to come as close as possible to the ideal of a laboratory experiment it is called *quasi-experimental*. Such studies are never conclusive in themselves, but if enough are conducted in a sufficient variety of "real-life" settings, if procedures are systematically improved, and if results remain consistent across studies, confidence in outcomes may eventually become high.

Appropriate Measurement

As noted at the beginning of this chapter, many investigators regard measurement to be the essence of all research that claims to be scientific. Improvement of measurement is necessary for improvement of research quality. Professional investigators therefore sometimes insist that complicated or highly technical measurement is better than simple, more obvious approaches. In research that is expected to be useful in treatment situations, however, this is not always true.

In the following example simpler is probably better. An investigator wishes to see whether the children of mothers who have been hospitalized for depression show more psychological disturbance than children of mothers who are comparable to the first group but were not hospitalized for depression. The design of this study includes two groups of *control* or *comparison* mothers: those who have not been hospitalized for any reason and those who have been hospitalized for conditions other than depression. The last group is needed because of the possibility that the psychological states of children are affected by the hospitalization of their mothers for any reason.

This feature of the research is not important now. The only matter of interest is how the severity of the children's psychological disturbances might be determined—no easy task, for children reveal psychological disturbance in many ways. Some may show it in behavior at school, others in behavior at home. Some may experience it inwardly but not show it in outward actions.

Many professional researchers would argue that the best way to approach a measurement problem such as this is to obtain many scores, each covering a different form of psychological maladjustment. That may be so, but a problem usually arises when the time arrives to analyze this type of data. The most obvious way to analyze such data would be to compare the scores for each form of psychological disturbance across group lines to determine which scores reveal differences between groups and which do not. But that approach is not likely to answer the research question. What if half the scores show expected differences between groups and half do not? If all scores were supposed to measure disturbance, then it cannot be said that the groups are different in *overall* disturbance. All the research would have shown is that the measurement of psychological disturbance is more complicated than it seemed to be at first. Recall, too, that this type of outcome may result from paying undue attention to unstable relationships.

A way out seems to be to get a *single* score for each child based on some combination of scores on all measures. With enough data, there are impressive ways to do this, one of which is called *factor analysis*. But what if the analysis shows (as it is likely to) that there is more than one good way to combine the numbers? Which way should be used?

What about the child who is seriously affected inwardly but not behaviorally? Scoring high on one factor and low on the rest, that child might emerge with a low total disturbance score. Meanwhile, another child might turn up with a high total score because this child "spreads out" his or her stress response.

In such a situation, the most practical solution to the measurement problem may be the much more direct one of presenting all available diagnostic information on each child to several qualified and experienced clinicians. Each would examine the data from every child and give each child a single rating as to degree of overall psychological disturbance, using whatever basis for judgment seems appropriate in a given case. Ratings from different clinicians could be checked for similarity (inter-rater reliability), and all ratings for each child could be summed to give a single value that represents the best combined judgment of the clinicians.

The investigator may wish to build other precautions into the rating procedure, such as keeping the judges ignorant (*blind* is the term researchers often use) as to which group each child came from. Other precautions will be considered in later chapters, but the main point is that this approach has the advantage of representing much more closely than the others the actual way in which diagnoses and judgments are made in clinical practice. Especially when judging behavior, clinicians rarely trust test data completely. They use tests as aids, but they often prefer to draw their own conclusions. Clinicians may disagree with each other, of course; the investigator can take this into account by giving different numerical weightings to the ratings made by judges of more or less experience or competence.

A current tendency is to design standardized interviews that may be used for diagnostic purposes in research. Such instruments have the advantage of consistency but each must be evaluated separately, as with any test, for its reliability, validity, and clinical applicability, and not accepted uncritically as the final diagnostic authority.

Names and Numbers

Clearly, the most complicated and technical approach to measurement is not always the best. Measures need not even be quantitative to be useful.

Investigators commonly speak of *nominal numbers*, numbers that serve as names or labels but that have no quantitative significance. Examples are telephone numbers and forms of identification, such as numbers designating players on a team, patients in a hospital, horses in a race, and social security accounts.

Such numbers may be handy as codes for purposes of tabulation. For example, in a physical medicine and rehabilitation setting, the prefix 01- might be assigned to all persons with spinal cord injuries, and suffixes -00 to -99 might be used to identify different types or causes of injuries. The well-known *Diagnostic and Statistical Manual of Mental Disorders, Third Edition (DSM-III)* (American Psychiatric Association 1980), which is used for making psychiatric diagnoses, provides an excellent example of just such a coding scheme. After a large amount of data has been collected, the frequency of use of any code number may be counted. That is, the data may be quantified. But even when that is done, the code numbers themselves usually have no quantitative significance.

Numbers and Meanings

The relationship between numbers and meaning may be clarified by two important principles: the use of numbers alone is no guarantee that results have any meaning, and numbers don't care what you do to them. Under some conditions, even nominal numbers may be subjected to mathematical analysis and the results interpreted.

Here is an improbable but instructive example. Suppose a high school coach announces that tryouts for the boys' basketball team will be held at the gym. Thirty boys appear, and they are asked to demonstrate their abilities on the basketball court in small groups so that the coach can choose among them. Because the coach does not know the boys' names, he distributes a t-shirt marked with a large two-digit number to each boy to wear. That way the coach can simply call out a number when he wants to give directions to someone on the floor. If the coach knew anything about statistics, he might say that as far as he is concerned the numbers are randomly assigned and their meaning is purely nominal.

When tryouts are over, the coach announces that he has picked 15 of the boys to be on the team. He calls out their numbers and tells the rest to leave.

Before they do, one of the more observant players says, "Hey, coach, that's unfair. The guys who got picked have higher numbers on their t-shirts than the guys who got cut. This tryout was phoney. Don't anybody leave the gym. I'm calling the principal." Which he does.

When the principal arrives (accompanied by the school psychologist), he lines the boys up, putting those picked by the coach on one side of the room and the rest on the other. He records the numbers on their t-shirts and, having a calculator on hand, quickly runs a statistical test (which happens by sheer coincidence to be called a *t*-test). He finds that the difference between the arithmetic average of the T-shirt numbers for one group and the arithmetic average of the T-shirt numbers for the other group is statistically significant. There is only one chance in a hundred that a difference as large as the one observed could have occurred by chance.

The student now maintains that his point is proven. The coach pleads innocent, claiming that the numbers are meaningless and that it makes no sense to use statistics on them. The school psychologist suggests that although the coach may have had the best intentions, he was influenced by the numbers while watching the boys play, unconsciously assuming that better ability went with higher numbers. Or, he adds, the coach may have judged each boy's appearance when he first saw him and unconsciously reached for a T-shirt with a higher number when he saw a boy who looked like a good prospect. Thus he biased the assignment of T-shirts without knowing it.

Fortunately, there is no need to decide what prompted the coach's choices because the scenario just described never actually happened. A statistician invented a similar story many years ago to show that a number in and of itself has no absolute meaning. A number takes on the meaning that the investigator and others are willing to assign to it. Therefore, one research study is not necessarily better than another just because it is quantitative.

The story illustrates a second principle that is especially important in the computer age: numbers are completely passive. Although someone might say, as did the coach, "You can't carry out a t-test on those numbers," the fact is that calculations can be performed using any numbers, regardless of their nature, as the principal demonstrated.

If the coach understood statistics he might have said, "A t-test on these data is meaningless because the figures are purely nominal and therefore violate necessary statistical principles that require at least an equal interval scale for the calculation of a t-test." This is harder to say, but it is more correct. Nevertheless, there is nothing about numbers themselves to prevent us from doing one thing or another with them. A long and involved computer program will perform a complicated factor analysis on random numbers just as quickly as on meaningful data, and it may even yield an apparently meaningful result. But remember the GIGO rule that was mentioned in this chapter. Remember also the basic principle that numbers don't care what you do to them. It will come up again and again in this book.

Uses of Statistics

When used in research, statistics serve two main purposes. They serve a descriptive purpose because they are used for condensing and summarizing data. The statement "the average score of this group of 500 persons on test X is 25.8" is certainly more useful to a reader than would be a listing of all 500 scores.

More important to many researchers is that statistics serve inferential purposes. The t-test, mentioned in the earlier example, is one of many statistics that are used inferentially. Usually inferential statistics enable an investigator to make a probability-based decision about the correctness of a particular statistical statement or its alternatives. Most often the statistical statement about which the decision is made is the *null hypothesis*, a hypothesis that says that the value of a particular statistic (such as a mean or a standard deviation) does not differ from a specified "true" value. The alternative to the null hypothesis is usually that the value of that statistic does differ from the hypothesized true value in some specified way. Inferential statistics may indicate that random variations among samples is an unlikely explanation for any discrepancy between the hypothesized true value and the value that is actually obtained in a research study. If so, the null hypothesis is rejected and its alternative is accepted, as we will see in the next chapter.

Forms and Qualities

If it is true that everything exists in some quantity, then it is also true that everything that exists has form. In numerical measurement, something that is to be evaluated is compared to a standard and assigned a number according to how much larger or smaller it is than the standard. The more exactly this difference can be stated the more *precise* the measurement is said to be. Numbers are easiest to understand when the thing being measured is *unidimensional*. Familiar examples of unidimensional variables are length, temperature, white blood-cell counts, and frequency of waves per second.

In psychology, intelligence was once thought to be unidimensional. The psychologist's job would be much easier if it were. The idea of the intelligence quotient (IQ) actually suggests that this is the case. However, because there are many kinds of intelligence— verbal, spatial, quantitative— intelligence is clearly not unidimensional.

Bearing in mind that numbers are passive, it is easy to see that someone has only to declare a concept unidimensional—and build a scale to measure it—to make it so. If everyone wants badly enough to measure something unidimensionally, no one may even think to ask whether doing so makes sense. Consider, for example, how you might measure marital compatibility, self-esteem, dominance, or psychological adjustment as a single number on a unidimensional scales. People have tried. How about beauty, love, morality, or truth? Nothing can stop you from doing it, if you are willing to overlook the general common-sense opinion that the beauty of a Van Gogh painting is of a totally different type than the beauty of a painting by Rembrandt and therefore incommensurate (not measurable on the same scale) with it.

Discrimination

The common denominator of all measurement is the comparison of one thing with another and the qualitative judgment that they are either alike or not alike. The basic operation of measurement is therefore *discrimination*, a yes-or-no decision. That is why modern computers, for all their complexity, can operate on the binary system, in which 0 can be thought of as meaning "the same" (or "no difference") and 1 as meaning "different."

Although simple discriminations can be built up or translated into numbers, the ultimate act of discrimination is not *quantitative* but *qualitative*. Complicated discriminations are not easily converted into numbers. For example, the difference between a symphony by Mozart and a symphony by Brahms is obvious but can hardly be stated as a number. The similarities among several of Shakespeare's tragedies are evident and describable in terms of something that might be called "style," but few would argue that all of his tragedies can be assigned places on the same one-dimensional scale. In clinical settings, similarities may be seen among certain types of patients (for example, patients who have been diagnosed as having different types of schizophrenia), yet one may not wish to say that they are comparable in all ways. Among 12 patients labeled paranoid, personality differences may be strong, yet a clinician may feel quite comfortable applying the same diagnosis to all of them.

When an investigator deals with complex issues, the problem often becomes one of describing form rather than measuring quantity. Such is the case with diagnoses, where it is not the amount of any particular thing, but the pattern of the symptom syndrome as a whole that matters. Again, *DSM-III* provides a good example of how forms of disorder can be described. A person may lack one or more features of a condition yet be diagnosed as having it, either because most of the other features are present or because the person lacks more of the features of other possible conditions than of this one.

Similar situations arise in research involving judgment of values, ethics, and meaning. Concepts like right-wrong, good-bad, beautiful-ugly can be treated as if they define unidimensional scales. People could be asked to use these scales to rate words like *love, war*, or *justice*, as is done in a technique known as the semantic differential. But scales like these are scarcely useful when it comes to deciding issues such as the morality of abortion or euthanasia, the desirability of divorce for a particular couple, or the necessity of war.

"Researchable" Issues

Some issues are not quantifiable, but they are researchable. The only topics that are outside the realm of research altogether are those that can be talked about only in terms of the supernatural. The phenomena examined by parapsychology, such as extrasensory perception (ESP), may or may not be "real." Nevertheless, para-psychology cannot be a suitable topic for scientific research if the investigator claims that it deals with unnatural or supernatural events or that it enters a separate reality that is put together differently than the one most of us know. The supernatural is researchable only if the investigator is willing to agree with the contradictory statement that it is natural, for science is the study of nature, whatever that may be. Many scientists might agree that research on ghosts would make sense if ghosts were real. But if ghosts are real, then they are not supernatural, and they should behave according to laws (perhaps as yet unknown) of the natural world.

Other matters that cannot be described with numbers seem unresearchable only because they are complicated and are not dealt with easily by unidimensional measurement. How do you describe a whole person with a single number? Other cases in point appear in the problems raised by *evaluation research* of all kinds. This type of research ranges from evaluating individual employees for "merit," as a way of determining salary increases, to evaluating the effectiveness of a publicity campaign or the operation of an entire institution. In a factory, a highly productive individual may be meritorious in that one respect, but if he or she has a high rate of absenteeism, another person who is more dependable may show at least equal merit overall. In a selling operation, a super salesman may increase a company's profits briefly but cost the company so much in good will in the long run as to be less meritorious than a salesman who sells less each week but upholds the company's reputation. In a medical setting, a nurse who has strong technical skills but gets along badly with patients or other staff may be highly meritorious in an operating room but not so meritorious on a ward.

A medical program that lengthens patients' lives may be highly successful in that one respect, but if it causes prolonged pain and loss of quality of life, it may be a failure in other ways. The question is not "Which is more important, length or quality of life?" Both are important but in different ways. A researcher can determine which type of outcome different treatment practices produce or different sorts of persons prefer. Or a researcher can assume that one type of outcome is more important than another and work to produce it. But no research can determine which type of outcome is "really" better. It can indicate that person A or treatment A, given a particular standard of value, is better than person B or treatment B. Or it can show that this standard of value leads us to prefer person A or treatment A, while another standard leads us to prefer person B or treatment B.

Such research should not be dismissed just because it does not yield simple solutions. Its contribution is to reveal the consequences of a variety of possible diagnostic, therapeutic, or administrative choices so that they can be made intelligently.

Given the tendency in American culture to demand that technology answer all questions, more may easily be required of research in the social, behavioral, and health sciences than research can reasonably be expected to deliver. Such expectations can lead to disappointment when simple answers do not appear, and the professional investigator may come to feel that research that is not perfectly controlled or quantified is not worth doing. What is needed, of course, is balance and perspective. This can be gained only by acquiring an appreciation of what can reasonably be expected of different kinds of research in different kinds of settings.

—2—

CARRYING OUT RESEARCH

General Principles

Designing Research

All research requires decision making. The very first decision is what problem to select for study, a matter of no small importance. The next step is to state specific questions that can be studied effectively within the limits of knowledge gained from past research, theory, and practical experience. The investigator must then choose among several possible research strategies or designs. Each will have advantages and disadvantages that must be recognized and weighed for importance in the overall plan. The ideal is to develop a research design that will answer the questions posed for study yet not make too many demands upon the subjects or the setting within which the study is carried out.

Experienced investigators realize that a properly conducted project is an integrated whole from start to finish. Changing one part will probably affect the outcome and meaning of the entire investigation. Therefore after the study has begun, procedural or design changes should be made with extreme caution, and only after their probable effect on the overall project has been considered.

Interpreting Outcomes

Another important principle is that no research study can be expected to answer questions that it was not designed to answer. This simple principle seems obvious, but it is easily forgotten.

Suppose that a study is undertaken to determine whether one particular drug reduces anxiety more effectively than another. A two-group research study using all the proper precautions is designed. These include, but are not limited to, selecting an appropriate group of people, or *population*, for study, devising a sampling plan for choosing the individuals, or *subjects*, to be studied, randomly assigning subjects to groups that are to be given one or the other substance, systematically adjusting dosage levels (taking care that the appearances of the capsules that contain each substance are identical), making sure that the investigator, the research staff, and the subjects do not know who is receiving which substance (this is called the *double-blind* precaution), and ensuring that all subjects cooperate by taking their capsules on time. The research design may also include a *crossover* feature. After a period of time, people taking drug A are shifted to drug B, and people taking drug B are shifted to drug A.

When the research is complete, the investigator analyzes the data and announces that substance A has been found to be better than substance B. Assuming that the investigator's statistical calculations are correct, the matter would seem to be settled. But is it?

A critic who prefers substance B may point out that this drug is more effective when taken just before meals than it is when taken between meals, which was the procedure used in the research. The critic claims that the study was therefore unfairly rigged against substance B. In all honesty, the investigator must admit that the research shows substance A to be superior to substance B only under the specific conditions of the study. Obviously, to determine whether A is superior to B when one of them is administered differently requires further investigation.

Another critic may believe that neither drug is effective. This critic claims that the patients would have improved if they had received no drug at all or had been given a *placebo*, a substance that has no active medical ingredients but is similar in every other way to the substances being studied. To answer this criticism also requires further research.

A pharmacologist may be willing to accept the general conclusion that substance A has been shown to be superior to substance B in reducing anxiety. But the pharmacologist may ask what the research shows about *how* the two drugs operate in the body: what physiological actions make one substance more anxiety reducing than the other?

With regard to the crossover part of the study, questions may arise about a possible carryover of effects from the first treatment condition to the second when the crossover is put into effect. On the basis of the study conducted, the investigator can say nothing in reply to these questions.

A lesson that should be learned early in research is that no study can answer all questions. And no study can answer questions it was not designed to ask in the first place.

Some studies do not even answer questions that were posed for them. But a distinction should be made between research plans that are effective, although limited in scope, and those with flaws so basic that the research cannot answer the question the investigator asked. The former can answer some questions, if they are properly asked in advance. New investigators (and some experienced ones, too) are often tempted to try to design the single all-inclusive project that will answer all questions in one fell swoop. It cannot be done.

It has been argued that the best research answers only one clearly stated question, however limited, but answers it with certainty. This is the ideal of much laboratory experimentation. But conducting such research in settings where services are actively being delivered is rarely possible, and sometimes not even desirable.

Although their arguments are too complicated and abstract to present here, philosophers of science now recognize that even the most precise and carefully executed laboratory experiment cannot produce absolute certainty of knowledge. It can contribute to developing a convincing argument, but absolute proof of anything is not possible in science (Rychlak 1981; Weimer 1979). Whether carried out in a laboratory, a mental health center, or in the community, research on topics important to the behavioral sciences and health professions has its limits. It cannot be expected to prove anything. What it can do is add weight to arguments for or against decisions that must be made, taking into account a host of other factors.

Nonstatistical Inferences

Although much is made of the desirability of quantifying research procedures, valid conclusions can be drawn from some kinds of research without relying on statistical significance or, for that matter, on numbers of any kind. Hendin et al. (1981) studied the structure of families of adolescent marijuana users. Conducted mostly through interviews, the research showed how young marijuana users fit into their family organizations. The initial research question was not quantitative, but it was certainly important in a practical, social sense: Do family relationships and interactions contribute to the use or abuse of marijuana in the adolescents studied?

Family members submitted to psychodynamic interviews, and psychological tests were administered to many of the adolescents. Data were integrated and summarized, and the investigators concluded that "marihuana abuse in all 15 cases ... appeared to be related to psychodynamic conflicts having their roots in the students' family experiences. Parents, in particular, were quite consistently and intimately tied up with these young people's sense of being caught in an impossible position regarding achievement and competition" (pp. 3–4).

Research of this type contributes to knowledge of personal and social behavior, but techniques for condensing data and for drawing conclusions from such naturalistic studies have not been standardized. Questions may be raised even about whether they could or should be, for too much standardization of procedure could destroy some of the main advantages of this approach: its flexibility and the opportunities it affords the investigator to examine natural phenomena with a minimum of interference and to describe things "as they really are." More is said about qualitative research like this in Chapter 4.

Statistical Inferences

In the ideal research study, all conditions would be so completely controlled that chance, or *random factors*, or error could not operate. The outcome would then be absolutely definitive. If such a study could be carried out, statements about probabilities would not be needed because there could be no variation in outcome. But no research is perfect; there is always the possibility that random or unknown factors will influence the results. Consequently, statistical inference is a matter of special importance in all quantitative research.

The concept of randomness. For the moment, a random factor may be thought of as an influence that affects the outcome of a research study but which varies in its effects in ways that are not controlled by the investigator. If the experiment were repeated again and again, random factors would affect the results strongly on some occasions, not so strongly on others, and not at all on still others, but always in unpredictable ways.

For example, differences in attitude may be a random factor that induces different responses to the same test from different subjects. Changes in mood over time may influence responses from the same person when he or she is tested on different occasions. Especially in the behavioral sciences and health professions, random factors often introduce considerable uncertainty into research outcomes.

At the end of a research study, an investigator likes to be able to say that the results cannot be explained by random variation. To say this, the investigator must be able to estimate in numbers just how much variation can reasonably be blamed on random factors. The investigator is then in a position to judge whether the outcome falls outside the limits of normally expected random variation, or as it is often called, *chance*.

Statistically speaking, even the outcome of a single experiment is a type of variation. In the simplest case, it is the difference between two numerical values. One value is the result that would be obtained if the systematically changed condition, or independent variable, were ineffective. The other value is the result that is actually obtained, influenced by the manipulated condition and random factors. As will be shown, the true difference between the two values is usually assumed to be null (zero) until research indicates that it probably is not. Random factors that cause the obtained difference to be something other than zero are referred to as *error* and their influence is called *error variance*.

If the investigator can estimate how much of a given outcome could be due to error, that amount can be allowed for when making decisions based on the result. What remains after error variance is accounted for can be said to be due to the change in the experimental factor alone.

A slightly more complicated procedure is followed in a two-group experiment in which one group is given some form of treatment while the other is not. Suppose a study is conducted to test the effectiveness of a form of training for medical students who are on their psychiatric rotation. In the new form of training, students are given full responsibility for several cases instead of being merely passive observers of others who are giving psychiatric care. The group of students that receives the usual form of training may be thought of as a *null standard*. Whatever is learned by this group during the training period cannot be due to the new method. There-fore, if the other group does not gain significantly greater benefit from training than the null standard derives, the new form of train-ing cannot be said to be superior. If the new form of training is not better, and if random factors are not a major source of variation, then the expected outcome is that there will be no difference between the two groups after the training period is over.

The null hypothesis. The reasoning that the investigator now applies is a bit tricky. First, by the logic described above, the in-vestigator assumes that after training by both methods has been completed the *true* difference between groups will be zero. In other words, the investigator states that the new method of training will be no more effective than the old. This is the *null hypothesis.* Then the investigator attempts to show that the null hypothesis is un-tenable (literally, cannot be held on to). This implies that the al-ternative hypothesis—that the difference is other than zero—is more likely to be correct. The investigator calculates an estimate of the amount of difference between groups that could be accounted for by chance. The investigator then argues that the difference actually obtained is so much greater than this that to say it is due to a deviation from zero caused by random variation alone is unreason-able.

Usually the investigator's argument is supported by some sort of ratio. In one such ratio, the t-test, the obtained difference between groups is divided by an estimate of the difference that can be ex-pected on a random basis. If the obtained difference (numerator) is less than the difference that can be said to be due to chance (de-nominator), the quotient will be less than 1.00. This result is taken to mean that the null hypothesis is *tenable*—although not neces-sarily true.

If the ratio is greater than 1.00, the obtained results must be greater than the results that can be explained by chance. The in-vestigator then uses mathematical formulas, or (more likely) looks up the ratio in a special statistical table, to determine how frequently a ratio as large as, or larger than, the one obtained could be expected to appear at random. If the ratio is large enough and the probability is low enough, the null hypothesis can be rejected at the appropriate level of statistical significance.

Remember: the investigator, not the statistics, rejects the null hypothesis; statistics are only mathematical tools. This book deals extensively with the use of statistics because an understanding of

Table 2.1. Types of Errors and Correct Inferences About the Null
Hypothesis

| | True State of Affairs: Null Hypothesis (NH) is actually | |
Inference	True	False
True (Accept NH)	Correct	Type II Error
False (Reject NH)	Type I Error	Correct

how these tools are used is important. But statistics are only part
of the story of research. Not all good research can be interpreted
statistically, and not all studies that are analyzed statistically are
good research.

Two kinds of error. Suppose that the numerical results of a
study could have occurred by chance fewer than 5 times in 100 (once
in 20 times), that is, at the so-called 5 percent level of significance.
In such a case investigators would usually regard as proper a decision to reject the null hypothesis, to conclude that the outcome did
not occur by chance. (Later chapters show how such probability
statements are arrived at mathematically.)

Conclusions drawn at this decision level of 5 percent (*alpha* level),
or $p < .05$, may be right 19 out of 20 times, but they will also be
wrong an average of once in 20 times by chance alone. Such a wrong
conclusion drawn from chance occurrences is called a *Type I error,
alpha error,* or *error of the first kind.* The investigator is claiming
a difference to be nonrandom that is really random, seeing a difference where there is none.

A *Type II error, beta error,* or *error of the second kind* occurs when
analyses of data suggest that a result actually did take place by
chance, although in fact it did not. In this case, the investigator fails
to reject the null hypothesis when it should be rejected.

Unfortunately, the logic of statistics is such that investigators can
calculate that a certain proportion of errors in decision making will
occur on the average, but they cannot determine exactly when errors
will occur or which type of error will occur in a given study. Keeping
the two types of errors clearly in mind can be rather difficult until
one becomes more familiar with the logic of hypothesis testing. Table
2.1 may be of some assistance. Notice that a Type I error is like
"capitalizing on chance"; it can be made only when the null hy-

pothesis is rejected. The probability of making a Type I error is determined by the decision level *alpha* (α).

A Type II error can be made only when the null hypothesis is not rejected. The likelihood of making such an error is inversely related to the *power* of the experiment. The more powerful an experiment is, the more sensitive it will be to real differences and the less likely the investigator will be to make an error of the second kind.

Example. Suppose that a drug manufacturer sponsors 20 studies by independent researchers to evaluate a newly developed medicine. The manufacturer does not know that the medicine is really not effective; however, by the magical process of supposition available to all textbook authors, we do. When the results of all the studies come in, the manufacturer finds 19 showing that the drug did not have statistically significant effects. The twentieth shows favorable results, significant at the .05 level. Considering how much money usually goes into product development and how much could be made if the product were effective, the manufacturer might be tempted to believe that the significant study was the only valid one. The manufacturer might then decide to accept the significant study and disregard the others.

If he does, researchers who read the single favorable report will probably be led to commit a Type I error. They will believe that the medicine is effective, although it actually is not. In this case, the one significant research outcome may be due to a peculiar arrangement of uncontrolled factors, factors of just the sort that could be expected to occur randomly about once in 20 times. That means that the probability of this outcome occurring by chance is 5 percent, and that is exactly how often the favorable outcome occurred in this run of investigations.

Now suppose that the same manufacturer has a new product that is effective. Its effects are not very strong, and no one is certain exactly when or how to administer it to get maximum therapeutic benefit. Again, 20 independent studies are run, but for various reasons only one comes out significant at the .05 level. Design faults that might cause failure of significance include giving the drug in doses that are too small or poorly scheduled, administering the drug improperly, having too few subjects, or selecting the wrong types of subjects for study.

The manufacturer, who took a course in statistics but not one in research design, examines the results of all the studies. He does not detect the flaws in the experiments and concludes that the one significant research outcome could have occurred by chance. He judges the drug to be ineffective and decides to cut the company's losses by halting its development program. In point of fact, the study that yielded significant results may have been the only one with a research design powerful or sensitive enough to give the medicine a fair test. Clearly, the manufacturer has made a Type II error because a real difference has gone undetected.

Textbook examples like these are easily constructed because the author determines whether the substance is or is not effective. In the world of everyday affairs, however, no one knows in advance whether a substance is or is not effective. If they did, research would not be needed to find out.

The manufacturer was faced with the same set of outcomes to both sets of studies: 19 unfavorable results and one favorable result. In each case a different decision was made, and in both cases the decisions were wrong. Type I and Type II errors do not come neatly labeled, and investigators cannot know for certain when they will occur.

Another important point is that neither the 5 percent level of statistical significance nor any other level has any special magic about it. Levels of statistical significance are sometimes called *confidence levels*, but the confidence lies in the investigator, not in the statistics. Some feel confident saying that a result that could have appeared only five times or fewer in 100 by chance did not occur by chance. Others feel confident only if the result could have occurred by chance fewer than once in 100 times. Still others, perhaps the majority, adjust their personal feelings of confidence to the probability level, feeling more confident as the level decreases. The 5 percent level is a customary cut-off point for decision making, but it is not a hard and fast boundary.

Testing Theories

In some circles, the testing of theories is regarded as being the most honorable of research activities. One of the main uses for statistical procedures is as an aid to drawing inferences about the truth or falsity of hypotheses that come from theories. Yet in order to use statistics as an aid to reasoning about theories, an investigator must take many things for granted.

Since at least the time of Aristotle, science has been a matter of applying reason to explain and understand observations. Reason involves logic, and the most highly developed form of logic is mathematics. Therefore, many feel that the use of mathematics is absolutely essential in research.

According to this view, the results of an ideal experiment could be described completely by one or more mathematical equations. The terms on one side of such an equation are the *independent variables*, or predictors, and the term on the other side is the *dependent variable*, or outcome.

Very few examples of ideal experiments or precise mathematical laws are to be found in the behavioral sciences, so the next point will be illustrated by borrowing from another field. Consider this example from high school physics. Within a simple electrical circuit, Ohm's law states that

$$I = E/R,$$

where E is electromotive force, measured in volts; R is resistance, measured in ohms; and I is current, measured in amperes. Theoretically, if an experiment is carried out in which a known voltage (E) is applied to a known resistance (R) in a closed circuit, the resulting current (I) will measure exactly E/R amperes. If the theory is correct, the mathematical formula can be used to predict outcomes to any desired degree of precision.

That last phrase about desired degree of precision is important. While the ideal (Ohm's law expressed as a mathematical formula) and the real (voltage, ohms, and amperes as read on meters) can be brought very close to each other, their identity can never be exact, and so the theory can never be proved absolutely. Even in a simple physical situation like the one described earlier, no meter can be made that will measure any of the quantities with absolute accuracy. All that can be assumed—and it usually suffices—is that in view of the outcomes of many experiments, using the most accurate and precise instruments available, the probability of Ohm's law being incorrect is so low that all qualified experts agree it must be true.

Definitions

In the above example, Ohm's law was treated as a theory that could be tested for its "truth value" by experiment. One may object (rightly) that Ohm's law is not a theory but a *definition*. It is a purely logical assertion: if one number is divided by another, the result is the quotient. As a mathematical statement, Ohm's "law" can never be proven wrong. Whatever number of volts is applied to whatever resistance, the result is defined as being exactly the number of amperes specified by the equation. If your meter reads differently, you had better get your meter fixed. But if Ohm's law is just an arbitrary statement, then it should not be discussed here because it is not researchable, and this is a discussion of research.

Taking a cue from a popular form of behavior research, Ohm's law could be thought of as an *operational definition*. A clinician says that a fundamental law of psychology is that reinforcements shape (or cause) behavior. Therefore, the clinician continues, I can change person X's behavior—overeating, for example—by withholding or administering reinforcements in a treatment program. If George Jones completes this program but does not lose weight, the clinician can draw one of two conclusions.

One is that the conditions of the operational definition were not met. The clinician can say, "Well, I guess I didn't find the right reinforcers, or I did not properly manage the ones I used. I'll have to try again." The clinician has defined reinforcement as anything that changes behavior. If behavior does not change, it can only be because reinforcement did not take place. This is not a researchable proposition because it cannot be tested. The clinician could treat a thousand people. In each case where weight was lost, a success could be counted for reinforcement theory. In each case where weight was not lost, the clinician could argue that reinforcement was not operating.

The other possible conclusion is that the "law" of reinforcement is wrong. This means that the clinician's original statement about reinforcement was a theory rather than a definition and as such could be tested by experiment. In that case, failure to reject the *null hypothesis* that food intake is not affected by treatment would require giving up the theory.

The example makes two critical points. The philosophical point is that there will always be a gap between the ideal and the real. The ideal is described in theories, mathematical formulas, and statistical assumptions. The real is never perfectly known. Similarity between the real and the ideal can only be assumed or judged from observation. When conducting or evaluating an investigation, we must be aware of the assumptions or inferences that are being made and of how far the real is likely to differ from the ideal in each case.

The second critical point is that the judgment involved in making assumptions or drawing conclusions is always human judgment; it is always open, by conscious or unconscious processes, to human error. This point may not be so essential in physics or chemistry, where standards and limits are well established and generally accepted. But it is crucial in research on health and behavior. In evaluating the effectiveness of a treatment program, a great deal may depend upon whether reinforcement is a "law of behavior" or a theory to be tested and discarded if it fails.

It could be said that the frequency of many forms of undesirable behavior—such as smoking, drug consumption, excessive eating, unusual sexual activity, and noncompliance with medical regimens—can be reduced by proper management of reinforcement contingencies. That statement alone could be either a definition or a theory. Therefore, it may or may not be open to question by research. The person who applies it may slip back and forth, regarding every successful outcome as proof that the theory of reinforcement is true and every unsuccessful outcome as a sign that proper reinforcement procedures were not followed in that particular instance. Nothing new will ever be learned that way.

The possibility of endless waffling led to the idea, proposed by the philosopher of science Karl Popper, that no theory is an acceptable research topic unless it can be *falsified*. Put another way, a research question is not really a question if things are set up so that only one answer is possible.

At this point the bewildered reader may well ask whether anything can be proved absolutely. In a word, the answer is no. But by using accepted research methods and logic based on statistical assumptions and reasoning, very convincing arguments can be constructed. Those that are most convincing to the scientific community will be regarded as correct, according to the standards of the times.

Correlation and Causation

Students of research methods are often told never to confuse correlation with cause. Usually this means simply that the mere fact that two things happen together regularly does not prove that one causes the other.

Mistaking correlation for cause is sometimes said to be the basis for the rise of superstitions. Suppose that in a prescientifc age a tribe believed the common cold to be a sign of possession by spirits. One day when a man caught cold, the witch doctor told him to undergo a ritual that was to last for 10 days. Perhaps it involved saying a certain special prayer three times a day. At the end of the prescribed time, the symptoms were gone, and the members of the tribe concluded that the spirits had been driven away by the prayers. From then on, everyone who caught cold was required to undergo the same ritual. Correlation of completion of the ritual with symptom relief was taken as cause.

In modern times we know better. When somebody sneezes we only say *Gesundheit*, probably a carryover from a time when people believed it kept the person's soul from being snatched by the devil.

The rule against confusing correlation with cause has a certain wisdom, but it also has a drawback. No one can avoid confusing them because correlation is really all there is to work with. Causation is a logical conclusion, not something that can be seen under any conditions. Even in the simplest case of one billiard ball striking another and "making it move," the observer does not see a cause producing an effect. All the observer sees is one billiard ball striking another and the resultant movement of them both. From this the observer may conclude that the first event caused the second, but no one can prove with certainty that it did. No one knows absolutely that the next time one billiard ball hits another the second won't simply disintegrate, refuse to move, or turn into a canary and fly away.

Causation—like Ohm's law, the principles of reinforcement, a regression equation, or the normal curve—is a concept or idea. It is something that scientists believe in, often very strongly to be sure, but it is not an object or an observation. In the final analysis, the only things any investigator can work with directly are correlations, or associations between one set of recorded observations and another. Anything else is inference and open to argument.

One way to try getting around the problem is to state the conditions under which scientists agree that causation can reasonably be inferred. Clearly, there is a difference between correlations that are reported in everyday life and those that are observed in laboratory experiments, but there is no obvious reason to find the latter more closely aligned with cause than the former.

Think, for example, of the Newtonian laws of gravity that state that objects exert attractive forces on each other by virtue of their mass. To be asked to believe that energy is directly carried from one billiard ball to another when they strike is one thing. It is quite another thing to be told that the same type of energy is carried over great distances in empty space from, say, the moon to the earth. Yet the idea of gravity operating through space seems like a good one because it works. At least it seems like a good idea until someone suggests that gravity is not really a force but a deformation of space itself that occurs in regions around large masses. Now the mind boggles.

Turning to the behavioral sciences does not help much, for things do not seem much clearer there. Most people understand someone who says, "I eat because I am hungry." The statement even sounds like a causal explanation. Hunger causes eating. But looking more closely, the meaning of the statement becomes unclear because no one can describe exactly what hunger is. Furthermore, even if the physiology and psychology of hunger were understood, we could still not explain how a body state becomes converted into the subjective feelings of hunger or the complicated acts of eating. Not only does science lack causal explanations of human eating, it does not even have stable correlational data that promise to provide causal understanding.

How much more complex, abstract, and unrelated to direct observation things are when a psychiatrist explains the neurotic behavior of an adult by saying that the cause lies in the person's childhood, in forgotten events that took place before the age of six. How can an effect observed in a patient of 25 be caused by things that happened 20 years before?

This is not to suggest that research has nothing to offer because it can never absolutely prove causation. Far from it. But we are best able to evaluate what has been and can be accomplished by research methods when we understand their inherent limitations.

Pragmatics. Science and technology have always been associated in the public mind with problem solving. The pragmatic attitude is characterized not by the question, how does it work? but rather, does it work? The fact that scientists do not yet have definite, precise physiological explanations of how tranquilizers operate or carcinogens cause cancer may not matter. For many purposes it is sufficient to know that a certain substance seems to calm people down or that the rate of development of cancer in groups exposed to a certain chemical for a period of time is higher than in groups who are not so exposed. In short, problems can often be solved even when causes are not known.

The accumulation of knowledge through observation often enables us to predict and control events. Referring to a large body of past experience, we can accurately predict not only that the sun will rise tomorrow but at what time and in what location on the horizon it will appear. These predictions can be made—and were made for many centuries—without an understanding of why the sun appears to rise and set.

Of course knowledge of sunrise and sunset patterns does not enable one to change the sun's motion. But it does enable farmers to control the growth of crops by planting according to rules based on the movement of the sun at different times of the year. This, too, can be accomplished with no knowledge of biology, plant chemistry, or photosynthesis.

A psychologist applying for a job at an orphanage was told by the administrators who interviewed him that the number of runaways had increased lately. The administrators said they wanted to know the reasons for the increase. Indeed, part of the new psychologist's job would be to conduct research on the problem and to come up with an explanation.

To examine a problem like this in enough detail to understand fully why the children were running away could require years of research. The investigator would need to exercise virtually complete control over institutional operations and conditions. Research design might require assigning children at random to living arrangements deliberately designed to either increase or decrease the rates of running away.

The psychologist soon discovered that what the administrators wanted was not research but a quick fix. The increasing number of runaways was making the agency look bad. At this point, the psychologist said, with more than a touch of sarcasm, "If all you want is to stop children from running away, why don't you just lock them up?" Needless to say, the administrators were not amused, and the psychologist did not get the job. The last I heard, he was writing a textbook on research methods.

Somewhere between the impossible ideal of causal explanation and the equally impossible demand for immediate solutions there is a middle ground in which most people who read this book must operate. Some may be in a position to approximate fairly closely the best of all possible research conditions; they may at least hope to arrive someday at causal explanations. But most who work in service delivery settings must settle for far less well controlled research conditions. That does not mean they should give up research altogether.

There are compromises that can be made between undertaking a five-year study to understand runaways and simply locking them up or administering tranquilizers to them. As one possibility, the investigator could set up a program of testing and interviewing to compare a group of children who had run away (and been retrieved) with a group that was comparable in age, sex, and other factors but had not run away. Even simpler would be a survey of children and staff that asked for opinions and suggestions. While not perfect, simple studies like these could rather quickly uncover correlates of running away that would lead to useful ideas about causes and remedies. For example, it might emerge that runaways have histories of getting into trouble with teachers and cottage parents more frequently than nonrunaways do. The studies would not definitively explain why children run away, but they might identify certain types of children who are at risk and should therefore be watched more closely in the future.

In the final analysis, all research, however complicated or simple, seeks correlations, that is, dependable associations among observations. The more systematic the search is, and the more thoroughly controlled or measured the conditions under which it takes place, the more confidence one may have in the outcome.

Practical Considerations

Feelings About Research

People who have worked in service delivery settings for a long time may develop mixed feelings about research, especially if they have tried to carry out research in their agencies. As students, they were probably taught to believe that research is highly desirable. They have probably been trained to take it for granted that scientific research is the only source of reliable and dependable knowledge upon which clinical practice can be based. Possibly their teachers also suggested to them that research is a highly technical undertaking that should be carried out only by persons with extensive training in statistics and experimental design.

For many reasons, most of them good, research activity has high prestige value in settings where services are administered to clients or patients. Those who work in such settings commonly say they would like to have someone carry out research at their agency; at least few are ever heard to say they would be totally against it. But the high value that is placed on research is sometimes more abstract than real, inspiring more discussion than action. In fact clinical settings often prove to be rather poor places to perform complicated or highly technical investigations.

The next few sections describe why this is so. They are not meant to discourage service-oriented professionals from undertaking research. Quite the contrary: they are written in the hope that a realistic awareness of problems will forewarn and forearm students to face realistically the difficulties that are likely to arise.

Economics

Money usually gets in the way of research. Despite their apparently favorable attitudes towards research, practitioners commonly feel that research is too expensive. The main purpose of many agencies is to provide services, and people who provide them almost always feel that money is in short supply. Funds that are spent on research are easily perceived as being funds taken away from patient care.

One way to solve this problem is to obtain grants for research from other organizations, especially government agencies. Most institutions favor this approach because a government grant generally furnishes an allowance for indirect costs as well as the funds to cover direct costs of a research project. Indirect costs are the hidden expenses a hospital or university incurs just to provide and maintain the space, equipment, and services (like heat, water, electricity, and housekeeping) required by any investigation.

A grant may seem like a sure cure for ailing research budgets, and often it works well. But even if the supply of research money in this country was not rapidly dwindling, the matter would not always be quite that simple.

A Fly in the Ointment: Technical Difficulties

Few strictly service-oriented agencies have the equipment, facilities, or personnel needed for research. In this highly technological age, the most advanced forms of research can be carried out only in places that are already suitably equipped to design, organize, and conduct them. With regard to the physical requirements, this may mean laboratories, computers, office space, and often some additional expensive and highly specialized pieces of equipment, not all of which can be used for patient care when the research is completed.

Before a grant application is written, the institution should have at least one person on the staff who has the training and expertise to produce a sound research design. Ideally this person should also have a good scientific reputation; he or she should have published several research papers on the topic of interest and be well known and respected by other scientists in the field. Review boards play a large part in deciding who gets money for research. Having professional colleagues on the board helps ensure that the agency's proposal is taken seriously. Many strictly service-oriented institutions, however, do not have a staff member with these qualifications.

Evidence that the investigator can depend on cooperation from other agencies and the community at large is sometimes vital if an agency is to attract research money. An investigator may wish to carry out a study designed to identify potential or actual drug abusers among school children. If the investigator cannot prove to a granting agency that the school system is willing to cooperate, a reviewing board will judge the proposal to be impractical.

These difficulties suggest some of the reasons why grant money seems to go to the same places again and again—places that have deliberately promoted research by finding the money to build up-to-date laboratories, purchase special equipment, hire promising or well-known scientists, and provide support in the form of secretarial, accounting, and other services. Often such places are associated with universities as special institutes, perhaps within schools of medicine. Universities and medical schools are likely to have staff with the needed expertise, and they may already have some of the equipment and facilities needed for conducting research.

Control groups. Unfortunately academicians sometimes have little appreciation of the problems that can arise in treatment institutions. A common example is trained scientists' insistence that the research design must include a nontreated control group if a new form of treatment is to be tested properly.

Responsible professionals in a treatment agency are likely to object to this. The logic of the experimental need for a nontreated control group is not the issue. What if the treatment turns out to be effective? Individuals in the control group who could have benefited from it will have lost an opportunity to do so. Isn't it unethical to deprive a patient of treatment? On the other hand, if the treatment turns out to be ineffective, the hopes of patients will have been built up by their participation as subjects in the research only to be destroyed by failure or even by a worsening of their conditions. Finally, what if the treatment turns out to be actually harmful?

"Waiting-list" controls. One proposed solution to the control-group problem is to use a waiting-list control group rather than a completely untreated one. A waiting-list control group is made up

of subjects, selected at random from among available candidates, whose treatment does not start until after the other subjects' treatment has begun or even finished. A strong argument in favor of this type of research design is that all subjects are eventually treated.

Ethically, however, the point may be made that treatment delayed is still treatment withheld. A hypothetical response to this charge might be that because the facilities of the agency are overcrowded and half the patients cannot be treated immediately anyway, a delay is inevitable. It could be argued in reply that when treatment facilities are limited, care is ethically given first to those who need it most. The logic of research requires random assignment of patients to the waiting list, but random assignment is certain to withhold immediate care from subjects who need it very badly. The investigator may not find it acceptable to follow normal clinical practice, which is to treat the first 20 patients who show up and place the next 20 who appear on the waiting list, because this system does not produce a truly random set of assignments.

Informed consent. A number of solutions to problems of this type have been proposed. The most popular is the application of the principle of *informed consent*, which states that people may be used as subjects in an experiment only if they are fully informed in advance about the risks and possible benefits of the procedures and then willingly consent to participate. This is a good solution in theory, but in practice it can create problems. Despite all assurances some patients, especially those in institutions, feel pressured to consent whether they wish to or not. They may believe (even if they are not told this, and even if it isn't true) that they will receive poorer care if they do not participate. The language of the information given to potential subjects may be so technical and complex that the ordinary person cannot understand it. How would the investigator know if that happened?

Anonymity and confidentiality. The preservation of subjects' anonymity is a related issue that can sometimes raise sticky problems for research planners. In any study in which very personal or even incriminating data are collected, precautions must be taken to prevent subjects' names from being disclosed. Ideally each subject in a research study of this type is given a code identifier and is never again referred to by name. Lists connecting codes to subjects' names are kept in locked file drawers and are accessible only to authorized project staff.

Use of identifier codes ensures confidentiality in most cases. But what if the research concerns a topic like the use of illicit drugs, and a judge decides to subpoena all research records? Recently I spoke to a researcher who said, "That's easy, I wouldn't turn them over. I'd go to jail rather than do that." Let us hope her resolve is never tested. Another researcher said he knew of someone who kept all the code lists for his projects in Canada, where presumably they are less accessible to U.S. authorities. Even if that solution were to guarantee the safekeeping of the lists, it would make for problems if the investigator often needed to refer to them; under the circumstances a generous monetary allowance for travel would be required. When a research problem is deemed to be important enough to society, courts in the United States will sometimes help out by granting immunity to data in studies on sensitive topics. That possibility should be examined before the research is undertaken.

Concealment of lists relating codes to names also causes trouble in any research that requires testing persons more than once. As a rule subjects cannot be depended upon to remember arbitrary or meaningless code identifiers. They would probably remember meaningful identifiers, such as their own social security numbers or telephone numbers, but these are obviously poor choices as codes to ensure anonymity. When codes are arbitrary, each retesting requires breaking the code and exposing subjects' identities to data collectors, thereby destroying anonymity or strict confidentiality or both.

Under the best of conditions, data loss may be high in repeated measure studies, especially those requiring long-term follow-up of subjects. Adding the requirement of anonymity makes the likelihood of loss greater and makes tracking subjects in experimental and control groups more difficult. Good research planning requires consideration of matters of informed consent and of anonymity and confidentiality.

Problems such as these cannot be solved simply. Yet they arise whenever people in a service delivery setting decide, or are requested, to undertake a tightly designed program of scientific research.

Another Fly in the Ointment: Changing Established Procedures

Suppose that all of the problems of a technical, legal, or ethical nature have been resolved. The experts have constructed a satisfactory, if not ideal, research design. The facilities and the research subjects are ready, and the money needed to support the project has come through.

There is still this other fly in the ointment. Trouble may follow if the study threatens to disrupt familiar service delivery routines, if it changes or disturbs accustomed treatment schedules, or if it shows any signs of being an attempt on the part of the administration to "spy" on personnel. Staff members may agree that research is good and that the proposed project is worthwhile. Yet they may still have reservations and a good many searching questions to ask about the study.

Therapists typically place a high value on the time they spend treating patients. After all, that is their job, and they usually feel that the treatment they offer is beneficial to the people who are receiving it. Therapists will therefore want to know how much treatment time will be lost because of the research and to what extent the research will change current practices. They will also want to know what demands will be made upon them for such tasks as collecting data or rating patients. Treatment personnel may feel that they are already overworked, and they may not take kindly to being assigned additional responsibilities. If the research involves a new form of therapy, they may wonder where room is to be found for it in treatment schedules that are already overloaded. They need to be convinced that, whatever its cost in time and trouble, the research is important and worthwhile.

In the face of these questions and possible difficulties, a conscientious investigator is likely to feel frustrated. If research procedures are not agreeable to the therapists and staff and do not fit reasonably comfortably into the usual practices of the agency, the project cannot be completed. Yet if too many changes are made in the research plans to accommodate the wishes of the staff, necessary control in the design might be sacrificed. Worse yet, if pressure is brought to bear on staff to participate in a research study they do not approve of, they may superficially cooperate, but they are likely to provide poor data.

Reading these cautions we might be inclined to conclude that research and treatment cannot be carried out at the same time in a single agency. Exceptions might be made for certain research hospitals and university medical schools, but they may be the exceptions that prove the rule.

Fortunately such pessimism is unwarranted. While it is true that research studies that have been designed to be executed in well-equipped laboratories employing rigidly controlled data collection techniques and highly sophisticated analytical procedures may not fare very well in treatment settings, many types of research can be performed effectively in such settings. Qualitative and quantitative studies can be conducted to serve both descriptive and theoretical purposes.

Case studies. Descriptive case studies could be devised to follow specific patients through the treatment process. These studies could show how the agency carries out treatment and how those who are treated experience the agency. Carefully collected and summarized, good case studies can be shaped into training materials for staff or used as a source of information that may stimulate people to think of ways to improve service delivery. In some instances, case descriptions may even be used to see how well general theories about behavior apply to individuals. They may be used to examine or identify possible causes of patient distress, relapse, or improvement. Such case studies are often publishable (Shontz 1985).

Surveys. If breadth of sampling rather than in-depth detail is needed to answer a research question, a survey can be carried out to learn about patient and staff attitudes, beliefs, or opinions. Survey findings may be of interest not only locally but regionally or even nationally. If surveys are efficiently designed and not overly long and if the number of forms to fill out is limited, surveys can be administered with little disruption of ongoing services and familiar practices.

Predictive studies. Predictive research is nearly always of interest to clinicians or therapists, whether it takes place in large institutions, small clinics, or even private practice. Those who deliver services would like to know in advance which persons who seek care are most and least likely to benefit from it. With experience, nearly every clinician or therapist develops a more or less conscious set of beliefs about which types of clients or patients are likely to gain most from care. Research can test these beliefs and provide a basis for improving their accuracy.

Predictions of outcomes may be useful in ensuring that facilities and personnel are used most effectively. Predictions have many other uses, however. They can aid in assigning persons to the particular type of treatment program that is most likely to benefit them. Furthermore, predictive studies have descriptive value. By correlating descriptive data about clients with later evaluations of treatment outcome, an investigator can learn quite a lot about the client population, the general rate of success of care, and how the agency is functioning.

Like case studies and surveys, predictive research can often be designed so that it does not greatly interfere with normal agency operations. Much of the information that is needed may be collected routinely. The investigator may wish to add a few special measures to the array of available information, but these need not be excessive or time consuming. In the ideal situation, predictive research would demand little more than the collection, organization, and statistical evaluation of data that are already on hand in agency files.

Monitoring. Predictive research has two possible benefits other than improvement of prediction, although they are probably not exploited as often as they should be. A predictive study can be used to monitor ongoing agency operations on a continuous basis. The ideal predictive study would not produce a list of correlation coefficients or cut-off scores and then stop. It would be a regular part of a practitioner's professional activities, a bit like quality-control procedures in industries. Not only would it show changes in outcome rates, but it also would show changes in patient or client characteristics and in what factors predict success.

This information is valuable in itself, but there is a second benefit: predictive research findings can be used to evaluate agency policies and practices and to stimulate people to think about how these might be changed. Suppose an investigator in a vocational rehabilitation agency found that its greatest percentage of successes in job placement was with clients who were young, married males. This information could be "fed back" to the counselors at the agency for their reactions. They might decide that since young, married males seem to need rehabilitation services least, this type of client should be processed more quickly in the future so that counselors could devote more time to helping people who need more careful attention. Of course they could decide something quite different on the basis of the same information. They might feel that to keep the agency's success rates as high as possible, the proportion of young, married men in the client population should be increased and the proportion of less successful clients reduced.

The possibility of disagreement over which course of action is best illustrates a significant point that has been made before: research does not make decisions; people do. In fact, as this example shows, research may stimulate thinking about alternatives that no one has thought about before and thereby cause decision making to become more difficult than it would be otherwise.

An important feature of this way of carrying out research is that the process of investigation never ends. Even as one set of results is being obtained and summarized another is being generated. Data collected during one time period can be compared with data collected during another. Or the entire history of agency operation can be reviewed as a whole. When enough data have been accumulated, *time-series analyses* can perhaps be performed to detect trends over time or to evaluate the effects of changes in institutional policies or practices on later success rates (Shontz 1972).

The Value of Appreciation and Understanding

Although much important research can be carried out in treatment settings, they may not be the best places for testing hypotheses that are of primarily theoretical interest. This does not mean that service-oriented professionals should have no interest in, or appreciation and understanding of, how that type of research is carried out. A broad although not necessarily deep or technical knowledge of the basic principles of research of all kinds can be useful in several ways.

If you are thinking about carrying out research, it can save you a lot of grief. Much time, expense, work, and worry have been spent trying to set up and carry out research projects that are simply not feasible. Many investigators who have conducted research in academic environments know very little about the possibilities and limitations of service-delivery settings as places to perform research. Perhaps some investigators of this type will read books such as this and gain a clearer overview of the whole situation. Whether they do or not, however, people in service-delivery settings should certainly gain such a perspective.

Without some general knowledge, a person in a service setting can be bluffed, if not intimidated, by someone who comes around talking about multiple regression, factor analysis, quasi-experiments, mixed-model designs, and degrees of freedom. This book should help dispel the mystique that surrounds them. Well-informed professionals can judge for themselves what studies and procedures are feasible in their own service-delivery settings.

Even those who never plan to make their livings using the principles of research design and statistics will find that knowing something about them is advantageous. Such knowledge enables a person to read the scientific literature more intelligently. Too many readers are at the mercy of the research report authors when it comes to evaluating the importance or even the meaning of a particular investigation. They read the introduction and the conclusion and ignore the rest because they cannot understand it.

The Place of Criticism

Research is crucial to science, but criticism is equally so. An investigator may dream of collecting data, interpreting results, and writing reports so effectively that everyone who reads them is convinced that the investigator is right. But if there were no challengers, science would soon grind to a halt.

A scientist reading a research report is more or less consciously trying to tear the research apart. He or she looks for flaws in the design, procedure, data analysis, or interpretation. Sometimes this is done in a hostile way, as if the point were to demolish the opposition. Ideally, however, the intention is constructive. The primary purpose of criticism is to ensure that false conclusions are recognized as such and that research continues to improve. If an investigation is criticized because it lacks certain necessary controls, the study should be repeated with those controls. Intelligent and constructive criticism requires almost as much knowledge and skill as research itself.

Research is valuable. It is essential to the development of new knowledge and the testing of old knowledge. But it is not sacred; it is a human activity (Kneller 1978). No research is above criticism, and no knowledge is absolute (Kuhn 1970; Polanyi 1962). Research is a tool, an instrument that may be used well or poorly. Whether or not they carry out research, all professionals in the behavior or health sciences should be prepared to understand and appreciate the special problems and skills of those who do.

READING AND WRITING RESEARCH REPORTS

Communication in Science

Governments (especially their military services) and industries that sponsor or conduct research sometimes choose to keep the results confidential. Research findings may be kept from other scientists or from the public because they contain information that gives their owner an advantage over rivals, enemies, or competitors. If a research study is interpreted to forecast a dangerous situation, it may be considered too anxiety provoking to be revealed to the public. The outcome of a research project might have such dangerous or revolutionary significance that its discoverer prefers, or is compelled, to keep it under wraps.

Most of the research and development for the purpose of creating the first atomic bomb was carried out in secret. Many project workers did not know the purposes of the research they were doing or how their work related to the work of others. Half a century later, governments with conflicting political and economic systems continue to discourage or prevent scientists from communicating some types of information across political boundaries.

Many scientists resent restrictive policies that are based on political or economic value judgments. They argue that knowledge is separate from values and that science can be effective only in a society that permits, even encourages, the open exchange of ideas and research results.

Clearly, people can benefit from research only if they are aware of its findings. Data filed away in drawers or computer memory banks are of no use to anyone—nor are they open to criticism—unless they are written up and published. Communication is therefore as essential a part of research as advance planning, careful collection of data, and analyses of results.

The two fundamental and closely related requirements for communication are *condensation* and *organization* of information. Especially in these days, when information is accumulating at an ever more rapid pace, effective condensation is critical. People do not have time to read long, elaborate descriptions of procedures and outcomes of scientific research. They look for brief summaries and are frequently more concerned with the bottom line, the practical significance of a set of findings, than with information about how the results were obtained. The tendency to concentrate on outcomes and ignore procedures may do no harm, as long as the reader is willing to trust that the investigator has done everything right and to follow the investigator's recommendations without question. But skepticism, not uncritical acceptance, is the traditional spirit of science, and skepticism requires that every research study be open in its entirety to inspection.

No one expects an investigator to describe in a published report every detail of every step taken and every bit of data that was collected. The ideal report contains the maximum possible amount of the most necessary information in the least possible space. To help a person who is writing a report decide what information should be included, a fairly standard outline has been devised. It provides a formal structure that helps the writer select and organize material for presentation. The use of conventions in report writing also helps readers know what to expect and where to look in a report for various types of information. If the outline is followed, the contents of the report are carefully chosen, and the text is clearly written, the reader will gain a picture of the entire project from start to finish. Learning how a scientific report is put together is therefore important not only to those who actually plan to write such reports but also to those whose primary contact with the research literature will be as concerned readers.

The task of communication does not end with publication of a written summary report. The investigator is expected to keep complete details of the project on file and to make them available upon request. The purpose of this is not only to make criticism by others easier but also to help those who wish to carry out similar research compare methods and learn details of techniques. It also makes the data available for supplementary analyses, a practice that can be especially important in survey research, where investigators may collect far more data than they need to answer a specific question. Often these data can be valuable to investigators pursuing answers to other research questions. For example, an investigator who collects data about drug use in a certain population may also collect information about dietary habits, illnesses, recreational activities, criminal records, and work and family history. Much of this information may not be used in the data analysis for the original project but would nonetheless be of value to investigators who are studying aspects of human behavior other than drug use.

The Research Report

Title

The title of a research report, like one's personal appearance, is the first thing, and sometimes the only thing, a potential reader encounters. The title creates an immediate impression, which can be very helpful if the impression is accurate and very difficult to overcome if it is wrong. Like all scientific writing, the ideal title is short yet accurate and informative.

Titles of scientific reports should not be journalistic. A report on a survey of the schools in the United States, issued in 1983, was called *A Nation at Risk*. This title is catchy, but it is unacceptable as scientific communication. The scientific report of an experimental test of a therapeutic agent for schizophrenia should not be entitled "Has Science Found the Cure for Mental Illness?"—even if the test was successful. That sort of title belongs to the tabloids, and no editor of a respectable scientific journal would accept it.

Neither should titles be too long. To describe in a journal that publishes only experimental reports an experimental study of the effects of a drug on a certain pathological condition, it is probably sufficient to write "The effects of treatment X on condition Y." Any title that begins with "An experimental investigation of" can immediately be cut by four words.

Readers of research reports should be aware that a catchy or important-sounding title is no guarantee of scientific merit. It may, indeed, be a cover-up for the poor quality of the research. Readers should realize also that titles do not always accurately reflect the contents of reports.

Inaccuracies or misrepresentations in report titles may become increasingly troublesome as searches of the scientific literature are more frequently conducted via computer. Electronic searches of computerized bibliographic databases frequently operate on the basis of titles or key words. A reader trying to track down the literature on a specific topic could overlook relevant and important studies while wasting valuable time searching for copies of inappropriate articles that have been misleadingly titled. Clearly, if a scientist wants to be sure to gain proper recognition, it is in his or her own best interest to devise the best possible titles for all communications.

Author Identification

With a few exceptions, authors do not publish anonymously in science. Sometimes research results "stand on their own" so well that it makes no difference who obtained them, but this is rarely the case, especially in the social, behavioral, and health sciences. For several reasons, a reader needs to know who takes responsibility for an investigation and where that person can be found. The main one, communication and correspondence, has already been mentioned. In addition, investigators and institutions gain reputations not only for the type of research they conduct and support but also for the general quality of their work; knowing the author's credentials assists the reader in evaluating the report. A reader has a right to be skeptical about a paper on the theory of social work that was written by a professor of physics at MIT, even if the professor has an excellent reputation in the study of subatomic particles.

Of course names and reputations can be misleading. An apparently appropriate paper by an apparently well qualified person at a well-known institution can be of poor quality. The point is not that the merit of a research report should be judged entirely by the background or reputation of its author, but only that the author's name and address often communicate important information and should be examined.

An investigator bears personal responsibility for reports that appear under his or her name. This makes possible one of the most important forms of peer influence and control that science exerts over those who carry out research. If an investigator is found, just once, to have used false data or to have deliberately misrepresented research outcomes, his or her entire research output may be called into question and reputation and career ruined. An investigator in the field of parapsychology was found by members of his own research team to be tampering with equipment and altering results. Editorials in the *Journal of Parapsychology* (Rhine 1974, 1975) reported the incidents and announced that all work that appeared under this scientist's name was suspect and should henceforth be ignored.

Abstract

Many journals require authors to submit a brief summary, or *abstract*, of their reports. This summary is usually expected to be approximately 150 words in length (about half of a double-spaced typed page) or less, and in journals it is usually printed just below the title of the article and the identification of the author. Abstracts help readers decide very quickly whether reading the entire article seems worthwhile. Abstracts are also collected by some organizations for storage in data banks, where they may later be called up in computer assisted searches of the scientific literature.

Many researchers find it difficult to write a good abstract. In fact, there is probably no better self-test of one's understanding of the essential information in a scientific report than to try to write an abstract of it. A properly constructed abstract contains all of the most important information that is elaborated upon in the balance of the report. The abstract omits details that are not absolutely essential, and it adds nothing to the content of the report itself.

Introduction

The body of nearly every research report begins with an introduction, although it is often not labeled as such. The introduction consists primarily of a brief historical review of work that has already been done on the research problem. The unspoken reason for this is that most scientists think of science as progressive, as a continuously growing fund of information in which every new research study builds upon what is already known. Therefore the introduction to the research report is expected to lay the foundation for what follows.

The historical review often has a critical tone. It identifies knowledge that is taken for granted to be valid as well as areas of uncertainty and doubt. It points out weaknesses in the work of others and argues that certain types of studies are needed to settle those issues or to advance knowledge by another step or two. In this way the introduction also defines the current research problem and usually contains a *statement of purpose* that lists the specific goals of the project.

The elements of an introduction may appear in any order. An investigator may try to gain the readers' attention by stating the purpose of the project in the first sentence. This can be helpful because readers can sometimes follow the argument of a historical review more easily if the text at the outset gives at least a hint of why the research was conducted, a function also served in part by the abstract. If the purpose of the research is to test specific propositions, these may appear in a list at the end of the introduction, frequently along with the statement of purpose. Indeed a report will sometimes state, "The purpose of this research was to test the theory that. . . ."

Method

The use of terms varies, and some investigators speak of *methods of procedure*, or use the terms *method* and *procedure* interchangeably. This usage is most likely to be seen in reports of research in the physical sciences. In sciences that use animals or persons as subjects, the term *method* is commonly applied in a more general way and may include as many as four categories of information— subjects, apparatus, measures, and procedures—with subdivisions created within each as needed.

Experimental studies of animals or persons are likely to call the organisms they examine *subjects*. Survey research is likely to refer to the subjects who respond to questionnaires collectively as a *sample*. Sometimes these terms are combined; for example, a group may be called a *sample of subjects*.

In the methods section of a research report, look for a description of the pertinent characteristics of the organisms that were examined, including the number of each type that was tested. If several groups are used (two treatment groups and a control group, for instance), look for evidence that the groups were matched, or at least equivalent, on factors that might influence the outcome.

Descriptions of samples or subjects often suggest something about the *generalizability* of results to other groups or other types of subjects. They may also give some indication of the sensitivity of the research as a whole. For example, a university professor may study college students' reactions to false information that they have just failed a test that predicts how well they will do in their chosen careers. (Incidentally, no test can do this, but college students who serve as subjects in experiments apparently don't know that.) The published report of this study may suggest that the findings can be generalized to reactions of all kinds of persons to all kinds of stressful situations. Until those generalizations have actually been tested, however, a wise reader will be cautious. One who carefully examines the subjects section of the research report will be skeptical, even if the author of the report is not.

A description of apparatus is necessary whenever special equipment is used. The term *apparatus* includes such technical equipment as timers, computers, recorders, meters, and automated stimulus-presenting machines. In a study of a psychoactive substance, it would also include a description of that substance and any other substances, such as placebos, that are used in the research.

In much psychological research and in most survey research, the main apparatus consists of tests or questionnaires. In reports of this type of research, the section that is usually called apparatus may be labeled instead *measurements* or *instruments*. If the tests or questionnaires are standard and have been described in detail by others, relatively little need be said about them, although references to reports containing fuller descriptions will usually be cited. If an instrument is newly devised, the report may contain information about its content, construction, reliability, validity, and correlation with other tests.

This section of the report should only describe instruments, apparatus, or tests; it should not go into detail about how the materials were developed or actually used in the research. This principle may be hard to follow in practice. Sometimes—especially in survey research—the research project itself includes a test development phase. To make the research more efficient, data collected during this phase may be used not only to check out the instrument but also to test theories as well. The investigator might then write one research report to describe the instrument-development phase and another to describe the theory-testing phase. Often, however, both are combined into a single article, and such reports can be quite lengthy and difficult to follow.

In some experimental research, the subsection called *procedure* may be the most important part of the report. If the investigator used a customary type of subject (for example, white rats) in a standard type of apparatus (a so-called Skinner box), readers who are familiar with the approach used may skip over these details very quickly. They are most interested in finding out what the experimenter did to the subjects to affect their responses. A research study may test the rates of response (lever presses) of white rats in a Skinner box as related to dosage level of a drug, such as methamphetamine. The subjects and apparatus in this familiar, almost conventional, laboratory setup need not be described in detail to others who carry out similar research. What they will want to know is how, at what physiological sites, and in what dosages the substance was administered and whether any other special manipulations of conditions were involved, such as varying the levels of food deprivation in different groups of animals or varying the amount of time that passed between drug administration and performance testing. These are matters of procedure, and they lie at the heart of most classical experimental investigations.

In reports of survey research, the subsection called *procedure* may have a different tone and cover quite different matters. It might describe how questionnaires were administered: to groups, on an individual-by-individual basis, face to face, or by telephone. If data collection was by mailed questionnaire, this section of the report might describe the follow-up procedures that were used to contact nonresponders in order to obtain the highest possible rate of return.

Ordinarily, descriptions of samples or subject selection are not presented under the heading of *procedures*. Under certain circumstances, however, information about subjects may appear here. In some types of research, subjects are pretested for certain physical or psychological characteristics. For example, they might be pretested to determine whether they are enrolled in one or another type of health care program, whether they regard themselves as Republicans or Democrats, whether they participate in certain types of recreational or vocational activities, whether they have ever had a certain disease, or whether they have graduated from college. The subjects would then be divided into groups according to the results of the pretests. The researcher probably expects that the various groups will respond differently to experimental manipulation.

For instance, subjects with a history of regular consumption of alcohol may be expected to react differently to consuming a certain quantity of the substance than will subjects who have a history of little alcohol consumption. In a research study in which people are divided into groups on this basis, the investigator might feel that the assignment of subjects to groups is part of the experimental procedure. The way it was done would then be described in the procedures section rather than in the section on samples or subjects.

Another type of information that is sometimes found in the procedures section is a description of the types of analyses applied to the data. In field or survey research, the report may include a description of data preparation, coding, or factor analyses of scores on many tests. It may also include a description, or at least a listing, of the types of computer programs used and the choices that the investigator made about the various options these programs offered. This takes a little more explaining.

One use for a computer in the analysis of research data is to provide a series of weighted scores on several independent variables that will best predict a specific criterion. Unless told to do otherwise, the computer program may supply weights for all possible predictors, even the ones that are not statistically significant or that, in statisticians' language, account for only a small proportion of the variance in the dependent variable. The computer operator may insert into the program some decision values that say, in effect, "do not insert a weighting value for scores on a variable that accounts for less than X percent of the variance in the criterion or does not account for a proportion that is significant at probability level *alpha*." The reader of a research report needs to know what the values of X and *alpha* are, and they will probably be found in a description of the research procedures.

Results

Results should be the payoff, the bottom line, the climax of the research report. In this section the investigator summarizes the data, often using tables and graphs, and describes the outcomes of the various analytical procedures that were applied to the data. In an experiment that tests specific hypotheses, the results are often presented in the order in which hypotheses were tested.

To be strict about it, this section should only describe results and not draw conclusions—another rule that may be very hard to follow in some instances. The results section of the report usually contains statements to the effect that the results favor or support rejection of the null hypothesis at a certain level of confidence. However, the results section should not contain statements that the investigator's theory—the proposed alternative to the null hypothesis—has or has not been confirmed. That decision can be expressed only after other possibilities have been considered, in the next section of the report.

The results of more purely descriptive research may be difficult to condense unless they can be organized around a set of specific

questions. Sometimes when a research study involves very complicated data arrays, such as correlation matrices, the best an investigator can do is summarize the general features of the data and
state in a footnote where interested readers may obtain a copy of
the full set of correlations. It is nearly always understood that an
interested reader has the right to contact the investigator and obtain
a copy of the raw data on which the tables and figures were based.
(A small fee is sometimes charged for copying and mailing.)

Graphic presentations of data. This section of the chapter examines briefly some of the types of graphs that are frequently used
to present data in condensed form in the results section of a research
report. Although a number of clever ways have been devised for
graphing data (Wainer and Thissen 1981), special attention is paid
here to the most familiar types of graphs: scattergrams, line graphs,
and bar graphs.

Most graphs in scientific reports are used to illustrate relationships between two or more variables. Usually these graphs have
two dimensions. The one represented by a vertical line is called the
ordinate (or, informally, the Y axis). The one represented by a horizontal line is called the *abscissa* (the X axis). When a vertical and
a horizontal line cross, they produce four areas, or *quadrants*: upper
right, lower right, upper left, and lower left. Some graphs show all
four of these quadrants, but the graphs that are probably most familiar show only the upper right quadrant. The place where the two
lines come together, their *intersection*, is usually called 0. Convenient scale values or labels are placed along the ordinate and abscissa.

In nearly all such graphs, the values on the ordinate represent a
continuous variable, such as weight, height, or probability, or a
variable that is treated as if it were continuous, such as frequency
of occurrence of some event or score.

The abscissa may also represent a continuous variable, or it may
represent *discontinuous* or *categorical* data, such as male or female;
normal, neurotic, or psychotic; Treatment Group I or Treatment
Group II; or Ward 3A, Ward 3B, or Ward 3C. When both variables
are continuous, the curve that is drawn to represent the relationship
between them is nearly always a continuous line.

Simple line graphs. Figure 3.1 shows a simple line graph in
which measures of a psychological trait, such as scores on an aptitude test, are related to final grades earned in a training course.

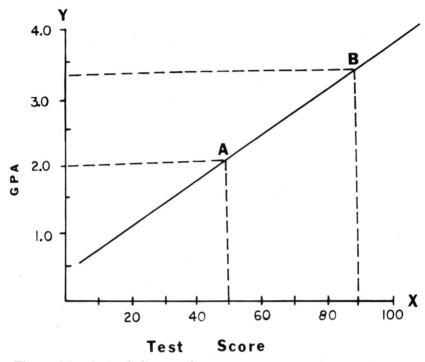

Figure 3.1. A simple line graph.

The data are hypothetical. The X axis might be students' scores on an entrance examination in engineering school, and the Y axis might be their final grade-point averages (GPA) on graduation. Figure 3.1 shows a straight line (continuous) relationship in which higher scores on the aptitude test are associated with higher grade-point averages. Drawing a straight line up from the abscissa and a straight line over to the ordinate shows that person A, with an aptitude test score of 50, is expected to have a grade point average of about 2.0 (a C average). Person B, with an aptitude test score of 90, should have a GPA above 3.0 (better than B).

The graph seems to say that final grade-point averages can be predicted perfectly (without error) from aptitude test scores in every case. Wouldn't it be nice if that were true? But of course it is not. No test is that good. The graph may show an ideal relationship or an average relationship between aptitude and grade-point average, but it cannot represent the actual relationships on a subject-by-subject basis.

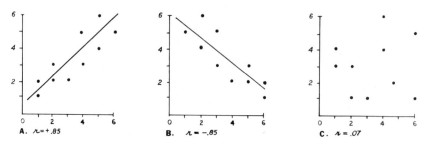

Figure 3.2.   Scattergrams of 10 pairs of scores.

Scattergrams. A more complete way to picture the data that enter into such correlations is to use a *scattergram* (Figure 3.2). A scattergram visually displays the data that are used in computing a *Pearson product-moment correlation coefficient*, otherwise simply known as *r*. The basic data in a scattergram (the points indicated by the circles on the graph) are *discrete*, or discontinuous. In behavior research, each point can usually be thought of as representing a person. The location of the point is found by plotting a pair of scores for the same individual, one score on a test that is represented by the *X* axis, the other on a test that is represented by the *Y* axis.

When both scores in a pair are low, the point falls near the *X* and *Y* values 0,0: the intersection of the ordinate and the abscissa. When both are high, the point falls high and far to the right. A scattergram that is made up of points like these, along with some points in the middle of the graph, shows a *positive* correlation, in which *r* is close to +1.00 (Figure 3.2a).

If the *X* score is low and the *Y* score is high, the point falls high and to the left. If the *X* score is high and the *Y* score is low, the point falls low and to the right. A scattergram which is made up of points like these, along with some points in the middle of the graph, shows a negative correlation, in which *r* is close to −1.00 (Figure 3.2b).

A scattergram containing a mixture of all four types, along with points in the middle of the graph (Figure 3.2c), shows no correlation (*r* = zero, or close to it). As a general rule, the more widely scattered the points, the closer the value of *r* will be to zero. The more the points tend to converge around a diagonal straight line, the closer the value of *r* will be to ±1.00.

Figures 3.2a and 3.2b contain two continuous straight lines. These lines are not drawn directly from the data but are arrived at by applying certain mathematical procedures to the data. They are called *regression lines*, and they represent a kind of complicated average of all the points in the scattergram. The line that represents the regression of Y on X shows the best guess one can make of an individual's score on Y, knowing that individual's score on X. Figure 3.2c contains no regression line because the relationship between X and Y is practically random, so prediction is impossible. Techniques for calculating r and plotting regression lines will be taken up later.

Bar graphs. When the factor represented on the abscissa is discontinuous or categorical, special graphing techniques are required. Strictly speaking, in that case the abscissa itself should probably not be a continuous straight line, but should be broken into parts, one for each category. That is not usually done, however. A continuous straight line is drawn, but it is divided into sections. The same practice is followed when the variable on the ordinate is discontinuous.

The most familiar way of representing the number of cases in each section of the abscissa is with a vertical rectangle that rises to an appropriate height, as indicated by the index values of the ordinate. This type of figure is called a *bar graph*.

Figure 3.3a is a bar graph showing the expected frequencies of occurrence of various combinations of heads and tails in 160 fair throws of five coins. It is drawn as a bar graph, rather than a continuous curve or a single line, because the categories on the X axis are discrete. There is no possible way to throw 4.5 heads and .5 tails, for instance.

The graph could be made to look continuous by finding the center point of the top of each bar, erasing all the bars, and then connecting the center points. But the continuous graph would not convey the discreteness of these categories and is therefore not preferred.

Another way to handle the graph would be to draw six vertical lines, one through the center of each rectangle, again erasing the rectangles themselves (Figure 3.3b). Although this type of graph is acceptable, it is used less frequently than the bar graph.

Notice that in Figure 3.3a the bars are right up against each other. Each shares a boundary with the one on either side of it. That suggests to the viewer that some sort of quantitative connection exists between categories that are next to each other. The number of heads in each combination decreases from left to right, while the number of tails increases from left to right.

If the categories differ only qualitatively, the bars should probably be separated from each other. For example, a graph showing the

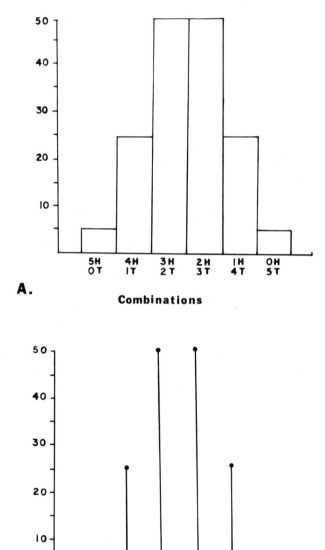

Figure 3.3. Two ways of showing expected frequencies of combinations of heads and tails in 160 throws of five coins each.

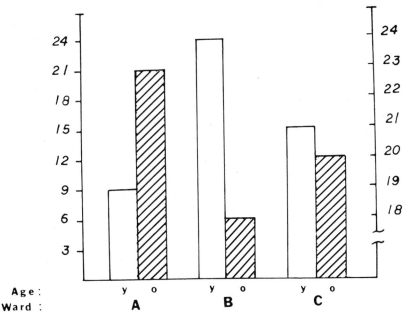

Figure 3.4. Hypothetical comparison of admission rates of older and younger patients to three wards.

number of admissions to three wards of a hospital might look like Figure 3.4. In this graph, admissions are broken down further into two subcategories, depending on ages. Each ward is represented by two bars. One shows the count of admissions of older patients; the other shows the count of admissions of younger patients. These bars are connected, but the bars representing the various wards are not. Crosshatching distinguishes the bars representing the number of older patients to make it easier to compare age groups from ward to ward.

According to the admissions indexes, shown on the Y axis at the left of the graph, Ward A seems to be getting most of the older patients while Ward B is getting the younger ones. Ward A admits 15 more older patients than Ward B and 15 fewer younger patients than Ward B. Meanwhile, Ward C admits a fairly even mix of old and young patients.

But graphs are like numbers: they don't care what you do to them, and they can be manipulated. Look at the second ordinate, on the right, with a different set of numbers on it. Those two little squiggles with the space between them at the bottom are not easily noticed, but they are extremely important. They mean that the ordinate has been deliberately broken. The intervals along it are not equal. In fact, the values from zero to 17 have been eliminated. If we now interpret the graph according to this ordinate instead of the one on the left, Ward A receives only five more older patients and five fewer younger patients than Ward B. Out of a total of 42 admissions to each ward (19 + 23 for Ward A; 24 + 18 for Ward B), these differences are not great compared to those measured by the left-hand ordinate. Yet the impression that is conveyed by strictly graphic means has not changed.

The deception works because people tend to respond only to the pictorial part of graphs. They often ignore, or pass over very quickly, the technicalities implied by the scales on the ordinate or abscissa, and they will seldom read the notes that may accompany graphic presentations.

Bar graphs can also be used to display proportions or percentages. To show how an agency's resources are used, for example, the ordinate can be made to represent the percentage of overall budget. Various bars can then be drawn to show what percentage is allocated to or has been spent in each budget category.

Pie charts. A common device for accomplishing the same purpose is the so-called *pie chart*, a circle that has been divided into wedge-shaped segments. In a circle that represents 100 percent of an agency's budget, the area of each segment is proportional to the percentage of resources devoted to an individual program administered by the agency. Pie charts are not usually used in highly technical reports, although they sometimes appear in reports of descriptive surveys, and they are prominent in the popular press. One problem with them is that it is even easier to create a false impression with a pie chart than with a bar graph.

Suppose at an annual meeting the administrator of an agency with a total budget of $20 million displays a pie chart indicating that only 1 percent of the pie is allocated to his salary (the tiny protruding slice that measures 3.6 degrees of the circle in Figure 3.5), while the rest of the budget (356.4 degrees) goes to other expenses. From the pie chart it appears that the director is being paid very little, and most people will not take the trouble to figure out that the actual salary of $200,000 does not represent quite the personal sacrifice it seems to at first glance. As one of my professors once said, figures don't lie, but liars can draw figures.

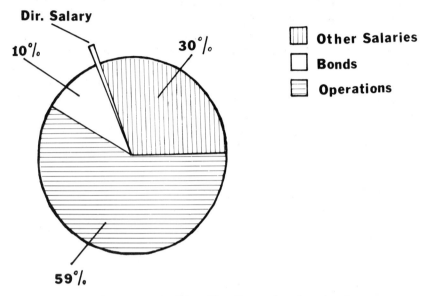

Figure 3.5. A deceptive pie-chart. The director's salary has been extended beyond the circumference.

Discussion and Conclusions

Following the account of results, the *discussion* or *discussion and conclusions* section states whether hypotheses were confirmed or, in a purely descriptive study, summarizes the findings. Typically the discussion also relates the current findings to those of other investigators, noting consistencies and inconsistencies. When inconsistencies are apparent, differences among studies in subjects, instruments, or procedures are examined as possible ways of explaining them.

This section of the report usually spells out the theoretical and practical implications of the research findings. Recommendations for additional research are almost always included here as a way of completing the process that begins in the report's introduction. The introduction anchors the research in the past; this portion of the discussion section thrusts it into the future.

The discussion section is a particularly important part of the report. It is the investigator's forum for convincing readers that the study should be taken seriously. It is also one of the only sections that some readers will see. Those who are less interested in what was done or how it was done than in "what the study means" are likely to go immediately to this section after reading the abstract.

Only the serious critic—a graduate student who is writing a paper or another investigator actively conducting research on the same topic—is likely to read the report in great detail. This is unfortunate because, especially in the social and behavioral sciences, investigators are sometimes inclined to overstate their cases when discussing results. As indicated earlier, it is always appropriate to be skeptical in science. Nowhere is skepticism more in order than in evaluating an investigator's conclusions and recommendations.

References

The last section of a report is usually a detailed list of the sources of all statements or conclusions that have been made by others. Usually these are published articles or books, although some references may be made to talks at conferences or personal communications, such as letters or even informal conversations. All citations must be accurate because many readers rely upon reference lists to direct them to additional information on the research subject.

In the past, reference lists tended to be quite long and thorough, attesting to the completeness of the investigator's knowledge of the field. Today, however, very long reference lists are usually found only in masters' theses, doctoral dissertations, and articles written to summarize the literature rather than to report on the results of an individual investigation. The modern author of a research report is usually expected to cite only the most important sources, not more that 10 or 12, if possible.

Deciding which sources are most important can be a tricky business. Despite their claim to being completely objective and rational, scientists are human beings with human pride, and none like to feel that their work has been ignored. A reader who has carried out research on a particular topic and is examining a published report of another research study on the same topic may turn to the reference list right away to see whether his or her own work has received appropriate recognition. Failure of an author to refer to work that others regard as important can prejudice a journal editor or reviewer against an article. The investigator who writes research reports on a popular topic and cites only six or eight references is therefore bound to offend someone. Such an investigator should keep in mind Oscar Wilde's (or somebody's) warning that one cannot be too careful when choosing one's enemies.

—4—

QUALITATIVE AND QUANTITATIVE ASPECTS OF RESEARCH

Qualitative Data

Research data come in two general forms: qualitative and quantitative. Qualitative data commonly consist of words, that is, of descriptive statements or text, although drawings, photographs, charts, and objects (for example, potsherds) may also be considered qualitative data. They are most useful when the research subject matter is structural rather than dimensional, as when an investigation deals with forms or patterns instead of quantities or amounts. Qualitative information tells what something is like, rather than how much of it there is.

A painting, a piece of music, a civilization, an industrial organization, or a family system cannot easily be described by a single numerical indicator. Even finely worked descriptive texts fall short of the mark in many cases, although they may be far superior to numbers in describing patterns or forms. If words are chosen carefully enough, some characteristics of a human relationship, emotion, or other complicated experience, object, or structure can be described well enough to suit many research purposes. But even when a verbal description is thorough and thoughtful, the reader or listener often feels that something essential has not been fully communicated. The best way to describe a painting is, after all, to show it to someone, not to present a list of numbers or write an essay about it. The best way to understand a feeling is to feel it.

A description is considered *formal* if it follows a set of agreed upon rules. Scientific reports, described in Chapter 3, are formal descriptions of research projects. Other examples of formal descriptions of qualitative topics are orchestral scores, scripts of plays or television shows, computer programs, architectural drawings, and maps. Flow charts showing networks of authority in hospitals or in industrial, governmental, or educational organizations are also good examples of descriptive information. Other types of qualitative information that may be valuable as research data are diagnoses, personality descriptions, and interview transcripts.

Some researchers seem to feel that qualitative data are somewhat less valuable, precise, or "scientific" than numbers, although few would say that qualitative investigations are worthless. If research were restricted to the study of things that can be quantified, scientific knowledge would be limited indeed. Many topics of considerable importance can be approached only qualitatively; some examples are human and animal societies, institutional forms and organizations, history, personality structures, and even physical phenomena such as anatomy and geological, geographical, and astronomical formations. Additional topics of interest are less obvious, such as quality of life, job satisfaction, and the effectiveness of a treatment program with multiple or complex goals that differ from patient to patient.

Identifying Types

Qualitative research attempts to describe meanings and processes; draw "maps"; and identify types, classes, and genres. Some of the greatest thinking in science has been in terms of types. The concept of disease is a typology, implying as it does recognizable qualitative similarities and differences among clinical entities. Biological schemes for classifying plants and animals are typologies. Everyday descriptions of people as introverts or extroverts, leaders or followers, friends or enemies, Republicans or Democrats, Christians or Moslems are typologies, although they are often rather informal, inconsistent, and unreliable. Everyone knows that there are two types of people: those who divide people into two types and those who do not.

With a little thought, everyone also realizes that while the members of a single type, class, or genre are similar in some ways, they are different from members of other types, classes, or genres. Qualitative research is often directed toward, and is better at, identifying and describing similarities among members of the same type or class. Quantitative statistical analysis is more typically used to test for, and specify differences between, groups or classes.

For example, when Spotts and Shontz (1984c, 1984d) described qualitatively the subjective states produced by barbiturates and cocaine, each description was published as a separate research report. The reports did not contain any statistical analyses comparing one group with the other. Their purpose was to describe each state by itself, not to contrast the two or say how they differed on specific variables. However, when Spotts and Shontz (1983) wished to demonstrate that users of one substance are psychologically different from users of other substances, they drew graphs, computed means and standard deviations, and performed analyses of variance and other conventional statistical operations to show the differences and support their conclusions.

Qualitative Data and Research Variables

Particular components of a complicated system, like a treatment program or its outcomes, can sometimes be treated as variables; that is, they can be separated for quantitative study in isolation. In fact, this is done very often. For example, an investigator may invent a single, simple numerical measure of treatment success that can then be used to evaluate overall program effectiveness.

Although this practice makes data analysis more convenient, it disregards the effects that other aspects of patients' lives may have on their treatment and vice versa. A physical therapist may be pleased to learn from a research study that a new schedule of exercises or piece of equipment quickly increases most patients' ambulation skills. What the study probably does not take into account, however, is that the therapist's patients may not have any place they care to ambulate to once they have learned how. A vocational training program may effectively improve clients' average job skills, but research that evaluates the program may fail to consider whether the clients are motivated to be employed, whether they know how to look for a job and will do so, and what jobs will be available when they have completed the program.

Of course, such factors are nearly always considered when a particular therapist or counselor works with an individual patient or client. But that is exactly the point. Quantitative research, of the sort that is usually undertaken in service-delivery systems, typically gives up the clinically essential appreciation of the qualitative complexity of individual cases to gain the apparent purity, precision, and objectivity of quantitative measurement. Even highly technical multivariate techniques of statistical analyses cannot substitute for qualitative description. As the name implies, *multivariate techniques* handle many variables in a single analysis and may therefore seem to offer a means for handling complexity. Nevertheless, this type of analysis does not take the qualitative features of the individual human being into account. Like most popular statistical tools, it requires that data be collected from large population samples so that averages can be calculated and differences among individuals smoothed over. Except in very special types of research on individuals, the complexity of multivariate methods is not the complexity of a person or other organism but the complexity of relationships among several *variables* in mathematical equations that describe groups or classes as wholes.

Once again, remember that variables are ideas in the minds of scientists: thoughts, not things; abstractions, not objects. Investigators define variables as dimensions so that numbers can be used to describe them. In behavior and health sciences, variables are not persons, just as persons are not variables. To say that an individual's body temperature is 103 degrees Fahrenheit does not describe that person but one aspect of that person. Moreover, a body temperature of 103 degrees Fahrenheit has quite a different meaning in a child of two than in an adult of 40. Research on factors that affect body temperature is therefore not a research on people but on a set of variables. That principle applies whether the research includes only one variable (univariate research) or, say, 30 variables (multivariate research).

Converting Qualitative to Quantitative Data

Most mathematical statistical operations that lead to decision making cannot be performed directly upon qualitative data. An intermediate step is usually necessary. As might be supposed from what has already been said about quantification, this step typically consists of defining one or more variables that are expected to be useful and setting up dimensions along which they can be measured.

The dimensions need not be complicated or finely differentiated. They may be as simple as two numbers: 0 if a specific trait is absent, 1 if it is present. For example, a child's drawing gets a score of 1 if the arms of the drawn figure are attached in the correct place at the shoulders. Other points are added if hands, fingers, and other predetermined features are shown, and so forth. The result is a very satisfactory scale for measuring the intelligence and cognitive maturity of children (Harris 1963).

Coding

This approach is commonly used in dealing with interview material, which is often extremely complex in content and not open to statistical analysis until it has been translated into numbers. In psychosocial research the procedure is usually called *coding*. Typically, coding first requires establishing some type of scheme for breaking interview information down into classes. The scheme may come from a theory that tells the investigator what to look for, such as references to parents, expressions of anger, and reports of antisocial activities.

Alternatively the scheme may come from the material itself. The investigator may examine the material for suggestions about how the statements it contains might be classified. A classification plan or coding scheme is then set up, and statements are assigned to categories within it. Coding operations are usually checked for *interjudge*, or *inter-rater*, *reliability* by presenting a coding manual to several other persons and having them code the data independently. Ideally these judges should have no knowledge of the purpose of the research, or at least have no interest in its outcome.

A high level of reliability is taken as evidence that the coding procedure is objective. The assumption is that if the classes are "real" (somewhat in the way physical objects such as rocks and trees are real), then different raters can use the coding scheme and come up with the same—or very similar—results. Using a reliable process of coding may be likened to having several raters count the number of people in an audience or the number of chairs in a room. The procedure is considered objective because it assumes that only one set of codings is correct and that every competent judge should be able to come up with the same results.

This technique is used in many psychological tests, including the well-known Rorschach inkblot technique. Like many other psychological tests, the Rorschach technique is essentially a carefully structured and highly formalized interview. The person being examined reports what each of the standard 10 blots looks like and then is asked certain questions about his or her responses.

This information is carefully recorded and coded according to one of several available schemes. Each response is coded according to whether it uses the whole blot, a usual part of it, or an unusual part of it. The response (or *percept*) is also coded according to whether the subject says it was influenced by the shape, color, or shading of the blot and whether the perceived object was seen to be in motion. Coding is available for type of content (human, animal, clothing, clouds, for example), and the response is rated for whether the content is commonly seen, how well it fits the actual shape of the blot, and how tightly organized it is. These codes are often called *scores*, and clinicians may talk about scoring a Rorschach even though the use of the term is not exactly correct.

When coding has been completed, the clinician counts the frequencies of different types of locations, determinants, and contents. Then a number of ratios and percentages are calculated, each of which is regarded as being interpretively important. For example, an active fantasy life is suggested if the person reports seeing a large number of human beings doing energetic things.

Counting

As suggested by the preceding discussion, the basic operation for converting qualitative data to quantitative data is simply counting. Suppose a ward supervisor believes that patients of a certain ethnic group (hypothetically, southern Europeans) are more likely to be complainers or management problems than are patients of another ethnic group (for example, northern Europeans). To find out whether this belief has any basis in fact, the ward supervisor must define a total of three dichotomous (two-part) variables. The first is southern European ancestry: yes or no. The second is northern European ancestry: yes or no. The third (which in this case would probably be called the dependent variable) is "complainer" or "management problem": yes or no. The subjects who are to be classified might be all the patients on the ward during a given time period, all the patients in the institution, or samples drawn from either of these populations.

The task of finding and identifying all the people who are either of southern or northern European ancestry is a matter of defining classes and counting the number of members of each class. After this is completed, one of two things may be done with the data. Those people who are of some ancestry other than southern or northern European may be dropped from the study, and the remaining composite independent variable may be redefined as "southern *vs.*

northern European ancestry" (scored 1 and 0 respectively). The other possibility is to use all available subjects by defining a three-category (trichotomous) composite independent variable: southern European ancestry; northern European ancestry; and "other."

The first option makes possible a test of the originally implied null hypothesis, namely, that people of southern European ancestry do not complain more (or are no more frequently identified as management problems) than people of northern European ancestry. However this option does not permit the investigator to determine whether either group contains more or fewer complainers than would groups of patients of other types. Suppose that people of southern European ancestry were found to be called complainers significantly more often than were people of northern European ancestry. Is that because people of southern European ancestry complain more than everybody, or is it because people of southern European ancestry complain about an average amount, while people of northern European ancestry complain less than almost everybody? Only by including the group of "others" can these question be answered.

Whichever option the investigator chooses, the next step is to classify all of the subjects in the study according to the dependent variable: complainer (or identified as a management problem) or noncomplainer (not identified as a management problem). If this can be reliably (that is, objectively) accomplished, the result will be another set of frequency counts.

Of course the principles of good research require that the classification of subjects on the dependent variable be performed by judges who do not know the persons' ethnic origins. This requirement in itself may prove to be nearly impossible because the judges who identify certain patients as complainers or management problems are almost certain to know the patients' names, and names are usually good clues to ancestry. For this and other reasons, the classification of people on the dependent variable will be difficult to accomplish, and if it cannot be done satisfactorily, the investigator might need to reconsider whether the original question is researchable.

Comparing Counts by Inspection

For the sake of example, let's assume that the investigator in this case can classify subjects on the dependent variable and thereby acquires two sets of numbers: a set of frequency counts of ancestral origins and a set of frequency counts of complainers and noncom-

Table 4.1. Data from a Hypothetical Study of Ethnic Origins of
Families of Complainers

Family Origin	Complainers	Non-Complainers	Totals
N. Europe	12	38	50
S. Europe	6	21	27
Other	25	67	92
Totals	43	126	169

plainers (or management problems and non-management problems). The specific research question (not the null hypothesis; remember the difference) may now be stated in one of two ways, the first of which is the form most commonly used: 1) Are there significant *differences* in the proportion of complainers or management problems coming from families of different geographic ancestry? 2) Is there a *correlation*, or association, between geographical ancestry of patients' families and the classification of individual patients as complainers or management problems?

Cross-classification. What is needed to answer these two questions is a special kind of table called a *cross-classification table*. It shows the independent variable (ethnicity) on one axis, the dependent variable on the other, and frequency counts in the cells. Table 4.1 is a cross-classification of the hypothetical data from this study.

A glance at the first vertical column of numbers in Table 4.1 suggests differences among groups. Most complainers (25) are in the "other" category. Twice as many complainers are in the northern European group (12) as are in the southern European group (6). A look at the second column of numbers, however, shows that the distribution of noncomplainers is somewhat similar in general proportions to that of complainers. Most noncomplainers are also in the others category (67).

The totals on the right side show that the overall proportions of people from families of different ancestral origins are also similar to those for complainers and noncomplainers; that is, 50 is about twice as large as 27, and the ratio of 2 to 1 is about the same in the other two columns. Furthermore, 50 is about half as large as 92, and that ratio is about the same in the other two columns as well.

Looking across the rows horizontally, the proportion of complainers in each sample is about the same, approximately 1/4 or .25 in every group: in the top row, 12/50 or .24; in the second row, 6/27 or .22; and in the third row, 25/92 or .27. The totals in the row at the bottom of the table indicate that the total sample contains 43/169, or about 25 percent complainers.

The null hypothesis seems secure even though none of the operations mentioned actually tested it statistically. What has been done so far is a preliminary step that is sometimes called inspecting, or "eyeballing," the data. In this case the eyeball test suggests that further statistical analysis is unnecessary because there are no differences or correlations worth examining more closely.

Group equivalence. But suppose differences had been found in the distributions of frequencies in these samples. Suppose a relatively large proportion of complainers had come from the group of people whose family origins were in southern Europe. Would the investigator have shown that people from such families are more likely to complain than people from other families? Certainly not. Many factors other than ancestral origin could account for the differences.

The investigator might strengthen the case for rejecting the null hypothesis by running additional statistical tests that compared complainers and noncomplainers on variables such as age, sex, education, and socioeconomic background, or on other variables that might be suggested to explain the results. The purpose of these tests would be to show that the samples do not differ on these factors. Eliminating them as possible explanations of the outcome reinforces the argument that ancestral origin alone accounts for the outcome. But of course the point can never be proven absolutely because no matter how many variables are examined, someone can always think up another one that has not been tested and that just might be the true cause of the observed differences. Absolute proof, remember, is unattainable.

Quantitative Data and Qualitative Classes

In the example just described, preset criteria—country of ancestral origin and current behavior—were applied to separate subjects into groups. Often, however, it is not so obvious how subjects should be grouped or typed. When this is the case, the investigator may employ any of several types of quantitative research that will suggest how, according to their scores on a number of tests, individuals can be classified.

One form of research used in the behavioral sciences for this purpose employs a highly technical multivariate procedure called *discriminant function analysis*. Suppose that an investigator has a number of scores from various tests. The tests were given to all members of a large group of patients, subgroups of which had already been labeled with different psychiatric diagnoses. The investigator may use discriminant function analysis to find the best way to combine scores on the various tests to identify which persons should be assigned to which diagnostic subgroup.

Discriminant function analysis nearly always must be performed by a computer because it is much too time consuming to be done by hand. It examines all possible correlations among measures, including as a criterion a variable that represents group membership. The discriminant function analysis produces a list of equations. Each equation contains a series of weights or multipliers that are associated with scores on the various tests. These weights are applied to the scores of each person, and the products are added up. If every person is then assigned to the diagnostic group indicated by the results of the calculations, the discriminant function analysis guarantees that these assignments will be as mathematically accurate as possible in matching peoples' original diagnoses.

For example, an investigator might divide a sample of physicians into groups defined by specialization. One group would be composed of surgeons, another of radiologists, yet another of internists. All members of all groups would be given the same set of tests. Suppose that physicians in one specialty were relatively more introverted, had lower mathematical aptitude, and demonstrated greater stress tolerance than members of other specialties. In the group-membership equation for that particular specialization, discriminant function analysis would assign especially heavy weightings to the tests that measure these variables. Different test scores would be weighted more heavily in the equations derived from the distinctive patterns of performance of other groups.

Later, the investigator might administer the same battery of tests to a group of medical students. Each student's scores would be plugged into each of the discriminating equations that had been derived from research performed earlier with practitioners. Students who scored high on tests measuring introversion and stress tolerance and low on those measuring mathematical aptitude would obtain their highest totals from the equation representing the specialty discussed above.

The investigator could use the test results to predict that each student would enter the specialty corresponding to the particular equation that gave him or her the highest total. Students whose test scores did not resemble those associated with any specialization would not obtain remarkably high totals from any of the equations, and no predictions could be made for them. The accuracy of the predictions could be checked by following up the study group after several years to see which students had actually entered the specialties for which they seemed best suited. Or the investigator might prefer to make immediate use of the results in order to advise current students about specialties that would probably be appropriate for them.

One might say that the series of equations produced from discriminant function analysis represents the results of an attempt to discover the *functional relationships* between a series of independent variables and the dependent variable (group membership). The investigator may wish to think about the equations that describe these relationships in order to tease out the underlying factors that may explain why a person belongs to a particular group. Or the investigator may simply use the equations actuarially, as a way of attempting to predict group membership in the future. Of course both purposes may be served simultaneously.

This type of research may appear to take the individuality of persons into account because it enables the investigator or clinician to derive a separate prediction for each person, based on that person's unique totals for several equations. Bear in mind, however, that the primary data analysis, the calculation of discriminant functions, is an analysis of grouped data. It averages individual patterns to arrive at overall sets of relations among variables. The investigator's ultimate purpose was to arrive at equations that increase the overall probability of making correct predictions about large groups of persons. To find these equations, the discriminant function analysis ignored differences between subjects in order to describe functional relations among variables. The actual outcome of the research is the set of equations, not the predictions that may be obtained later by using them. Predictions represent an application, or perhaps a cross-validation, of the research findings.

If the functional relations obtained from this research study are tested for validity in a subsequent study, a new variable must be set up in that study as a way of testing the equations. The new variable will probably be called "success in prediction," and individuals will enter it as tallies on the plus or minus side, as "hits" or "misses." This type of research, examples of which are presented in subsequent chapters, does not search for functional relations but tests their usefulness or accuracy.

Another quantitative technique, *cluster analysis*, is designed to solve a different kind of classification problem. It is used when the persons tested have not been grouped ahead of time. The investigator's task is to search a complex set of data to identify statistically recognizable groups of individuals. Cluster analysis sorts people according to the degree of similarity in their performances on several tests. Following decision rules specified by the investigator, the procedure puts into the same clusters people whose test-score profiles resemble each other but are different from other profiles. Like discriminant function analysis, cluster analysis must be performed on a computer. Not only is it quite complicated, but it also usually requires several computer runs before a satisfactory grouping of individuals appears. Cluster analysis is insensitive to differences among patterns in persons who are placed into the same group.

Factor analysis is a particularly well known quantitative procedure for revealing similarities. By analyzing a group of product-moment correlation coefficients this procedure shows which variables among a large set of variables are closely enough associated with each other to suggest that they can be combined into a single class, or factor. Usually the variables are tests or items on tests, and the resultant factors are interpreted as being underlying traits or variables.

Suppose, for example, that an investigator wishes to construct some self-rating scales to assess the trait of dominance. The investigator suspects that dominance expresses itself in several different ways—that it is multidimensional. To discover what its dimensions are, the investigator constructs a questionnaire containing, say, 60 self-report items. These represent as many different kinds of dominance as the investigator can think of. Some items might describe dominance through the use of physical strength; others might describe dominance through argument, deceit, or even affection. Items might also describe dominance as it could occur in different types of interpersonal relationships and settings, such as at home, in the office, or in sports.

After administering the questionnaire to a suitable sample of persons, the investigator correlates scores on the 60 items with each other. The resulting correlations are then subjected to factor analysis. This procedure produces a new set of correlation values. They are constructed along perhaps three to six dimensions, or factors, according to which items tended to be answered in similar ways.

Each factor will contain several items with high factor *loadings*. By examining the contents of these items, the investigator may infer what the different kinds of self-perceived dominance are. This information can be helpful in guiding the construction of an improved version of the instrument. Examining how closely the factors that emerge correspond to those described by theory will also be of value in judging the content validity of the questionnaire.

Redundancy and Meaning

To say that factor analysis reveals *redundancies* in a set of data is actually more correct than to say that it reveals similarities. A similarity is a resemblance. A redundancy is a repetition or duplication. If I call scarlet fever an illness and you call it a disease, we are probably not disagreeing. In this example at least, the terms *illness* and *disease* are identical for all practical purposes. In other words they are redundant. Because they are merely different names for the same thing, we may as well throw out one of the words and use only the other. That is what most quantitative techniques for classification do. They reveal redundancies. They do not say what the redundancies mean, only where they are. The investigator must discover what they mean.

A well-known test of personality, the *Sixteen Personality Factors Questionnaire*, was constructed on the basis of extensive factor analytic research (Cattell et al. 1970). This research revealed that 16 basic personality traits can be identified—but that is all the research did. It revealed redundancies in the data, but the investigators had to take responsibility for examining the items contained in each factor, to decide what underlying traits those factors represented and how they should be named. When the research was completed and the final version of the personality questionnaire was constructed, the product was a set of 16 subtests, each presumably measuring one variable or factor.

A clinical psychologist may now use this questionnaire to assess individuals, but after it has been administered and scored quantitatively, the tester still has the task of relating the meanings of the 16 scores to each other. To produce a description of an individual's personality, the test findings must also be integrated with everything else that is known about the individual. In other words, like the outcomes of cluster analysis, factor analysis, and other similar procedures, the test results are an aid to description but do not constitute a description in and of themselves.

Recently computer programs have been written that not only administer and score this test but also write reports that appear to describe each person who took it. These reports are based on a formalization of the clinical judgments of one or more trained professionals who are familiar with the test and with the research that is based upon it. Such reports are valuable because they describe the inferences that these experienced judges feel are justified from the data. However, the reports are not guaranteed to be accurate simply because they come from a computer.

The Development of Theories

Similarities Within Classes

Suppose that I say scarlet fever is a disease, and you say that arthritis is also a disease. Now we are in a far different situation from the disagreement about names described earlier. We are not talking about two different names for the same thing—that is, redundancy—but about two qualitatively distinct things that must be similar because they share the same name: *disease*. We are talking about different members of the same class.

Or suppose I read a computer report from a psychological testing and say that the examinee is maladjusted; in fact, the person has a psychosis. Then I read a computer report about another person and say that this person is also maladjusted but has a hysterical personality disorder rather than a psychosis. The question is: what is there about these apparently different conditions that permits me to use the same term, *maladjusted*, when talking about them?

The best way to find an answer to that question is not merely to look for redundancies, that is, common elements, between psychosis and hysteria but to define the abstract concepts of disease or maladjustment. The definition of the term *maladjustment*, for example, should enable us to recognize the similarities among all forms of maladjustment, not just the two that are of current interest. In the same way, *disease* must be defined so as to apply to scarlet fever, arthritis, and measles, as well as to any other apparently different, but fundamentally similar, conditions that now, or in the future, seem to belong to the same class.

Defining a term like *disease* may seem fairly simple because the work of abstraction and definition has already been done for us. Defining the term *maladjustment* is bound to cause more trouble. The task of definition is not at all easy if one wishes to speak of such things as ways in which someone can belong to the class of persons who are in an ideal state of mental health, different characteristics of just and unjust actions, good and evil intentions, or symbolic meanings of human thoughts and experiences.

Relations Among Classes or Types

The discussion thus far suggests that while quantitative research may aid in constructing a set of classes, the main task of understanding and describing types or classes is conceptual, or qualitative. Furthermore, a complete and useful typology must contain more than just a list of definitions of separate classes. It must also specify how the classes relate to each other.

The phrasing of that last sentence is important, especially when the topic is the human organism or human behavior. The sentence does not refer to descriptions of how members of the same class are alike but to descriptions of how classes are related to each other. A useful class or type is not just a pigeonhole or compartment. It is more like a geographical feature in a landscape.

A vivid description of a landscape may be partly quantitative, providing information about distances, altitudes, and directions. However, it must also distinguish in a graphic way between foothills, plains, ponds, lakes, and rivers. It must reveal something about what the mountains and lakes in a region look like, but more importantly it must show where they are in relation to the forests, rivers, and other features of the countryside. In short, a good description of a landscape is not just a list of similarities and differences among classes of geographic features, but a map. Analogously, in the study of human behavior or of people as whole organisms, the most useful typology is more than a set of numbers or a list of descriptions of classes. It describes relationships.

An ideal diagnostic scheme not only defines each disease within it quantitatively and qualitatively, it also describes relationships among them by comparing and contrasting their important features. As a device for classification alone, psychiatric diagnosis is made observationally more precise by describing in detail the specific symptomatologies of, say, obsessive compulsive personality disorder and paranoid schizophrenia. Increased precision helps standardize diagnostic procedures—perhaps so effectively that diagnostic procedures will ultimately become routine clerical operations.

However, this way of describing diseases does not describe the relationship between obsessive compulsive personality disorder and paranoid schizophrenia. It does not explain why these conditions may appear similar in some ways yet quite different in others. It does not tell how or why these conditions develop in individuals, what the other features of the personalities of people with these diagnoses may be like, or why people with these conditions can be expected to respond in different ways to different forms of treatment. In short, a detailed list of symptoms, whether expressed qualitatively or quantitatively, aids in classification but it does not promote explanation or necessarily produce a useful map or typology. That requires seeing relationships among classes, something that cannot be satisfactorily accomplished in numerical terms alone.

Analyses and Theories

Maps and organizational charts are good examples of diagrams that reveal relationships among items and types. They do not simply list the characteristics of all the various components. Rather, they provide an *analog, metaphor,* or *model,* a special kind of picture or likeness of traits and the relationships among them. Let's consider them to be theories.

When reading a road map, a traveler does not expect the actual highways to be colored red and the secondary roads, blue. Or when reading an organizational chart, a bureaucrat does not expect a real vice-president to look like a rectangle radiating arrows, although this is the way vice-presidents may be represented. Similarly, to say that the ego of an obsessive compulsive person is rigid, while that of a hysterical person is brittle, is to metaphorically characterize a relationship between certain features of the two diagnostic categories, not to describe actual physical entities or properties. To be sure, this particular metaphor can be understood only if the listener knows what the word *ego* means and how the terms *rigid* and *brittle* are used in psychiatric terminology. The same is true for maps, organization charts, and computer programs. Unless we know the terminology and conventions associated with models, we cannot understand them.

Relationships communicate and imply meanings. One of the main things a theory does is specify meanings by defining terms and the relationships among them. What it means to be the administrator of an institution can be learned in part by examining the position occupied by the administrator on an organizational chart of the institution. Much can be learned about the difference between what it is like to live in New Hampshire as compared with southern

California by studying maps and reading descriptions of the two states. In personality theory, the meaning of the word *anxiety* can be learned at least in part by examining the variety of conditions in which it is and is not prominent as a symptom.

For individuals, life events tend to take on meanings as they relate to everything else that is going on from day to day. Graduation has a different meaning for the 30-year-old convict who is just completing high school than it does for the 18-year-old youth who is thinking of a career in medicine. It is not easy to imagine how that difference in meaning could be captured by defining a single variable and measuring the two graduates along it.

Processes

Research often involves processes. A good example of a metaphor, model, or theory of a process is a flow chart. Flow charts serve many purposes. For example, the flow charts for a manufacturing operation may diagram the steps that transform raw material into finished products. In a complicated institution—such as a military service, an industrial firm, or a health service-delivery agency— flow charts may show how orders are transmitted downward and reports of results are transmitted upward. Computer programs are often developed from, and may be thought of as, flow charts that "instruct" the computer how to handle various types of input and what output to produce at the end.

Parts of complex processes may be measured and described quantitatively, or the output of the process may be examined or counted. But monitoring single variables does not describe the process itself. Continuous records of body temperature show whether, or to what extent, measurements of that variable are changing in response to therapy. But they do not show what is happening to produce the response or how the response is to be interpreted. That information must be described qualitatively or examined directly if it is to be understood.

In statistics, a procedure called *path analysis* uses formal diagrams to depict theoretically derived patterns of numerical relationships among variables. Suppose an investigator thinks that schoolchildren's grades can be explained by several variables, including the children's scores on a test of intelligence and their parents' educational levels.

Before collecting data, an investigator might set up a model like the one shown in Figure 4.1 to represent a likely pattern of caus-

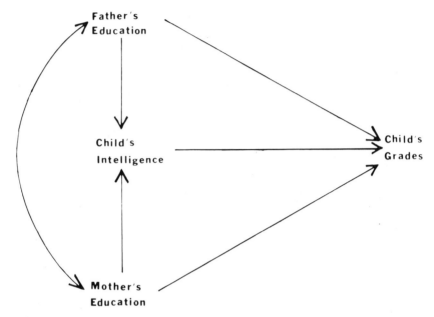

Figure 4.1.   A possible model of some factors predicting school grades.

ation. The lines drawn into the model say that the researcher expects to find correlations between all possible pairs of the four variables. The upper and lower straight lines, which point to the right, indicate the investigator's belief that parents' education has an effect on children's grades, possibly because better-educated parents are likely to provide a stimulating or helpful environment for the child or to put pressure on the child to succeed. The vertical straight lines represent the effect, possibly genetic, of parental intelligence on children's intelligence, assuming that better-educated parents are probably more intelligent than less well educated parents. This effect is an indirect factor in the child's academic performance. The curved line shows that the investigator also expects mothers' and fathers' educational levels to be correlated, but does not see that relationship as having causal significance.

The diagram in Figure 4.1 is a theory, analog, model, or chart of an expected causal pattern. The investigator must test it by actually collecting data from numerous parents and children. These data will be put through a mathematical analysis that provides a numerical indication of how strong each relationship is within the *causal model*.

Scarr (1985) has provided an interesting account of how the same sets of correlations may be used to support several different causal explanations of parent-child relationships. Using actual data, Scarr showed that the obtained patterns of correlations may be interpreted as showing that a mother's ways of controlling her child's behavior determine the child's social adjustments. The same data also seem to show that how a mother controls her child's behavior is determined by her own IQ. In turn, a mother's IQ is strongly related to her educational level. So according to this interpretation, a mother's IQ or educational level determines her child's social adjustment. That seems reasonable enough.

By "turning the data around" and looking at them in another way, however, the same set of correlations can be repatterned to suggest that a child's behavior determines the mother's educational level, which in turn seems to determine the mother's IQ. Of course this alternative causal model is rejected. But it cannot be rejected on the grounds that statistical analyses fail to support it. This model is rejected because, according to our conception of causality, it does not seem like a plausible description of the real course of events.

The choice of interpretations is not dictated by data alone. It is arrived at by applying logic and reason to statistical outcomes. Even this process is constrained by what is currently regarded in the community of scientists as being reasonable or acceptable explanations of results.

Integration

This discussion should not be taken to mean that either qualitative or quantitative considerations are primary. Nor should it be taken to mean that qualitative and quantitative research never can or never should be combined. Quite the contrary. A good qualitative description should always include quantitative information of many kinds. The more precise and accurate the numerical data, the more complete and useful the qualitative description will be. Including available quantitative test data in a descriptive case study enables readers to judge on an objective basis how similar their cases are to the one described in the report.

Similarly, the report of a study that is primarily quantitative is almost always improved by including qualitative descriptive material of the sort that cannot be communicated by numbers alone. For example, quantitative data show many important and necessary things about how effectively a program of service delivery is operating. What they do not tell is what a particular patient or client is likely to experience when going through the program. Quantitative reports of this type can often be improved by providing, when possible, descriptions or pictures of the exterior and interior of the building or treatment facilities, along with background information on some of the staff. Qualitative information such as this helps give the reader a better understanding of the context within which data were collected.

Qualitative and quantitative approaches always work together. Scientific research begins qualitatively. An investigator observes or thinks about something that seems interesting and important enough to justify closer examination. A research plan is devised that typically provides for the quantitative assessment and analysis of natural events. The research is carried out, and the results are interpreted qualitatively. These interpretations often serve as a stimulus to further thought and more research. The continuous interplay of qualitative and quantitative approaches is essential. Attention should not be directed to trying to decide which is better but to learning how to integrate them most effectively.

—5—

ESTIMATING
PROBABILITIES

Logical and Empirical Bases

Probability is basically a simple idea, but it is used in so many different ways and in so many different types of situations that a newcomer to this way of thinking may have difficulty seeing what they all have in common. Perhaps the easiest to understand and most familiar examples of probability are connected with gambling and games of chance. In a crap game, the bettor wants to know the odds on throwing a second eight before throwing a seven. In poker, what are the odds on drawing successfully to an inside straight? On a roulette wheel, what are the odds on winning if you place a bet on either red or black? Given that there is the same number of black slots as red slots on a roulette wheel, the last example would seem to be an even bet. However, roulette wheels contain at least one number—zero—(and usually double zero as well) that is neither red nor black. If that comes up, the house wins and you lose, no matter which color you bet on.

The mathematical values of these probabilities can all be calculated with a high level of precision, and they can be used as aids in decision making, if one is willing to make a few assumptions about real-life situations. For example, the mathematical probability of turning up a specific number when throwing a single die is 1/6 because a die is a cube, and a cube has six faces, only one of which can be on top on a single throw. But the logically correct probability applies in real life only if the die being thrown is a perfect cube, its internal mass is evenly distributed, and it is thrown in such a way that each face has an equal chance to fall face up. Any deviation from ideal conditions when the die is thrown introduces bias into the outcome. Bias causes mathematically calculated probabilities to misrepresent actual states of affairs.

Minor deviations from ideal conditions are unavoidable, of course, and most people are willing to overlook them. Or benefit from them: by keeping a careful record of which bets pay off most frequently, a skilled and experienced gambler may be able to detect the bias in a roulette wheel that is not functioning properly. If the bias is strong enough to cause wide deviations from mathematically determined long-run expectancies, the gambler may use knowledge of it to advantage by making only the type of bet that wins more often than mathematical probability suggests. To overcome or counteract at least some kinds of biases, a player may insist on frequent changes of dice or on using new decks of cards. A casino may substitute roulette wheels if the management feels that the bias in one wheel is too great or has been discovered, or simply as a matter of routine to cancel out biases and cover all possibilities.

In examples like these, mathematical probabilities can be calculated because the total number of possible outcomes is known exactly. If you draw a single card from a shuffled standard deck of playing cards without the joker, exactly 52 different outcomes are possible. Of these, only thirteen are spades, only four are aces, and only one is the ace of spades. The mathematical probability of drawing any spade is therefore 13/52, or 1/4. The mathematical probability of drawing the ace of spades is 1/52.

These fractions express the ratios between the number of ways a specified outcome, such as "any spade," can occur (this number is the numerator of the fraction) and the total number of different outcomes that can occur (this number is the denominator of the fraction). The fraction can be divided out and made into a proportion (1/4 = .25) or a percentage (25 percent). Expressed as a percentage, the mathematical probability of drawing any ace is about 8 percent. The mathematical probability of drawing the ace of spades is .019, or about 2 percent.

As indicated earlier, if an assumption is violated—that is, if a bias is introduced—the actual probability is not the same as the mathematically calculated probability. A crooked dealer may shuffle all the aces to the bottom of the deck, thus eliminating the possibility that anyone who cuts the cards somewhere around the middle of the deck will draw an ace.

Suppose we observed that when a certain person shuffles the cards, the long-term probability of a heart card appearing when the cards are cut is less than 1/4; let's say it is 1/5 or 1/6. Does that prove the person is cheating? Obviously not. Does it prove that the mathematical probability of cutting a heart should really be 1/5 or 1/6 instead of 1/4? Perhaps, if, unknown to the observer, extra cards that are not hearts were slipped into the deck, but it does not prove that either.

In an experiment on behavior, a pigeon that is placed before two stimuli is observed to peck more often at the stimulus on the left side than at the one on the right, or more frequently in response to the presentation of one stimulus card than the other, no matter on which side it appears. In other words, the response probabilities that are observed are not exactly 50-50, as mathematics suggests they should be. Does that prove that the pigeon has learned something? Under certain carefully controlled experimental conditions, the answer might be at least a qualified yes. But the "bias" could appear for other reasons. It could result from some peculiarity of the apparatus that makes one response easier than the other, or from some innate preference on the part of the bird, or from cues or signals given by the experimenter.

These examples suggest two important principles. First, the more observations that are made, and the more stable that results are from trial to trial, the more confidence can be placed in an outcome. The more times deviations from expectancy are observed, the more certain one feels that the deviations are reliable (that is, can be depended upon to appear in the future) and valid (that is, accurately represent the true state of affairs that are of interest). Notice that this discussion uses the same terms, *reliable* and *valid*, as were used in Chapter 1, where the topic was scores on psychological tests. In actual research reports, the words *reliability* and *validity* are often used to refer to all types of research data, but their meanings are not always as exact or clear as they are in this text.

Second, starting from mathematical or theoretical probabilities obtained by logic alone is basically different from starting from empirical probabilities that come directly from observations. The difference is most obvious in the contrast between the types of betting situations described earlier and the types of situations that involve forecasting the weather or that require actuarial prediction, such as determining life expectancies of different groups of people.

The probabilities of rain or snow used in weather forecasting and the probabilities that insurance companies use in establishing rates and charges are based mainly on the study of historical records. Scientists may use these empirical probabilities, or experience tables, to help develop theories about the causes of rainfall or the reasons for life expectancies, but the probabilities themselves are not theoretical. To use them in forecasting requires only a willingness to believe that the best way to guess about what will happen in the future is to use mathematical models to project over time the knowledge of what happened in the past. Incidentally, this belief seems justified in many applications, including the forecasting of human behavior.

Most research of interest to service-delivery professionals in the health and behavioral sciences begins with *empirically based* rather than *mathematically derived* probabilities. The investigator starts with a set of observations. Statistical reasoning enters the picture when the investigator assumes that the collected data can be appropriately described by certain mathematical models of probability.

This reverses the procedure of the gambling examples. When tossing coins, spinning roulette wheels, throwing dice, or drawing cards, the player starts with a mathematical theory about the probabilities involved. Then the player makes decisions based on the assumption that the theory can be applied to observations made under real-life conditions.

Imagine a simple two-group study of treatment effects. One group is given treatment; the other is not. The reason a no-treatment group is included in the research study is that the investigator has no sound way of knowing exactly how many patients would improve without treatment. Sometimes past experience with a treatment can provide an empirical basis for comparison. Data from earlier observations may supplement data obtained from a no-treatment group. Or, in clinical studies that examine only treated subjects, data from the past may serve as the only available standard. In such instances, the investigator reports, say, a 50 percent improvement rate in the clinical series and notes that this is 20 percent higher than the previously recorded improvement rates at the agency or with other drugs.

Generally a better practice is to run a comparison group at the same time and place that the treatment group is being examined. Purely historical comparisons are best avoided unless there is good reason to believe that rates of improvement without treatment have not changed over time. Even in the absence of treatment, improvement rates may go up or down with variations in such factors as diet, climate, levels of environmental pollution, availablility of over-the-counter treatments, changes in disease-causing agents themselves, and shifts in levels of public confidence and trust in the value of professional care. Improvement rates may also vary among agencies, and comparison groups tested simultaneously by the same staff are preferred to comparison or control groups that are tested by other people in other settings.

In the research examples outlined above, probability estimates describe a set of observations. They are not based on theoretical knowledge or mathematical calculations that are made beforehand. Empirical estimates like these become useful as aids in decision making or hypothesis testing when the investigator selects and applies an appropriate statistical model to analyze them.

Frequency Distributions

The most familiar and commonly used mathematical statistical model is the *normal curve*, the symmetrical, bell-shaped curve shown in most textbooks on statistics. The normal curve is the model for a type of *frequency distribution*. It shows, in a highly abstract but very convenient way, how often different sets of numerical values may be expected to appear in an infinitely large array of randomly selected numerical values, all representing variations along a single dimension.

Actually, the normal curve is not usually a distribution of frequencies, as the term *frequency distribution* suggests, but of proportions. Because a frequency can always be converted to a proportion in a given sample, however, the terms are practically interchangeable. Also, because in reality there are no such things as either a free lunch or "an infinitely large array of randomly selected values," the normal curve is a theoretical mathematical ideal, not an empirically derived set of values.

An example of a theoretical frequency distribution appears in Figure 5.1. This figure may look familiar because it shows the same type of information as was shown in Figure 3.3, which represented expected frequencies of combinations of heads and tails in 160 throws of five coins. Now imagine that six unbiased coins are being tossed all at once in an unbiased way many, many times. The seven possible outcomes of each toss—from six heads (H6) to six tails (T6)—are shown along the abscissa. The graph again makes evident the fact that these are discrete possibilities. The distribution of outcomes is

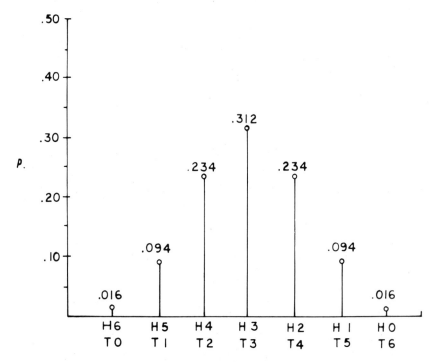

Figure 5.1.   Probability distribution for a series of tosses of six coins per toss.

discontinuous, so the lines representing proportions for each out-come are not connected to each other at the top.

Although the number of possible outcomes for any given toss was said earlier to be seven, the coins can actually come down in a total of 64 different ways. A single coin can fall in either of two ways. For each of these two ways, a second coin can fall either of two ways, making a total of four possibilities for two coins. For each of those four, a third coin can fall either of two ways, making a total of eight possibilities. The discussion can either go on like this for awhile or we can note that for every additional coin, the total must be mul-tiplied by 2 again. Eight times 2 is 16 (fourth coin); 16 times 2 is 32 (fifth coin); 32 times 2 is 64. Or, more simply, $2^6 = 64$.

Out of all these ways the coins can fall, only one way will produce six heads: all the coins must turn up heads. So the chances of getting all heads (a one-directional probability) is only one in 64 ($p = .016$). The chances of getting all tails (the opposite one-directional prob-ability) is also only one in 64. However, the chances of getting either all heads or all tails (a two-directional probability) is two in 64, or 1/32. This way of thinking about one-tailed or two-tailed tests of probabilities will be quite important in understanding more complicated problems of inference from statistics.

Outcomes

A bit of confusion may be avoided at this point by explaining the difference between the two uses of the word *outcome* in the preceding discussion. The seven possible outcomes of each toss of the six coins were said to be shown on the abscissa of Figure 5.1. In that statement, the properties of an outcome do not depend on whether any particular coin comes up heads or tails. Any combination of coins that adds up to five heads and one tail qualifies as an H5T1. That is why this "possible outcome" can appear in six ways. Coin A can be heads and the rest tails, or coin B can be heads and the rest tails, and so on through all six possibilities.

Binomial Expansion

This type of problem in probability is neatly handled by use of a procedure called *binomial expansion*. A binomial is a mathematical expression made up of two terms connected by either a plus or a minus sign. In this case, the terms represent possible outcomes in a *binary* situation. The word binary means double, and here it applies because each coin can fall in only one of two ways, heads or tails. It is convenient to label the sides of the coin H (heads) and T (tails), each of which is equally probable on any single toss of any single coin.

This binomial must now be raised to some power: that is, it must be multiplied by itself a certain number of times. To elaborate, $(H + T)$ times $(H + T)$ is $(H + T)^2$, and $(H + T)^2$ times $(H + T)$ again is $(H + T)^3$. In the coin-tossing example, $(H + T)$ is raised to the power of 6 because we are tossing six coins. The expansion needed requires finding a more complete way of writing out the value of $(H + T)^6$.

Most algebra courses teach students how to expand binomials so that, for instance, from $(H + T)^2$ they can get $H^2 + 2HT + T^2$. This, however, is not a course in algebra. The primary concern here is with how a fully expanded binomial ties in with the example at hand. Therefore the actual procedure for expanding $(H + T)^6$ will be discussed only briefly. An easy way to start is to make a list of all the ways Hs and Ts can appear in any single toss of six coins. Look at the labels on the X axis of Figure 5.1. Change all the numbers to exponents, do a little rearranging, and put plus signs between the terms, as shown below. (The exponent 1 is not actually written but is understood if no other exponent is present. Terms at each end, with exponents of 0, are dropped.)

$$H^6 + \_\_H^5T + \_\_H^4T^2 + \_\_H^3T^3 + \_\_H^2T^4 + \_\_HT^5 + T^6.$$

The blank spaces above are for another set of numbers, called *coefficients*. (Again, a coefficient of 1 is understood for the terms at the two ends, where there is no blank left for coefficients.) The coefficients may either be calculated by methods taught in algebra courses or copied from tables that are published in many books on statistics, such as the one by Hays (1973). Inserting the appropriate values here gives

$$H^6 + 6\ H^5T + 15\ H^4T^2 + 20\ H^3T^3 + 15\ H^2T^4 + 6\ HT^5 + T^6.$$

Notice that the sum of the coefficients $(1 + 6 + 15 + 20 + 15 + 6 + 1)$ is 64, which is 2^6 or the total number of possible outcomes for any toss of all six coins. Each coefficient represents the number of different ways the particular outcome that is associated with that coefficient can occur. Three heads and three tails (H^3T^3) can occur in exactly 20 ways; six heads can occur only one way, and so on.

Dividing 20 by 64 gives the probability of a single toss of all six coins turning up three heads and three tails $(20/64 = 5/16 = .312)$. The probability of obtaining only one head or only one tail is $1/64 = .016$. The probability of turning up four or more heads is the sum of the probabilities of turning up four heads $(15/64)$, five heads $(6/64)$, and six heads $(1/64)$. That comes to a total of $22/64$, or $.344$.

In the simpler case, where only two coins are tossed, the binomial expansion is

$$H^2 + 2HT + T^2.$$

The total number of possible outcomes is $(1 + 2 + 1) = 4$. The probability of two heads appearing (H^2) is $1/4 = .25$. The probability of 1H and 1T is $2/4 = .5$. The probability of at least one head is $.25 + .50 = .75$.

As an exercise, you might wish to refer back to the graph of probabilities for tosses of five coins at a time (Figure 3.3). These values were obtained from the expansion of $(H + T)^5$.

The binomial expansion may also be used to analyze probabilities in many more complicated types of situations. It is one of the techniques that is taught rather early in nearly every course in statistics.

Permutations and combinations. The discussion so far has used the term *outcome* in two ways. In the six-coin example, there are seven possible outcomes, but the coins can fall a total of 64 different ways. This suggests that 64 outcomes can appear, rather than only seven—a true statement only if differences among individual coins are taken seriously. The outcome in which coin A is heads and the rest are tails must be considered to be different from the outcome in which coin B is heads and the rest are tails, even though both these outcomes can be called H1,T5. Technically, this meaning of the term *outcome* deals with *permutations* rather than *combinations*. Permutations include every outcome of any kind that could possibly appear; combinations refer to all the different outcomes of a particular class.

In some cases, the distinction between the two terms can be important. Suppose one develops a simple six-item questionnaire to test patients' or clients' opinions about various aspects of the care they receive. If an opinion about any aspect of care that is covered by the questionnaire is favorable, the item concerned with that aspect of care is given a score of 1. If the opinion is unfavorable, the item is scored 0. Translate favorable into *tails* and unfavorable into *heads,* and Figure 5.1 can be seen to portray this situation.

T6, on the right end of the abscissa, becomes a total score of 6 on the questionnaire. The only way for a patient or client to get a score of 6 is to be favorable about all aspects of care that are covered on the survey items. The score of 0 (H6) can also be obtained in only 1 way. A score of 3 can be obtained in many ways, 20 to be exact.

Note that all items are given equal weight when the total score is added up. All contribute either 1 or 0 to the total; none contributes more, none less. Therefore, the scoring procedure is based on the assumption that the topics covered by the different items are equally important. Equal weighting is not absolutely necessary, but it is certainly most convenient and is generally used in test construction.

A peculiarity of this type of test is that one person can be unfavorable toward the same three aspects of care that another person thinks are favorable. That is, one patient can give "favorable" responses to a completely different set of items (say, items 1, 2, and

100 FUNDAMENTALS OF RESEARCH

4) than that receiving favorable responses from another patient (items 3, 5, and 6). Yet they will both get the same total score of 3. In such a situation, the only way to justify treating all scores of 3 as if they mean the same thing is to invent an underlying dimension or variable that might be called "favorableness of opinion." All people with scores of 3 could then be said to be at the same place along this dimension (responding with equal amounts of favorableness), despite their possible disagreements on particular items.

When items are combined into a scale such as this one, the important shift in thinking that takes place is the shift from discontinuity of observation (scores that cannot have fractional or decimal values) to assumed continuity of underlying variables. Figure 5.1. shows a discontinuous distribution, but the underlying dimension of some trait or attitude must be thought of as being continuous.

Figure 5.1 and Figure 3.3 picture the same types of information, although Figures 5.1 and 3.3b use straight lines and Figure 3.3a is a bar graph. When a bar graph is used to represent a frequency distribution for a variable that is conceptualized as continuous, the widths of the bars represent what are called *class intervals*. The graph itself is called a *histogram*. For example, if the variable measured by this test were continuous, then the "true" value of an actual raw score of 2 could lie anywhere in the range between 2.00 and 2.99... (which is one way to define its class interval) or between 1.5 and 2.499... (which is another possible class interval definition for the same score).

Class intervals are also used for condensing data for tabulation or graphic purposes. If a set of scores ranges from 0 to 100, they are more conveniently put into a table or graphed by grouping them into class intervals of 10 points each than by plotting frequencies for every possible score value.

If the scale for this hypothetical test were continuous, then a score of 2.5 or 4.8 would have meaning, if anyone could possibly get such a score. A score on a dimension or variable can be said to "have meaning" if the investigator is sure that it represents more of the measured characteristic than lower scores do and less of it than higher scores do. This requirement may sound silly, but it is not. The next paragraph explains why.

On tests of intelligence, no psychologist can ever be certain that someone whose performance earns an IQ of 108 really "has" more intelligence than someone whose performance earns an IQ of 105. Scores on all tests, not just those used in psychology, always contain some portion of uncertainty or error. Psychometricians have even devised a special number that can be calculated from information about a test's reliability. It is called the *standard error of measurement,* and a test maker may use it to specify the limits of meaning of individual scores. Even on good tests of intelligence, the standard error of measurement may be as much as plus or minus 5 points. The standard error of measurement is an index of *variability*.

Variability

Thus far the words *difference, deviation, variation, variance,* and *variability* have been used somewhat loosely. Later discussions will be easier to understand if more precise distinctions among these terms are now drawn. Variation refers to change or difference. Therefore a variable is something that can change, that can have different values. Variation implies that many quantities are unequal. A variation between only two numbers is called a difference.

The situation becomes complicated when more than two values lie on the same scale. The number of possible differences between pairs grows rapidly as the list gets longer. A single pair of numbers has only one difference between them. All possible pairings of three numbers produce three differences (A minus B; A minus C; and B minus C). A list of four numbers can yield six differences, and a list of five numbers can produce ten differences. To find a useful indicator of variation within a long list of numbers, a single value must be discovered that can communicate how wide the spread is among them all.

The Mean as an Average Deviation from Zero

Actually, every series of numbers contains two sorts of variation. One is the obvious sort, described above. It is the variation among the numbers within the series. The other is not often thought about, but it is quite important to statistical thinking. It is the variation from 0 of each number in a series.

As a measured quantity, the number 6 does not merely mean six units of something. It means the difference between six units and no units at all. The average deviation (difference) from 0 of all numbers in a series is therefore a measure of variation. It is called the *mean* or the *arithmetic average,* and it is commonly represented by the symbol $\overline{X}$, called *X-bar*.

The average deviation from 0 of the numbers 4, 6, 9, and 11 is

$$\frac{(4 - 0) + (6 - 0) + (9 - 0) + (11 - 0)}{4} = 7.5.$$

The denominator, or divisor, in this calculation is simply a count of the number of differences in the calculation. Of course, the same result is obtained if the zeros are left out. Therefore, the usual formula for the mean is simplified and written

$$\overline{X} = \frac{SumX}{N}$$

where SumX means total (often written ΣX), X is an individual score, and N is a count of the number of values.

This formula can be described as follows: the mean of a distribution (that is, of a list, array, or series of numbers) equals the sum of all the numbers in the distribution divided by a count of the number of values in the distribution. As shown here, it can also be thought of as the average variation of all the scores from zero.

Central Tendency

Mean

From a research point of view, the mean is often said to be the best single estimate of the true value of a group as a whole on a variable. The true value is typically represented in mathematical formulas by the Greek letter *mu* (μ). Actual statistical operations do not use true values, only estimates, so the formulas presented here use $\overline{X}$ rather than μ.

If four people are 21, 28, 30, and 42 years old, respectively, the best number to use to represent the age of the group, as a group, is 30.25 years, the arithmetic average. If another group contains four people who are 18, 22, 28, and 33 years old, the best number to characterize their age as a group is 25.25 years.

The mean is one of several available measures of *central tendency*. In most distributions of scores that come from a single group of subjects, the mean is the best guess that can be made about the value toward which all numbers would probably move (or regress), if error were gradually removed from them. Think of statements made about characteristics of the second four-person group as being statements about all persons who are exactly 25.25 years old (assume that $\mu = \overline{X}$). Then you can see that the age of anyone in the group who is not 25.25 years old is in error by whatever amount it deviates from 25.25. This idea will come up again in a later chapter, in the discussion of *regression*.

A look at the two groups in the example suggests that, on the average, the first group is older than the second. The means of the groups differ by 5.0 (30.25 − 25.25) years. A more complicated, but nonetheless instructive, way to put this is to say that the average deviation of the first group from 0 years is five years greater than the average deviation of the second group from 0 years. This formulation reminds us that in research an investigator always deals with differences or variations and almost never with absolutes.

Remember, too, that merely finding a difference between means does not permit rejection of the null hypothesis. Means are influenced by error, although presumably not as much as are individual scores. Random factors in subject selection may have raised the mean of one group by 2.5 years and lowered the mean of the other by the same amount. If that happened, the true difference would be zero. A later discussion will show how variations within groups are used to obtain estimates of how much difference between means can be said to be caused by such factors.

Median and Mode

The other two commonly used measures of central tendency are the *median* and the *mode*. The *median* is the value that divides an array (list) of numerical values in half when the values are arranged in order from lowest to highest. If the array contains an odd number of values, the crude median is the one in the middle. For example, if five people are (in ascending order of age) 17, 20, 25, 30, and 32 years old, the median for the group is 25. When the number of values in an array is even, the crude median lies half way between the two scores in the middle of the list.

In the previously mentioned group of persons who are 21, 28, 30, and 42 years old, the median age is half way between 28 and 30, or 29 years. In the second group of persons 18, 22, 28, and 33 years old the median is 25: (22 + 28)/2. Notice that these are fairly close, but not exactly equal, to the means for the same groups.

There are ways to calculate more refined estimates of "true" medians and modes. These techniques use the idea, mentioned earlier, that each score is not a point but lies somewhere within a class interval. The techniques are not much used and are too involved to get into here.

The median is usually thought of as being a somewhat less precise, less elegant estimate of central tendency than the mean. The median is often useful, however, when precision is not required or when certain assumptions that underlie more sophisticated techniques are not met (for example, the assumption of symmetry, described later). Consider the following set of five bowling scores: 90, 180, 225, 230, 235.

The arithmetic mean of these scores is 192. The median is 33 pins higher, at 225. In this case, the median is probably a better measure of central tendency—that is, of the bowler's overall skill—than is the mean because the arithmetic average has been pulled down quite alot by one relatively poor game.

The *mode* is probably the least often used index of central tendency. The mode is simply the most frequently occurring value in a series. It is the least precise or elegant of the three possibilities. The mode is most useful when a data set contains a great many values. None of the arrays presented above actually has a mode because no values appear more than once in any of them. But in a survey research study it might be convenient to cite the modal age or income level of the residents in a neighborhood. Slightly stretching the concept of mode, one might even say that the illness or disability most frequently treated in a health or rehabilitation agency is the modal condition of patients treated there. This is certainly useful information for either planning or descriptive purposes.

Spread or Dispersion

The essential features of any distribution of data can be described by specifying only two values: the central tendency and some indicator of variability, which shows the amount of spread of scores around the central tendency. Because the mean is most commonly used to represent the central tendency of an array of data on a single variable or dimension, it is of particular importance in many statistical operations. When a mean is cited, it is usually accompanied by the value of the *standard deviation*, an indicator of variability that will be discussed shortly.

If the mode is used as the value of the central tendency, variability may be described merely by citing the *range*: the highest and lowest values in the series. For example, the modal stay of patients in an institution is 7 days. The range is 1 to 15 days, meaning that no one stays less than 1 day or more than 15, and the most common length of stay is 1 week.

When the median is used as the value of the central tendency, the range may also be cited, although some prefer to locate the *quartiles* (values that cut off 25 percent of the array at the top and bottom of the distribution), or even the *deciles* (which divide the array into tenths). The median is the point that separates the second quartile from the third quartile. Another way of saying the same thing is to say that the median is the point that separates the fifth decile from the sixth.

It follows that the tighter a distribution is, the less spread out it is and the more accurately the central tendency represents the group as a whole. If everyone in a group scores 30 on a test, then the variability is zero and the mean, median, or mode tells it all. If everyone scores between 28 and 32, the central tendency is still probably reasonably good as a measure of group performance, since no one scores more than two points away from the central tendency in either direction. But if the range is 0 to 60, the central tendency tells relatively little about individual performances. Naturally, when a measure of variability around the central tendency is taken to be an indicator of experimental error, the investigator wants it to be as small as possible.

The range is useful descriptively, but it is not stable or dependable enough as an indicator of variability for most statistical purposes. The more commonly used indicator of variability is the *standard deviation*, which is the square root of a value called the *variance* or *mean square*. Like all statistics, the calculated value of the standard deviation is presumed to be an estimate of a true value. The true value of the standard deviation is represented by the Greek letter sigma (σ), and the true value of the variance is represented as σ^2. The best estimate of the standard deviation is represented by the lower case letter s, or letters sd, and the estimate of the variance is represented by s^2 (or sd^2).

The standard deviation measures variability around the mean of a distribution of numbers. If $\overline{X}$ (the mean) = 42.5 and s or sd = 5.0, then roughly one-third of the scores fall between $\overline{X}$ and 47.5 (42.5 + 5.0), and another one-third fall between $\overline{X}$ and 37.5 (42.5 − 5.0). Another way of saying this is that two-thirds of the scores lie between $\overline{X} \pm 1\ sd$, or $\overline{X} \pm 5.0$.

For the standard deviation to be useful as an index of variability, the frequency distribution of scores must, within reasonable limits, be symmetrical about the mean. When shown as a graph, the right and left sides must look nearly like mirror images of each other. If half of the cases fall between 42.5 ($\overline{X}$) and 47.5 ($\overline{X}$ + 1 *sd*), but only one-tenth fall between 42.5 and 37.5 ($\overline{X}$ − 1 *sd*), the standard deviation (or its square, the variance) will be a poor measure of variability.

No firm or simple rules can be stated for determining when the *sd* is not usable, but the standard deviation is fairly *robust*. This means the data can violate the assumption of symmetry by a rather large amount without raising serious questions about inferences drawn on the basis of the *sd*. Usually the reader of a research report can take it for granted that a conscientious investigator will have considered this issue before analyzing the data.

Note that if about two-thirds of the values in a distribution of scores fall between +1.0 *sd* and −1.0 *sd*, then about one-third of the values must fall beyond ±1.0 *sd*. Moreover, if the distribution is symmetrical, one-sixth (half of that outside third) must be higher than the mean +1 *sd*, and the other sixth must be lower than the mean −1 *sd*. This way of thinking about variability becomes extremely important when reasoning about probabilities. For the moment, though, the standard deviation is being looked at more as a *descriptive* tool than as an *analytical* tool.

Finally, recall the basic principle that numbers are passive. Numbers do not care what is done to them, and they do not fight back when they are mistreated. No matter how asymmetrical (*skewed*) a distribution may be, one can always calculate a standard deviation. Whether it is useful as a descriptive tool in a given instance is not a decision made by the numbers; it is a matter of human judgment. Fundamentally, statistics are useful only when scientists agree that they are because formulas never make decisions; only people do.

Normal Curve

A shift was made before from thinking about discrete events (such as coin tosses or items on a scale) and discontinuous distributions to continuous scales and dimensions (such as underlying variables). Shifts like these are vital to the logic of a great deal of statistical decision making. They enable the investigator to take advantage of powerful mathematical models that can be used only if distributions are continuous. As noted previously, the most commonly used of these models is the *normal curve*.

A normal curve is shown in Figure 5.2. Notice that this figure is similar in some ways to Figures 5.1 and 3.3. For one thing, they are

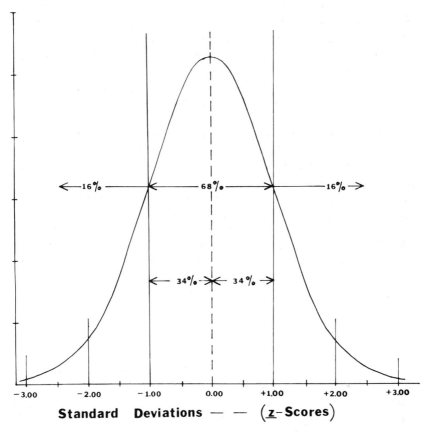

Figure 5.2.   A normal curve divided at ± 3.00 standard deviation units.

all symmetrical: their right and left halves are mirror images of each other. However, Figure 5.2 differs from Figure 5.1 in several important ways. Most obviously, the line on the graph in Figure 5.2 is continuous and is extended down almost to the X axis on the right and left. This expresses the assumption that however discrete the actual scores are, the underlying factor is continuous.

Another thing that indicates this assumption is the use of decimal points and following zeros along the abscissa. As shown in Figure 5.2, they seem to suggest that the investigator believes that differences as small as a hundredth of a standard deviation (two decimal places) would be meaningful, if they appeared in the data.

Standard deviation (or z) *scores* have been noted along the abscissa in Figure 5.2 because they are the conventionally used units for measuring variability within the normal-curve model of probability. Yet almost no research instruments yield scores directly in standard deviation units. Obtained values on tests are usually called *raw scores*, and they must be processed mathematically to be converted into standard deviation scores.

The scales on some tests, like the *Minnesota Multiphasic Personality Inventory*, are empirically normed. People have been tested, and standard deviations of their scores have been calculated by the developer of the test. All the user needs to do is to get the raw scores for a person who is tested. The user then converts them into standard scores by looking them up on tables of norms that are provided by the developer of the test (Greene 1980). When an instrument has no norms, the investigator must first calculate the size of the standard deviation (measured in raw score units) for the available data, then convert all raw scores to standard scores by an operation of division that will be described later.

Another difference between Figure 5.2 and Figures 5.1 and 3.3 is that the graph in Figure 5.2 has no numbers along its ordinate (the vertical line, or Y axis). Numbers have been omitted because they would look too much like probability values, and that could be confusing. The determination of probability values when using the normal curve is a bit more complicated than simply checking off numbers along the ordinate.

An important feature of the normal curve, besides its symmetry, is that neither tail of the curve touches the abscissa. The curve is *asymptotic* to the X axis, which means that it never reaches zero but can be stretched out to infinity in both directions. Therefore, it is theoretically possible to extend a normal curve until it contains an infinite number of standard deviation units. In actual practice, no more than about three on each side of the central point are needed to describe a single set of data.

Before learning how standard deviations are calculated, it is helpful to consider how probabilities are estimated when the normal curve is used as a model. The first thing to bear in mind is that the total area, or space between the curve itself and the abscissa, may be thought of as representing all possible outcomes. Each point in that space is one outcome (in the second, stricter sense of the term as defined in the coin-tossing example), and the number of outcomes is not countable because the curve never comes all the way down to zero.

Because the theoretical normal curve never comes to an end on either the right or left side, it has no zero point on the left at which to begin counting or measuring to get probability estimates. However, counting can be started, not at the end of the curve but in the middle. In terms of proportions, the total space under the curve, clear out to infinity on both sides, can be represented by the number 1.00 (or 100 percent, if you prefer). A vertical line down from the peak of the curve to the center of the abscissa (at a standard score, or z, of 0.00) cuts the space exactly in half because the curve is symmetrical.

Suppose an investigator decides to apply the normal-curve model to the variable or dimension that underlies scores on a test of the personality trait introversion-extraversion. Suppose also that the test is constructed so that all persons who are extraverts obtain standard scores greater than 0.00 on this test, while all persons who are introverts obtain scores below 0.00.

Finally, suppose that extraversion and introversion are believed to be normally distributed within the population of persons who have been diagnosed as having a certain condition, such as hypertension. The normal curve shows that half of all the people with hypertension should obtain scores somewhere on the right side of the center line, while the other half should obtain scores somewhere on the left side.

Following the logic described in Chapter 2, an investigator who believes that extraversion plays a part in hypertension might express such a supposition as a null hypothesis. Testing a group of hypertensive people might then show that the hypothesis is not tenable. In other words, significantly more than 50 percent of the group might obtain scores greater than 0.00.

The investigator must have some basis for stating an expected frequency in advance. In an actual research study, the investigator would probably be severely criticized if he or she were to assume that extraversion and introversion are equally common in the population. Suppose the investigator's research showed that 58 percent of the hypertensive group are extraverts. Could not 58 percent of the non-hypertensive population be extraverts, too?

This question can be answered only by testing two groups of people that are equivalent in every way—except that one contains individuals with hypertension and the other does not. This research design would use the empirically obtained frequency of occurrence of extraversion in the nonhypertensive group as the standard of comparison. It would test the null hypothesis (which the investigator would really like to reject) that the difference in extraversion scores between groups is zero.

To use the normal curve as a model for this analysis, the investigator must be willing to assume that a very long array of differences between groups, and not just the scores within groups, will be normally distributed. In most instances this seems to be the case. Even when scores within groups are not normally distributed, a long series of differences between the means of groups tends to be normally distributed anyway; so does a long series of means, medians, modes, standard deviations, or any other statistic. Stated more formally, this is called the *central limit theorem*. It is an important assumption behind many tests of statistical significance. Tests of null hypotheses about normal distributions of mean differences are crucial to many research designs.

If one line can be drawn to divide the area under the normal curve in half, there is no reason why other lines cannot be drawn to divide it into thirds, fourths, tenths, twentieths, or hundredths. In a normal curve, two vertical lines, drawn exactly one standard deviation on each side of the mean, divide the space under the curve into three parts: a central portion (about 68 percent of the area) and two end portions (each of which contains half of the remaining 32 percent $(100 - 68)$ of the area (Figure 5.2). Because the normal curve is symmetrical, the space between the center line (the mean of the entire distribution) and either of the two other lines must contain half of 68 percent, or 34 percent, of the distribution.

If you know that the average IQ of the population at large is 100 (its z score is 0.00 because the average *is* the mean) and that a single z of the distribution is 15.0 points, and if you believe that intelligence is normally distributed, you can be sure that about 68 percent of the population have IQs between 85 $(100 - 15)$ and 115 $(100 + 15)$. By reverse logic, you can say that the IQs of persons drawn at random are 68 percent likely to fall between 85 and 115, or that they are 32 percent $(100 - 68)$ likely to fall beyond either 85 or 115, or 16 percent likely to fall below 85, and so on.

The table in Appendix 5.A provides a partial listing of normal curve properties. It shows the proportion of the area that is included between pairs of standard scores (z scores) of various sizes. Note, for example, that the column labeled "0 to z" shows that only .5 sd on one side of the mean includes 19 percent of the total area (.192). Therefore twice as much area, or 38 percent (.384) must be included within the single sd that goes from $z = -.5$ to $z = +.5$. The table also shows that plus or minus 2 sds includes more than 95 percent of all the area in the curve (47.7 percent + 47.7 percent) and plus or minus 3 sds includes much more than 99 percent of the area. Tables like this one are quite important in statistical decision making.

Standard Deviation

As is evident in Figure 5.2, a standard deviation represents variability around the midpoint, or central tendency (usually the mean), of the distribution; that is, the midpoint is given the value of zero for convenience, and other points along the abscissa are measured from there. In actual research, most data do not have means of zero. The mean that is calculated from data is the central tendency of an *obtained distribution*. It is taken to be the best estimate of the value of the mean of the assumed, underlying distribution. The reason the obtained mean is only an estimate is that all measurement contains some error. True means can never be known with certainty.

Now *two* zeros must be considered: the absolute one from which every value in the array of raw data deviates and the new one that replaces the mean. One zero is enough, so the first can be eliminated by a basically simple, but somewhat tiresome, procedure. Subtract the value of the calculated mean from every value in the distribution of raw scores. The result will have a plus sign if the raw score is greater than the mean, and it will have a minus sign if the raw score is less than the mean. The result will be zero if the raw score equals the mean.

Hypothetical scores from the six-item test of favorableness of attitude mentioned earlier will serve the purpose. After administering the test to eight persons, we have the following array of raw scores: 0, 5, 2, 2, 4, 4, 6, 3. The arithmetic average of this array is the sum of these scores, divided by 8 (the number of scores):

$$\overline{X} = \Sigma X/N = 26/8 = 3.25.$$

This value represents the average amount by which the raw scores in the array deviate from a raw score of 0. Incidentally, the median is 3.5. The distribution has no clear mode.

Subtracting the mean from each score gives us a new array of *deviation scores* (Table 5.1). Some deviation scores have plus signs, and some have minus signs. The sum of all of the numbers with plus signs is $+6.00$; the sum of all of the numbers with minus signs is -6.00. The two totals balance each other out, showing that the overall deviation on one side of the mean equals the overall deviation on the other.

Table 5.1. Deviation Scores Derived from Raw Scores on Six-Item Test

Raw Score	(minus)	Mean	(=)	Deviation Score
0		3.25		−3.25
5		3.25		+1.75
2		3.25		−1.25
2		3.25		−1.25
4		3.25		+ .75
4		3.25		+ .75
6		3.25		+2.75
3		3.25		− .25

One problem in calculating some kind of average deviation is that the computed average of the deviation scores must be 0 because their sum is 0. This is true of any array of scores, no matter how many numbers it contains.

The accepted solution to this problem is to convert every deviation score into a positive value by squaring it. Negative values disappear because minus times minus is plus. The average of the squared values may then be calculated and the result may be reconverted to deviation score units by taking the square root (Table 5.2).

As already noted, the sum of the deviation scores (on the left) is 0. Therefore, any attempt to divide it by any other number gives 0 as an answer. The squared deviation scores total 25.5000, and their

Table 5.2. Calculation of Standard Deviation

	Deviation Score	(Deviation Score)^2
	−3.25	10.5625
	+1.75	3.0625
	−1.25	1.5625
	−1.25	1.5625
	+ .75	.5625
	+ .75	.5625
	+2.75	7.5625
	− .25	.0625
Sum	0.00	25.5000
Sum/N	0.00	3.1875
Square root of (Sum/N)	0.00	1.7854 (Not sd)
Sum/(N−1)	0.00	3.6429 (s^2)
Square root of (Sum/(N−1))	0.00	1.9086 s

average, using $N = 8$, is 3.1875. Taking the square root of that gives 1.7584, which is a value called the *root mean square.*

It might seem that this is the value of the standard deviation, but it is not. Why not? The answer lies not in our arithmetic but in statistical reasoning.

Degrees of freedom. In statistics, no values are absolutely correct. All are estimates, including both the mean and the *sd* (or *s*). Logic dictates that in order to estimate any value, outcomes cannot be fixed but must be free to vary. The probability of drawing an ace from an honest deck of cards cannot be estimated by drawing 50 times from a deck that contains only aces. Such a deck contains no freedom for outcomes to vary. A fair estimate can be produced only if any single draw could bring out any of the 52 cards in the usual deck. Each possibility for variation is called a *degree of freedom*, and every time a value is arbitrarily fixed, or made constant, one degree of freedom (*df*) is lost.

To calculate deviation scores, one must assume that the empirically obtained estimate of the mean is, in fact, the true mean. This amounts to arbitrarily fixing the mean at its calculated value, and that fixing results in the loss of 1 *df* for use in estimating the true value of the *sd*. To allow for this loss, the sum of the squared deviation scores (25.5000 in this example) must be divided by $(N - 1)$ instead of N. Dividing 25.5000 by 7 instead of 8 gives 3.6429, a slightly higher value than was obtained before.

The value 3.6429 is called the *variance,* or the *mean square,* of the distribution (typically designated s^2). Its square root is the *unbiased estimate* of the standard deviation (± 1.9086), the object of our quest.

To compute the standard deviation more easily, begin by calculating three values: the sum of all raw scores (ΣX); the sum of squares of all raw scores (ΣX^2); and the number of degrees of freedom. Previous calculations have shown that, in this case,

$$\Sigma X = 26.$$

Squaring all scores and summing them ($0^2 + 5^2 + 2^2 + 2^2 + 4^2 + 4^2 + 6^2 + 3^2$) gives

$$\Sigma X^2 = 110.$$

And $df = (N - 1) = 7$, as previously shown.

The formula shown below is for the *variance*:

$$s^2 = \frac{\Sigma X^2 - (\Sigma X)^2 / N}{df}$$

Substituting gives:

$$s^2 = \frac{110 - 26^2/8}{7}$$

The term $(\Sigma X)^2$ means the square of the sum of the raw scores. The square of 26 is 676, so the next steps in calculating give:

$$s^2 = \frac{110 - 676/8}{7}$$
$$= \frac{110 - 84.5}{7}$$
$$= \frac{25.5}{7} = 3.6429.$$

This is exactly the same value that was obtained by the more direct method. As always, the standard deviation is the square root of the variance, or mean square.

Standard Scores

If the supposition that the normal-curve model applies to these data is reasonable, what was said before about the normal curve leads to the expectation that 50 percent of the scores will lie above the mean and 50 percent will lie below it. The arithmetic mean is 3.25 and may therefore be said to be equal to a *standard score of zero*. A review of the original array of scores shows that, as expected, four are below 3.25 (0, 2, 2, 3) and four are above it (4, 4, 5, 6).

If 1 *sd* equals approximately 1.91 score points in this example, then 1 *sd* above the raw score mean equals 3.25 plus 1.91, or 5.16, and 1 *sd* below the mean equals 3.25 minus 1.91, or 1.34. Adding or subtracting successive values of 1.91 gives the raw score equivalents for standard scores +2.0 (7.07), +3.0 (8.98), −2.0 (−0.57), and −3.0 (−2.48).

Now the properties of the normal curve lead to the expectation that 68 percent of the scores will lie within 1 *sd* of the mean (plus or minus). Sixty-eight percent of eight scores is 5.44. About five cases should therefore lie between 1.34 and 5.16. Six scores clearly do so (2, 2, 3, 4, 4, 5), so this is fairly close to what is expected. Furthermore, three of these cases fall below the mean, while three are above it, and this, too, is what is expected.

The person with a raw score of 0 is more than 1 *sd* below the mean, and the person with a raw score of 6 is more than 1 *sd* above the mean. Neither is more than 2 *sd*s away from the mean in either direction, though. So all cases are within ±2 *sd*s of the mean (between raw scores of −.057 and +7.07). The properties of the normal curve are such that more than 95 percent of all cases (in an infinite number of cases) are expected to fall within ±2 *sd*s from the mean. Ninety-five percent of eight cases is 7.6, so the data do not appear to seriously violate these expectations.

Limitations. Before concluding too hastily that the normal curve adequately describing these data has been established, we should note two things. First, eight cases is never enough for drawing such a conclusion. When N is sufficiently large (30 at the very least), certain rather complicated mathematical procedures and statistical tests can be used to help an investigator decide whether use of the normal curve is appropriate. In most actual research, however, the appropriateness of the normal curve is simply assumed unless the data themselves are obviously different from what was expected.

Second, the normal curve in Figure 5.3 contains enough space on the X axis to include raw data values that cannot possibly be obtained on a six-item test in which each item is scored on 1 or 0. The raw scores for *sd*s of +2.0 and −2.0 and more would lie beyond the possible raw score extremes of 0 to 6. The test itself is so constructed that no one could possibly obtain a standard score beyond +1.44 or −1.70.

No test can have an infinite score range, as the theoretical normal curve would require. Still, it is possible to increase the range of this instrument. Two obvious ways to do this are to increase the number of items and increase the number of response categories for each item. Instead of asking people whether they agree with an item, they could be asked to state their level of agreement in units from +3 (strongly agree), through 0 (neutral), to −3 (strongly disagree). The results would be a seven-point spread on each item and an increase in the possible range of total scores from a floor of 0 to a floor of −18 and from a ceiling of 6 to a ceiling of +18. The possible range would therefore grow from 7 to 37 points, even without adding

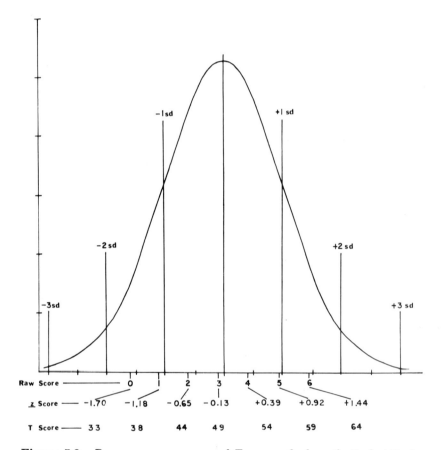

Figure 5.3. Raw scores, z scores, and T scores of a hypothetical attitude scale.

items to the scale. A simple rule of testing is that no subject can get a more extreme score than the instrument allows.

Calculating a standard score. Converting a raw score into a standard score is not hard, but it requires close attention. Read the following slowly and carefully.

If 1 *sd* on the normal curve contained 4.00 raw score points, then 1 raw score point would take up 1/4 of an *sd*. Similarly, in the present example, 1 *sd* contains 1.91 raw score points, so 1 raw score point takes up 1/1.91 (.524) standard deviations. A raw score that is 1 point above the mean (a raw score of 4.25) has a standard (z) score value of 0.524 (0 + 0.524).

But no one can get a raw score of 4.25 on this test. A score of 4 is possible, though, and it is only .75 points above the mean. Not to worry. Just divide .75 by 1.91. This gives .39, so a raw score of 4 is equivalent to a z score of 0.39 (0.00 + .39).

A raw score of 2.0 is 1.25 points below the mean of 3.25, and that takes up 1.25/1.91, or .65 *sd* units in a negative direction, so a raw score of 2 equals a z score of − .65. A raw score of 1 is 2.25 points below the mean and has a z score value of −1.18 (that is, of − 2.25/1.91).

Stated in mathematical terms, the procedure for converting raw scores to z scores consists of expressing the raw score as a difference from the mean (preserving the plus or minus sign), dividing that value by the *sd*, and adding the results to zero (which is the mean for all standard scores of this type).

$$z = \frac{X - \overline{X}}{s} + 0$$

For example, the z score for a raw score of 6 is:

$$\frac{6 - 3.25}{1.91} + 0 = \frac{2.75}{1.91} = 1.44.$$

Figure 5.3 shows the z scores corresponding to all possible raw scores on the six-item test of favorableness of attitude.

One final point. Some people do not like working with negative numbers so they transform z scores into yet another type of standard score. Several such transformations are in use. A popular transformation, which produces *T* scores, converts the mean from $z = 0.0$ to $T = 50$ points and the *sd* from 1.00 to 10. A score 1 *sd* above the mean ($z = 1.0$) becomes 50 + 10 = 60. A score 2 *sd* below the mean becomes 50 − 20 = 30.

Any z score can be converted to a *T* score by multiplying the z value by 10 (preserving the algebraic sign) and adding 50. So a raw score of 4 with a z score of + .39 becomes a *T* score of

$$50 + (10)(+ .39) = 50 + 3.9, \text{ or } 54.$$

T scores are usually rounded off to whole units. A formula for expressing this is

$$T = 50 + 10 \, z.$$

Therefore, a z score of -1.70 (corresponding to a raw score of 0) becomes a T score of

$$50 + (10)(-1.70)$$
$$= 50 + (-17) = 33.$$

T scores corresponding to all possible raw scores in our hypothetical example are also shown in Figure 5.3. Actually, *any* values can be substituted for the 50 and the 10 in this formula. The result will be a set of transformed z values. Transformations change nothing essential about the data. They are used simply for convenience.

Standard Errors

Just as scores vary in a single set of data, descriptive statistics vary from sample to sample. The expected mean IQ of 100 will probably not appear as the central tendency of a single set of scores on an intelligence test, even if the scores come from a truly random sample of the population. But if many adequately sampled groups are tested, the mean of all their means will probably be very close to 100. The same is true of the median, mode, standard deviation, and all other statistics. Furthermore, according to the central limit theorem, all these values will tend to be normally distributed. Each group statistic will differ from the "true" value, but the variance of each can be calculated over all the samples. The square root of any of these variances is called a *standard error*.

A particularly important measure is the standard error of a mean ($\sigma\bar{X}$ or SEM). Its value can be found by taking many samples and then calculating the standard deviation of the means of them all. Fortunately, there is an easier way to estimate it, which involves using a fairly simple mathematical formula. An estimate of the SEM is designated $s\bar{x}$, and the value of s, obtained from a single sample, is divided by the square root of the number of observations in the sample:

$$s_{\bar{x}} = \frac{s}{\sqrt{n}}$$

This formula always produces a lower numerical value than the standard deviation of the scores themselves because means from many samples will vary less than raw scores in a single sample.

Confidence intervals. The SEM is often used to set up *confidence intervals*. The upper and lower boundaries (the *confidence limits*) of a confidence interval describe the range within which the "true" population mean is likely to lie. In a normal distribution, the upper and lower limits of the 95 percent confidence interval are set at ±1.96 SEMs from the sample mean. The upper and lower limits of the 99 percent confidence interval are set at ±2.58 SEMs from the sample mean. The values 1.96 and 2.58 are determined by the properties of the normal curve.

Some investigators have adopted the practice of reporting the SEM, rather than the raw score standard deviation, as a descriptive statistic for a single group. Because this practice makes the data look more precise than they actually are, it can mislead a reader who is not knowledgeable about statistics or about how to examine research reports closely.

Another important standard error is the standard error of the difference between means. Any difference that is calculated between the means of a single treatment group and a single comparison group is not a "true" difference but an estimate. If more groups were run and mean differences between them were calculated, the differences themselves would vary from run to run. How great that variation would be can be estimated by combining the standard deviations of the two groups in another formula, which will be shown later. Confidence limits can then be set up for the standard error of mean differences, just as they are for a mean or any other normally distributed statistic. These limits can be used in a statistical test (the *t*-test) to determine whether the obtained difference is significantly greater or less than zero. The use of standard errors for statistical inference is taken up again in Chapter 8.

Appendix 5.A
Partial List of Normal Curve Properties (See also Figure 5.2)

z	0 to z	Beyond z
−3.0	.499	.001
−2.5	.494	.006
−2.0	.477	.023
−1.5	.433	.067
−1.0	.341	.159
− .5	.192	.308
0.0	0.000	0.500
+ .5	.192	.308
+1.0	.341	.159
+1.5	.433	.067
+2.0	.477	.023
+2.5	.494	.006
+3.0	.499	.001

The number in the column labeled "0 to z" is the proportion of the area under the whole curve that is included between the mean and the z score in the first column.

The number in the next column shows the proportion of the area that extends beyond the z score.

In every case, the numbers in the two columns on the right total to .500 because half the curve is on each side of z = 0. Numbers repeat themselves in each column because of the symmetry of the normal curve.

ANALYSES OF FREQUENCY COUNTS: CHI SQUARE

Frequency Data

As Chapter 4 explained, qualitative information is often converted into numerical data by a process in which classes or categories are set up and then the number of statements or other events that fall within each class is tallied. For example, one class of statements in interview material might be "expression of anger"; another might be "reference to own childhood." When frequency counts are derived by this method the investigator should have more than one person tally the data for greater reliability. Sometimes the investigator can take advantage of categories that appear naturally, such as gender, educational level (college graduate or nongraduate), and citizenship (American or other). Data that seem at first sight not to be categorical can usually be made so. For instance body temperature is usually measured on a continuous scale of degrees, but an investigator could classify patients with temperatures of 99 degrees or higher as febrile (having fevers) and all others as nonfebrile. A continuous scale of temperature is thereby made into a two-category classification scheme that is probably objective enough not to require checking for interjudge reliability.

IQs commonly range from about 70 to about 130, but an investigator or a clinician might prefer to classify persons with IQs of 90 to 110 as normal, 80 to 89 as low normal, less than 80 as subnormal,

111 to 120 as high normal, and over 120 as bright. In this way IQ could be simplified to a five-category scheme, and the investigator could obtain frequency counts in each category directly from individuals' IQ values.

Precision

Data that fall along continuous numerical dimensions can be converted—or "collapsed"—into categories in this or some similar way. However, conversion cannot take place in the other direction. If the only information available is in the form of frequency counts within categories, the data cannot be transformed into scores along a continuous dimension. Using the classification scheme in the preceding discussion, you know that a person of low normal intelligence has an IQ somewhere between 80 and 89, but you do not know exactly where.

The conversion from continuous to categorical data results in a loss of precision. To say that a person's IQ is 122 is obviously more precise than to say that the person is bright. As a general rule, more precise data can be converted to less precise data, but the reverse cannot be done unless more information is obtained.

Rankings are more precise than frequency counts but less precise than continuous measures. Exact scores enable us to say by how many points each person differs from every other person. Knowing patients' exact scores on a test of psychological adjustment, we can always find the best adjusted person (the one who ranks number 1), the next best (ranks number 2), and so on, down to the person with the lowest score. The resulting rankings say only that patient A is better adjusted than patient B, but not by how much. Consequently, given an original distribution of raw scores, we can always construct a rank ordering without further information. But given a set of ranks alone, we can know nothing about the level of precision or the shape of the distribution of raw scores. More is said in the next chapter about analyzing ranked data.

Because frequency counts are even less precise than ranks, rankings can be combined to produce frequency counts just as continuous data can. All persons above a specified rank may be classified as well adjusted, and all below that rank may be classified as poorly adjusted. A *median split*, according to scores on a particular test, will automatically divide any group that has an even number of scores in it into two groups of equal size.

Why would an investigator want to use imprecise data when the most sensitive statistical tests are those that use continuous data? There are at least three possible reasons. The simplest is that an effect seen in the research data may be so obvious and powerful that the investigator does not feel any need to use the most sensitive analyses available to prove a point. If a biased coin turns up heads 48 out of 50 times, statistical testing is hardly necessary to show that the coin, or something about the way it is thrown, is unfair.

The second reason is that precise data may not be available. No existing test produces a single completely accurate numerical indicator of overall psychological adjustment on a continuous scale. Nevertheless, people who know a certain group of patients well may be able to rank them from best to most poorly adjusted. If that is still too demanding, they may be able to categorize the patients into two groups as being grossly well or poorly adjusted. Some variables do not lend themselves readily to precise measurement, no matter what an investigator wishes. A patient is either on Ward 3B or not; he or she is either in a certain program or not. As is all too well known, no one can be 25 percent pregnant.

A third possible reason for preferring categorical data is that the statistical procedures applied to categorical data are more flexible than those used with ranks or with continuous data. For instance, in the example of the IQ categories, the investigator might try the five-category scheme and find that too few persons fall into the extreme categories to make statistical analysis of the data possible. The extreme categories may then be collapsed into the next two to produce a three-category classification of IQs that can then be analyzed. Alternatively, an entirely new set of three or four categories, based on a different set of upper and lower limits, could be defined for analytical purposes.

The flexibility of less precise measures comes in handy in exploratory research, which seeks to uncover relationships that were not anticipated. It can be a problem, though, in hypothesis-testing studies because it introduces some possibility that the investigator will "capitalize on chance" by defining categories only in ways that are favorable to producing the desired statistical decision. Therefore, the flexibility of categorical data should be utilized sparingly.

Properly handled, frequency data can be used for a variety of research purposes. They can test for "goodness of fit," that is, whether a set of data appears to conform to a specified frequency distribution. Frequency data can also be used for testing differences between groups or for examining changes in scores of the same group over time. Nearly everything that can be done with more sophisticated types of scales has a parallel in analyses that can be carried out on frequency counts, either with *chi square* or with other statistics, such as the closely related *likelihood ratio*.

Chi Square

To analyze a set of frequency counts, an investigator is likely to use a statistic called *chi square*. Chi square (χ^2) is based on a mathematical statistical model that bears a relationship to models like the normal curve. The family of curves of chi square can be used to tell how frequently random selection is likely to produce an array of differences between a set of values obtained from observations and another set of expected values obtained by calculation. It does not use standard scores directly, as do normal-curve statistics, but it does require calculating a ratio, which is evaluated for statistical significance. A special feature of chi square is that, under certain conditions, several ratios calculated in the same study may be added together to produce a figure that can be evaluated to test the significance of the data as a whole. Subsequent examples will show how this is done.

To calculate the simplest form of chi square, an investigator needs counts of observed frequencies in two or more categories and a logical way of guessing what those frequencies would be if random factors alone were operating. The guesses, or estimates, are called *expected frequencies*.

Rationally Determined Expectancies

In the examples that were drawn from games in Chapter 5, expected frequencies could be derived rationally. An unbiased die is expected to show each number 1/6th of the time in a large number of tosses. Random draws from an intact deck of cards, properly shuffled, are expected to produce aces 1/13th of the time, and so forth.

Most research in service delivery systems does not permit rational determination of expected frequencies in advance. Usually calculations must be performed on the data to obtain estimates of expectations in this type of research. The following example is of a hypothetical research study that could use rationally derived expected frequencies. It may seem far fetched at first, but it is a good starting place for developing important points that will be made later.

Imagine a situation in which a staff member says, "I can tell whether a patient is schizophrenic just by looking at him." To test this claim, patients are shown to the staff member in pairs. Those conducting the test know that one member of each pair carries the diagnosis of schizophrenia; the other does not carry that diagnosis. None of the patients has ever been seen by the staff member before, and all are dressed similarly and examined for the same length of time under identical viewing conditions.

All these precautions (and any others you can think of) should be taken to ensure that no bias is introduced into the test. The presence of bias, or even of possible bias, would raise doubts about the legitimacy of any analysis of the results that depends on using a statistical model based on the assumption that both choices are equally probable. For example, if the patient diagnosed as schizophrenic is always placed on the viewer's right, the possibility of bias may be raised later by a critic, especially if the viewer has a personal preference for guessing that the person on the right is schizophrenic. To evaluate the results statistically, the investigators must be willing to believe that if the staff member is merely guessing, the guesses will be correct half the time.

The problems of design in this rather unlikely research are actually much like those that arise in paired-stimuli learning experiments performed in psychological laboratories. They are also like those involved in carrying out a taste test of two cola drinks. Commercials reporting that Brand X cola was preferred by "more than half" the people tested do not tell what, if any, precautions were taken to overcome possible biases. Neither as a rule do they report whether the differences obtained were statistically significant or even very large. What does it mean to say that "more than 50 percent chose Brand X"?

Having done all that can be done to ensure a fair test of the staff member's skill, the investigators may wish to argue that the experimental situation is exactly like that of tossing a coin. *Heads* corresponds to a correct identification of a person with schizophrenia (a "hit"), *tails* corresponds to an incorrect identification of a person with schizophrenia (a "miss"). Stretch your imagination and think of the staff member as a coin that claims that it is biased (that heads and tails are not equally probable). Those administering the test of that claim are testing the null hypothesis that the number of hits and misses will not differ significantly from what the theoretical model leads one to expect, that is, 50 percent hits and 50 percent misses.

Suppose the test is arranged so that the person examines 50 pairs of individuals. Out of these, 35 patients are correctly identified as being schizophrenic—an obviously different finding from the ex-

Table 6.1 Hypothetical Data from a Study of a Staff Member's Ability
to Recognize Schizophrenic Patients

	Hits	Misses
Observed (o)	35	15
Expected (e)	25	25
[abs.(o–e) – .5]	9.5	9.5

pected 25 correct identifications. Does it differ enough, however, to
be statistically significant? To answer that question requires calculating a value for chi square and checking it against a table of
probabilities.

Calculations. Generally, to calculate one component of an overall
chi square, we find the difference between the observed and the
expected values (o − e), square that difference, and divide the result
by the expected value. For reasons that will be explained later, the
difference in this particular type of case between o and e is custom-
arily reduced by .5 before squaring. After all components have been
calculated, they are summed to get the final value.

Stated mathematically, the formula is

$$\chi^2 = \sum \left(\frac{[\text{abs.}(o - e) - .5]^2}{e} \right)$$

The *abs.* in the formula means that when the .5 is subtracted, the
algebraic sign of (o − e) should be ignored. Pay no attention to
whether it is plus or minus—just reduce the number by .5.

In the example of the shrewd staff member, at first glance the chi
square value seems to have only one part to it. The difference between the observed 35 hits and the expected 25, minus .5, is 9.5. Do
not forget, however, that the staff member also had 15 misses. The
difference between this 15 and the expected number of misses (25),
minus another .5, is also 9.5 (Table 6.1).

Chi square equals

$$\frac{9.5^2}{25} + \frac{9.5^2}{25} = 7.22$$

Significance. To check this value for significance, turn to the table of the chi square statistic (Appendix 6.A). You will find that the table reports probability values but that the first column on the left seems to require information about df, which has not yet been explained for the chi square statistic. In a previous example dealing with the calculation of the standard deviation, df was said to be "one less than the number of observations." The df in this example, however, does not equal $(N - 1)$, or 49.

Degrees of Freedom

In the case of chi square, degrees of freedom refers to the number of cells in the summary table that contain values that are free to vary. How many observations each cell contains does not matter. Our summary table consists of only two numbers, 35 and 15, and since the total of these was fixed at 50 by the research design, only one of the two values is free to vary. Given that the staff member made 15 misses, it must also be true that the staff member made 35 hits, no more and no less. Either the number of hits or the number of misses is free to vary, but not both. So the chi square value of 7.22 has 1 df. Look back into the chi square table at the row of figures for 1 df. The *critical value* at the .05 level is 3.84. That means that a chi square of 3.84 *or higher* will occur 5 percent of the time or less often in a set of truly random trials. The null hypothesis that the staff member was merely guessing (that the true difference between o and e is zero) seems untenable.

The investigators can draw one of three conclusions from the statistical results: this set of trials happens to be one of the 5 percent that occur at random (the staff member was just lucky); a biasing factor that has not yet been discovered was in operation; or the staff member really can tell the difference between schizophrenics and nonschizophrenics just by looking at them. Note that there is no way of deciding for certain which of these possibilities is correct.

Another Possible Research Design

This research could have been carried out in a slightly different way, which would have provided more detailed information about how the staff member went about making guesses. Instead of bringing people in for evaluation in 50 pairs, the 100 persons could have been brought in one at a time. The staff member would have been called upon to make twice as many independent judgments as in the preceding design. An important difference between the two re-

Table 6.2. Hypothetical Data from the Alternative Research Design

Guessed Diagnosis	Actual Diagnosis		
	Schizophrenia	Other	Sum
Schizophrenia	(A) 35	(B) 30	65
Other	(C) 15	(D) 20	35
Sum	50	50	100

search designs is that in the first, the staff member might well deduce from the procedure that 50 percent of the patients viewed (one in each pair) has been diagnosed as schizophrenic. In this revised study, the guesser has no way of knowing what proportion of the group actually carries the diagnosis.

The revised procedure has the advantage of being more like actual clinical practice, where patients are usually seen one at a time rather than in pairs. In fact, in this research design the staff member could be thought of as a diagnostic "test" or "indicator" of schizophrenia. The experiment could be considered to be an evaluation of this test's validity according to a concurrent criterion.

Assume again that the staff member correctly identified 35 patients who had been diagnosed as schizophrenic. Because the experiment was set up to contain 50 such persons, 15 of them (50 − 35) must have been misidentified as nonschizophrenic. These guesses can be called *false negatives* because the staff member labeled them minus on the schizophrenia dimension although they were really plus.

Fifty guesses are still unaccounted for. These are the guesses made about patients who were actually in the nonschizophrenic category. Suppose that the staff member did not do so well on these, correctly identifying only 20; 30 must therefore have been misidentified. These are called *false positives* because the staff member said they were schizophrenic, but they are not. (Actually, it does not matter which type of judgment is called positive or negative as long as usage is clear and consistent.) The outcome of this set of trials may be represented in the 2 × 2 table shown in Table 6.2.

For convenience, the cells in this table are labeled A through D. The diagonal cells A and D contain the number of hits, or correct guesses. Cells B and C contain the number of misses. Cell B contains the number of false positives, and cell C contains the number of false negatives.

The sums on the right of the table show something interesting: the guesses are somewhat biased; more people are labeled schizophrenic than nonschizophrenic (65 to 35, to be exact). We know, although the guesser did not, that the true proportion is 50 percent.

If you stop to think about it, you will realize that the guesser could have been right 50 percent of the time by calling all the persons schizophrenic. The guesser could also have guaranteed being right 50 percent of the time by calling everyone nonschizophrenic. The *base rate* for this set of trials is therefore 50 percent.

Naturally, base rates are not always 50 percent. The situation would be quite different if a person were trying to identify people who are likely to commit suicide in a population with a base rate of less than 1 percent suicidal individuals. Calling everybody suicidal would identify all the potentially suicidal individuals without error. It would misidentify all of the nonsuicidal individuals, producing more than 99 percent false positives. On the other hand, there would be no false negatives.

Estimating expected frequencies. The task at hand is to calculate a value for chi square. This requires estimating expected frequencies of the various types of correct and incorrect guesses. Because there are 100 data points altogether and four cells in Table 6.2, a reasonable guess would seem to be that expected values are evenly distributed, putting 25 in each cell. They would be evenly distributed—except for one thing: the known bias of the guesser. The guesser's tendency to overuse the schizophrenia label means there is reason to expect that correct identifications will be made more often than 25 times just by guessing.

No matter how often the guesser says "schizophrenia," half of those guesses are expected to be right because the true proportion of schizophrenic patients is 50 percent. The investigators proceed by finding out exactly what proportion of the time the staff member applies the schizophrenia label. Then they adjust the expected frequency for this tendency. The staff member uses the label 65 times (the sum of the numbers in cells A and B of Table 6.2) out of 100 (the total of the numbers in all of the cells), or 65/100 of the time.

Mathematically, it can be written

Table 6.3. Observed and Expected Frequencies for Data in Table 6.2

| Guessed | Actual Diagnosis | | |
Diagnosis	Schizophrenia	Other	Sum
Schizophrenia (o)	35	30	65
Schizophrenia (e)	32.5	32.5	65
Other (o)	15	20	35
Other (e)	17.5	17.5	35
Sum (o)	50	50	100
Sum (e)	50	50	100

$$\frac{(A+B)}{(A+B+C+D)}$$

or

$$\frac{(A+B)}{N}.$$

A, B, C, and D refer to cells in the table, and N is the total number of observations tallied in the table.

The actual number of schizophrenics is 50 (that is, cells A + C). The guesser can reasonably be expected to "hit" 65 percent of these 50, or 32.5. This can be written as

$$\frac{(A+B)(A+C)}{N}.$$

Getting the expected value for cell A by this procedure is called *estimating expected values from marginal totals.* The general rule for estimating expected values for cells in chi square tables that are not too complicated is as follows: for any cell of the table (that is, for any value in it), multiply the sum of its row (horizontal total) by the sum for its column (vertical total) and divide by the grand sum.

In our example, to find the expected value for cell D, multiply 35 (row sum) by 50 (column sum) and divide by 100 (grand sum). This equals 17.5. Similar procedures can be followed for each cell, but there is an easier way. Table 6.3 presents the data, which this time include expected values.

Table 6.4. Components of Chi Square for Data in Tables 6.2 and 6.3

Guessed Diagnosis	Actual Diagnosis	
	Schizophrenia	Other
Schizophrenia	$\dfrac{[\text{abs.}(35-32.5)-.5]^2}{32.5}$ $= 2^2/32.5 = 0.12$	$\dfrac{[\text{abs.}(30-32.5)-.5]^2}{32.5}$ $= 2^2/32.5 = 0.12$
Other	$\dfrac{[\text{abs.}(15-17.5)-.5]^2}{17.5}$ $= 2^2/17.5 = 0.23$	$\dfrac{[\text{abs.}(20-17.5)-.5]^2}{17.5}$ $= 2^2/17.5 = 0.23$

Chi Square $= 0.12 + 0.12 + 0.23 + 0.23 = 0.70$ *NS*

Table 6.3 shows that the marginal sums of expected values and the marginal sums of all observed values are equal. That will be true in chi square tables of any size whenever expected values are calculated from marginal frequencies. With fixed marginal totals (they are not free to vary), you only need to know the value of one o in one cell in the table and you know them all. The same is true for the values of e. Any cell will do.

Subtract the o or e value for cell A from the row total of 65, and you know the o or e value for cell B. Subtract the o or e value in cell A from 50 (that is, from A + C) and you have the value for cell C. Subtract C from 35 or subtract B from 50 to get D. This is another way of showing that although the table of observed data has four cells, the table of chi square that it yields is based on only one degree of freedom. The general rule for chi square tables of the type dealt with here is that *df* equals the product of the number of rows minus one and the number of columns minus one:

$$df = (r - 1)(c - 1).$$

If the table has only one row of cells, *df* equals one less than the number of cells in that row.

The chi square in this example has four components, one for each cell (Table 6.4).

Evaluated against the critical values in the table of the chi square statistic (Appendix 6.A) for 1 *df*, this chi square value (0.70) is clearly not significant. It is far below the critical value of 3.84 required at the .05 level of confidence.

Correction for Discontinuity

A moment may be taken here to comment on the adjustment term of .5 that was slipped into the equation for chi squares with 1 *df*. Notice that in the example the estimates of e are carried out to one decimal place. In practice, estimates are often carried out to several decimal places. Expected frequencies often are. Being logical or mathematical, rather than empirically real, they are *continuous*. However, observed frequencies can never have values beyond the decimal point. This feature of observed frequencies brings a bias into calculated values of chi square, especially when *N* is small and *df* equals 1. The bias can be so great that the recommendation is sometimes made that chi square not be calculated at all when any expected value is less than 10 in a 2 × 2 table, or less than 5 in a more complicated table.

The subtraction of .5 from o minus e is often called a *correction for continuity* (or Yates's correction). Actually, it is a correction for the fact that observed frequency counts are discontinuous, and it tends to overcome the bias that is introduced because they are. The greater the difference between o and e, the less the effect of the adjustment. The correction for discontinuity is not used in tables with more than 1 *df*. It is also not applied when a chi square table is used to arrive at a correlation value rather than a test of differences.

The *Phi* Coefficient

Suppose the staff member who presumably identifies schizophrenics by sight is replaced by a psychological test, or some other less personal diagnostic instrument. Usually a test that is used for decision making is developed from research that leads to setting up a *cut-off score*: a score on the test that is used to make decisions more or less automatically. Anyone scoring beyond the cut-off score on this psychological test is labeled schizophrenic.

Suppose that the test is somewhat more successful in identifying such persons than was the staff member. The data might look like those in Table 6.5.

Again the observed values for cells A and D represent hits. Cell B represents false positives. Cell C represents false negatives: people who have been diagnosed as schizophrenic but who were not iden-

Table 6.5.   Data for *Phi* Coefficient Example

Identification of Schizophrenia by Cut-off Score on Standardized Test	Actual Diagnosis		
	Schizophrenia	Other	Sum
	(A)	(B)	
Schizophrenia (o)	25	20	45
Schizophrenia (e)	15.75	29.25	45
	(C)	(D)	
Other (o)	10	45	55
Other (e)	19.25	35.75	55
Sum (o)	35	65	100
Sum (e)	35	65	100

tified as such by application of the cut-off score. The overall "hit rate" is 70 (A + D) divided by 100, which equals 70 percent. Calculated as before, including the correction of .5 for each (o − e) value, X^2 equals 13.5975. This value exceeds not only the 3.84 required for significance at the .05 level for 1 *df*, but also the 6.63 value required at the .01 level. The investigator feels safe in rejecting the null hypothesis that the overall variation of observed values around expected values in the table is not significantly different from zero.

To convert this analysis into one that deals with correlation instead of differences, chi square must first be recalculated without using the correction term in each cell. The (o − e) value in every cell is therefore 9.25, which becomes 85.5625 when squared. Divide 85.5625 by each of the e values in the table and sum the result to get 15.1959. (The uncorrected value of chi square will always be slightly higher than the corrected value.) The calculation may be summarized as follows:

$$(25 - 15.75)^2/15.75 \; + \; (20 - 29.25)^2/29.25$$

$$+ \; (10 - 19.25)^2/19.25 \; + \; (45 - 35.75)^2/35.75$$

$$= \; 9.25^2/15.75 \; + \; (-9.25)^2/29.25 \; + \; (-9.25)^2/19.25 \; + \; (9.25)^2/35.75$$

$$= \; 5.4325 \; + \; 2.9252 \; + \; 4.4448 \; + \; 2.3934$$

$$= \; 15.1959$$

The correction term of -0.5 is not needed here because the chi square value will be used only to help summarize what is actually in the data table. This is also the procedure to follow when calculating chi square as a test of differences when the *df* is greater than 1 because, as mentioned earlier, the correction for discontinuity is not used in such tables anyway. Right now the task is not to test differences but to obtain a correlation coefficient that represents the strength of association between classifying patients by actual diagnosis and classifying them by test scores. Chi square is not to be the end result of the calculation. It is only a step along the way.

Chi square for a 2 × 2 table like this can be made into a *phi* coefficient of correlation just by dividing it by N, the total number of observations, and taking the square root of the results.

$$\text{phi} = \sqrt{\frac{\chi^2}{N}} = \sqrt{\frac{15.1959}{100}} = 0.390 \text{ (rounded)}.$$

Being a square root, the *phi* coefficient could be either plus or minus. Whether it is positive or negative is only a matter of convenience. The strength of the association between test-based decisions and actual diagnoses is not affected by the sign of the coefficient.

If a high score on the test means "considerable disordering of thought processes," then a high score corresponds to a decision to label the person schizophrenic. The simplest course of action might be to call the correlation coefficient $+.390$. If, on the other hand, a high numerical score on the test means "good personal and social adjustment," then a low score corresponds to a decision to call the person schizophrenic. In that case, the correlation coefficient is perhaps more usefully called $-.390$.

The *phi* coefficient shows the strength of the relationship between two variables. It may range from as low as -1.00 to as high as $+1.00$. Do not think of it as a percentage, though. In actual research in the behavior sciences, correlation coefficients of 0 to .20 are generally considered low; .20 to .40, low to moderate; .40 to .60, moderate; .60 to .75, fairly strong; .75 to .85, strong; .85 to .95, very strong; and .95 or higher are almost unbelievable.

The grandfather of all correlation coefficients is called the *Pearson product-moment correlation ratio*, or Pearson *r*. Actually, the calculations shown for the *phi* coefficient are just a shortcut to the Pearson *r* in a special case. Imagine that every person in the study was given two scores of either 0 or 1. The first score represents the test-based label (1 for schizophrenia, 0 for other). The second represents the actual diagnosis (1 for schizophrenia, 0 for other). If the array of 100 pairs of scores were subjected to the calculations for Pearson r (described in a later chapter), the result would be identical to that obtained by way of the chi square value. Given the score assignments suggested, the sign of the result would be plus. Reversing either score would produce a coefficient with a negative sign. Reversing both scores would again produce a coefficient with a positive sign.

The Contingency Coefficient

A disadvantage of the *phi* coefficient is that it can be used only with chi squares based on 1 *df*. When working with more complicated problems, a different correlation value is often used. It is called the *contingency coefficient*, or *C*. The value of *C* is calculated in much the same manner as is the value of *phi*, except that an extra chi square is added into the denominator.

$$C = \sqrt{\frac{\chi^2}{\chi^2 + N}}$$

In this example:

$$C = \sqrt{\frac{15.1959}{15.1959 + 100}} = \sqrt{.1319} = .363.$$

The disadvantage of C is that the highest and lowest values it can possibly reach are not the same for summary tables with different numbers of rows or columns, that is, with different numbers of degrees of freedom. The maximum C for tables with 1 *df* is .71. This maximum increases as *df* increases. Therefore, values of C can be compared with each other only if the tables from which they were calculated have equal numbers of degrees of freedom. Moreover, Cs are not the same as Pearson rs, and they cannot be compared with Pearson rs for purposes of interpretation.

Change Scores

A special way of using chi square is required in situations in which the same subjects are tested more than once. Suppose an investigator

Table 6.6.   The Wrong Way to Arrange Data from a Study of Improvement

	Treatment A	Treatment B	Sum
Improved	75	90	165
Unimproved	75	60	135
Sum	150	150	300

decides to test the effectiveness of a treatment using only one group of 150 subjects, each "serving as his or her own control." For a period of time, half the subjects are given treatment A, half are given treatment B. Next all are evaluated for improvement. Treatment conditions are then reversed for an equal period of time, after which all subjects are again evaluated for improvement. In this type of crossover research design, each person is exposed to both treatments. The question is whether one treatment is better than the other.

A tricky thing about this crossover research design is that because everyone is tested twice, a total of 300 measurements of improvement are taken in a study that has only 150 subjects. The chi square must be based on 150 data values, not 300. Otherwise, it would appear that the N is twice as large as it is. Table 6.6 should *not* be used for data analysis.

The table shows that treatments A and B combined produced a total of 165 ratings of improvement out of 300 ratings, but it does not answer the research question—is treatment A or B superior?—because of the 90 patients who improved on B, 75 of them could be the *same* patients who improved on A. (Remember all subjects received both treatments.) The table can also be deceptive because as far as an uninformed observer can tell, the 150 persons who took treatment A could be a different group from those who were given treatment B. The actual research situation becomes clearer if the data are reorganized as in Table 6.7.

In this table each person is tallied only once. The table shows that 50 patients were judged to have improved on both treatments (cell A), and 35 were judged not to have improved on either treatment (cell D). Data from these 85 patients actually tell nothing about the comparative merits of the treatments, so they are discarded from the statistical analysis. What is left are 25 patients who did better on treatment A than on treatment B, and 40 who did better on treatment B than on treatment A. If the two treatments are not

Table 6.7.   The Right Way to Arrange Data from a Study of
Improvement

| Treatment B | Treatment A | | Sum |
	Improved	Unimproved	
Improved	50	40	90
Unimproved	25	35	60
Sum	75	75	150

different (the null hypothesis), these values should be about equal.
The question is whether they are different enough to support rejection of the null hypothesis and the conclusion that treatment A is
superior to treatment B.

The logic thus far been somewhat complex, but the statistics are
fairly simple from here on. The task is to test the null hypothesis
that the values 25 and 40 do not differ significantly from 32.5, which
is their mean. That is the value that would have appeared in both
cells if the treatments are exactly equal in effectiveness, and if the
experiment was run without error. This being a test with 1 df, a
correction for discontinuity is also in order, so:

$$\chi^2 = \frac{(\text{abs.}[40 - 32.5] - .5)^2}{32.5} + \frac{(\text{abs.}[25 - 32.5] - .5)^2}{32.5}$$

$$= 7^2/32.5 + 7^2/32.5$$

$$= 3.015.$$

This value is not quite high enough to justify rejecting the null
hypothesis at the .05 level for 1 df, so it seems that the investigator
must conclude from this research that the treatments are equally
effective, as far this research can tell.

But wait a minute! The situation may not be as simple as it seems
at first sight.

How many tails? Notice that exactly the same probability value
would have been obtained if the results had been reversed so that
treatment A had seemed superior to treatment B. The above statistical interpretation of chi square is based on a two-tailed probability
value, because it would be the same whichever treatment the results
favored.

What if the investigator had originally been interested in the outcome only if treatment B came out to be superior to treatment A? If the results had come out in the opposite direction, chi square would not even have been calculated. The clinic would simply go on using treatment A as it always had in the past. Under those conditions, this would be a one-tailed test, not a two-tailed test. The value of 3.84, tabled for the 5 percent level, would really be the 2.5 percent level. The proper figure to use for a one-tailed test at the 5 percent level is the value actually tabled for the 10 percent level. The required chi square for significance at $p < .05$ (one-tailed) is therefore 2.71. The results would have been significant.

If a decision regarding which type of test will be used is delayed until after the data are analyzed, the investigator may well develop a crisis of conscience at this point. Suppose the results had come out in reverse. Would the clinic really have been interested in knowing that treatment B is inferior to treatment A? If so, a one-tailed test would not have been appropriate, and the results would have been nonsignificant. One-tailed tests should be used only when it has been decided before data collection that results in one direction will be ignored, no matter how large they may be. Furthermore, once a one-tailed test has been decided upon, even contrary results that would have been significant with a two-tailed hypothesis must be ignored or, at most, treated as being merely suggestive.

A better way out is for the investigator to make no immediate decision, but to run 50 more subjects and see whether the trend shown in the first study holds up. If it does, the number 40 can be projected mathematically to increase to about 53 or 54, and the number 25 can be projected to increase to about 33 or 34. (To explain how these figures are derived would be beside the point, but you might try to figure them out on your own. It's not complicated.) If the projections are correct, chi square would almost certainly be significant at the .05 level even for a two-tailed test.

Calculate some chi squares for yourself. Assume several different sets of projected observed values. First calculate chi square assuming projected observed values to be 54 and 34, 54 and 33, 53 and 54, and 53 and 33.

In general, the same proportional difference between o and e will produce a higher chi square if N is large than if N is small. It makes sense. Proportionally speaking, 8 is twice as large as 4, but that is not impressive because the arithmetic difference between them is only 4. Eight hundred is also twice as large as 400, but the difference between them is much more impressive because it is 400 units, or 100 times as large as the difference between 8 and 4.

Table 6.8. Hypothetical Data for a Study of Three Treatment Conditions

	Treatment A	Treatment B	No Treatment	Sum
Much Improved	8	3	0	11
Improved	25	22	12	59
No Change	18	30	42	90
Worse	6	8	11	25
Sum	57	63	65	185

Final Example

Let's perform one last analysis with chi square using a more complicated example. An investigator applies three treatment conditions (or two treatments and a control) and evaluates the results by having each patient's progress rated: much improved, somewhat improved, showing no change in condition, or showing a change for the worse. The procedure produces the 3 × 4 table of data shown in Table 6.8.

The first thing to notice about the data in this table is that the number of persons rated as much improved is quite low. Calculating the expected frequencies for the cells in the top row, using marginal frequencies yields

for the first cell: $(57)(11)/185 = 3.39$;

for the second cell: $(63)(11)/185 = 3.75$;

for the third cell: $(65)(11)/185 = 3.86$.

All three values are less than the required five per cell for chi square, so the investigator collapses the table by combining the two top rows. This is a legitimate, although not completely desirable operation, as will be noted again later.

Now Table 6.8 is 3 × 3 and looks like Table 6.9, in which expected frequencies are shown on separate lines.

Table 6.9 has 2 (three rows minus one) times 2 (three columns minus one) df, or 4 df. The chi square value of 20.321 (calculated without the correction for discontinuity because df is greater than 1) is well above the value of 9.49 needed for significance at the .05

Table 6.9. A Collapsed Table of Chi Square Data

		Treatment A	Treatment B	No Treatment	Sum
Improved *or*	(o)	33	25	12	70
Much Improved	(e)	21.6	23.8	24.6	70
No Change	(o)	18	30	42	90
	(e)	27.7	30.7	31.6	90
Worse	(o)	6	8	11	25
	(e)	7.7	8.5	8.8	25
Sum	(o)	57	63	65	185
Sum	(e)	57	63	65	185

level. It is also above the value of 13.28 required for significance at the .01 level.

The significant overall chi square does not mean that any particular cell or group of cells in the table is significantly different from any other. By inspection, treatment A appears to be superior to treatment B, and both treatments appear to be superior to the no treatment condition, but chi square alone does not tell us this. In fact, if you extract from Table 6.9 the columns for treatment A and treatment B, then calculate a chi square based on a new set of expected frequencies and 2 *df*, you will find that the resulting value (4.099) is not significant at the .05 level.

A Disadvantage

One of the disadvantages of using chi square in more complicated research designs is that an investigator could rearrange cells in so many different ways that statistical significance would be bound to appear sooner or later. One arrangement may justify rejecting the null hypothesis; a different arrangement may not.

When chi square is used as a guide to inference, the investigator must be careful to clearly state relevant statistical hypotheses before analyzing data. In the preceding study, it would have been better, if possible, to have avoided collapsing the data table by obtaining more subjects, so that expected frequencies would have permitted data analysis to take place as originally planned.

Complicated research problems sometimes require the use of complicated chi square tables. If they are set up in advance, and if the investigator has decided which aspects of the data are to be tested, complex tables can be broken down into their components by using a special mathematical procedure called *discrete multivariate analysis*. As suggested by its name, discrete multivariate analysis is far too involved for us to get into here, so we won't.

Random Assignment

A note should be included about randomness. In a study like the one just described, subjects should be randomly assigned to treatment and control conditions. Fulfilling that requirement may not be as easy as it sounds. Almost every conceivable way to produce a random array of assignments has something wrong with it.

For example, an obvious technique when working with patients is to assign consecutive patients alternately to different research conditions: the first patient to treatment A, the second to treatment B, the third to A, the fourth to B, and so on. This procedure would not be acceptable if the study was one in which patients and staff had to be kept uninformed as to which patient was in which condition. If the assignment cycles regularly placed the first patient in treatment A, the next in treatment B and the next in the control condition, group membership of the patients could be figured out easily.

If several treatment groups were being made up and each successive patient were assigned to a different condition, but not necessarily in a fixed order, the staff would still know that consecutive patients probably did not belong to the same group. Although they might not know which conditions Mr. Smith and Mr. Jones were in, they could be pretty sure that the two men were in different conditions, and therefore they might look for differences in reactions and perhaps treat the patients differently as a result.

The most practical way to handle most problems of randomization is usually to use a *table of random numbers*, which is simply an array of rows and columns of digits from 0 to 9, so arranged that any digit is about equally likely to appear in any position. (A very small table of random numbers appears in Appendix 6.B.) The array can be entered anywhere, and the digits can be read in any direction; the result will always be close enough to being random to satisfy most investigators.

In this example, treatment A could be signified by the number 1, treatment B by the number 2, and the no-treatment condition by the number 3. Any assignment of digits to conditions should be equally good. To make matters easier, treatment A could even be assigned the numbers 1, 2, or 3; treatment B could be assigned the numbers 4, 5, or 6; and the no-treatment condition could be assigned the numbers 7, 8, or 9.

The person assigning patients to conditions then enters the table of random numbers at a position chosen as randomly as possible and moves in a direction that is also selected, if possible, on a random basis. If the first digit encountered is a 5, the first patient is assigned to treatment B. If the next digits are 6, 3, 8, and 4, the assignments of the next patients are B, A, No Treatment, and B, in that order. Obviously, it is important to keep careful records of the assignments, or the whole project would be ruined.

A table of random numbers is a useful research tool. As mentioned in preceding chapters, research designs that use statistical models require randomness as a way of reducing bias, that is, of helping to ensure that no factors other than the one of research interest are producing the results.

Suppose that someone realized later that nearly all the patients in the No Treatment condition had been treated by Dr. X, while nearly all patients in the other conditions had been treated by Drs. Y and Z. Such a deviation from apparent randomness could occur even with random assignments; after all, the improbable does happen sometimes. Should the investigator conclude that a possibly biasing factor was thereby introduced into the experiment? In all honesty, the answer is "yes," and the investigator will be called upon to interpret the data cautiously and consider seriously what steps should be taken to provide a more fair test of the research hypothesis in later studies.

Appendix 6.A
Selected Critical Values of Chi Square

df			Probability Levels		
	.10	.05	.025	.01	.005
1	2.71	3.84	5.02	6.63	7.88
2	4.61	5.99	7.38	9.21	10.60
3	6.25	7.81	9.35	11.34	12.84
4	7.78	9.49	11.14	13.28	14.86
5	9.24	11.07	12.83	15.09	16.75
6	10.64	12.59	14.45	16.81	18.55
8	13.36	15.51	17.53	20.09	21.96
10	15.99	18.31	20.48	23.21	25.19
15	22.31	25.00	27.49	30.58	32.80
20	28.41	31.41	34.17	37.57	40.00
30	40.26	43.77	46.98	50.89	53.67

Appendix 6.B
Some Random Digits

	Column		
A	B	C	D
3 0 1 6 8	9 0 2 2 9	0 4 7 3 4	5 9 1 9 3
2 5 3 0 6	7 6 4 6 8	2 6 3 8 4	5 8 1 5 1
3 8 0 0 5	9 4 3 4 2	2 8 7 2 8	3 5 8 0 6
0 0 2 5 6	4 5 8 3 2	1 5 3 9 8	4 6 5 5 7
9 2 4 2 0	6 0 9 5 2	6 1 2 8 0	6 7 6 5 8

—7—

ANALYSES OF RANKS

Properties of Ranks

If eight horses are racing, you will not be satisfied to learn that the horse you bet on came in "among the first four." On the other hand, if your horse wins, you probably don't care much whether it was by a nose or six lengths. An organization selecting persons to receive various monetary awards as "employees of the year" may first select those employees who belong in the top half, third, or quarter of the group, or perhaps even in the top 20. Eventually, however, further discriminations must be made so that the largest awards can go to the most meritorious persons.

One way to make these discriminations is to use ranks. Within the top 10 employees, the one judged to be best is ranked 1, the next best ranked 2, and so on. Discriminations among the people who occupy positions below the rank of 3 or 4 may not be important. The top-ranking employee gets the biggest award, the next gets slightly less, and the person in third place still less. The administrator gives everyone else in the top 10 a hearty handclasp and an "Honorable Mention" certificate (although ranks may be needed to determine the order in which even these are given out at the ceremony). When ranks are used for statistical analysis in research, as distinct from award ceremonies, they should cover the entire range of the variable on which persons or things are ordered.

Ranking very many entities along a single dimension can be tiresome, even difficult. A therapist could probably identify with ease the two or three best patients and the two or three worst patients who are in treatment, but distinctions often tend to break down in the middle of the range. In almost all competitive situations where the distribution of ability conforms to the normal curve, those who perform at each extreme can be readily identified, while the rest form a sort of lump of mediocrity in the middle—just what the normal curve, after all, leads us to expect.

Ranking procedures work best when the number of items being ranked is relatively small. Nearly always it should be less than 30. Usually it is far less than that, more in the neighborhood of 8 to 15. Ranking also works best when discriminations among positions are fairly easy to make; that is, when differences are fairly obvious.

Problems in Discrimination

The difficulty of making many types of discriminations, some of which can be quite important in practice, points out the main problem with ranks: they do not show how large or small the difference is between the things ranked. The only exception to this occurs when two or more things are so nearly alike that there seems to be no difference between them. Because they cannot be distinguished, they are given tied ranks.

The use of ties is usually an admission of lack of precision in judgment, or lack of discrimination. Sometimes, however, ties cannot be avoided. In statistical calculations a few ties within a listing of ranks usually have a minor effect on the outcome. But too many ties can seriously limit the sensitivity of an analysis, and they should be broken whenever possible. Special rules that have been agreed upon for assigning tied ranks to stimuli will be described later.

Suppose that six people apply for an important position in an agency. Each submits a résumé and comes for an interview. The administrator, medical director, and personnel manager then independently rank all six candidates. Table 7.1 presents the hypothetical results.

A glance at the array of rankings in the first three columns of the table shows that all three judges agree that Martha is the best and Ernest is the poorest of the candidates. The agreement is not as strong about Al, who is ranked second by the administrator, fourth by the medical director, and fifth by the personnel manager. The judges also disagree about Charley, whose ranks are 5, 5, and 2,

Table 7.1. Hypothetical Rankings of Candidates for Employment

Candidate	Administrator	Medical Director	Personnel Manager	Sum	Overall (Composite) Rank
Al	2	4	5	11	4
Bert	4	2	3	9	2
Charley	5	5	2	12	5
Martha	1	1	1	3	1
Ernest	6	6	6	18	6
Frances	3	3	4	10	3

respectively. Frances is rather firmly fixed in third place, while Bert's rankings cover the midrange from 2 to 4. (The midpoint is between 3 and 4 in each series of ranks.) The fairest way to determine the overall merit of each candidate seems to be to create composites (last column on the right in Table 7.1) by adding the ranks and then reranking the candidates according to the sums. On that basis, Martha comes out first, followed by Bert, Frances, Al, Charley, and Ernest, in that order.

If the job is offered to Martha and she accepts it, everybody will be happy. But if Martha is as outstanding as she appears to be, she probably has job offers from several places, and she might very well decide to go elsewhere. What should be done then? The mathematically correct course of action would be to offer the job to second-in-line Bert. But the administrator, who ranked Bert fourth, vetoes that option. He points out that as far as he is concerned, Bert, Charley, and Ernest are all unacceptable. For him, Martha was outstanding, and Al and Frances were both very good, but the gap in competence between Frances (rank 3) and Bert (rank 4) is far greater than the rankings themselves reveal.

Both the other two judges see the situation differently. For them, there was practically no difference between Frances and Bert. Both judges admit that their rankings of these two candidates could easily have been reversed, in which case Frances would have been ahead of Bert. Not wishing to upset the administrator and having no strong feelings against Frances, they agree to offer the job to her. Let us hope that she accepts because choosing a third person for the job will certainly not be easy.

In this example, ranking procedures were not sensitive enough to reveal that the difference between Bert and Frances was minor for the personnel manager and medical director, while it was of major

Table 7.2. Combining Ranks When Certain of Differences Between Subgroups

Patients	Ranks of "Sicker Patients" (in Smaller Rooms)	Overall Ranks (Regardless of Location)
A	1	1
B	2	2
C	3	3
	Ranks of "Less Sick Patients" (On Ward)	
D	1	4
E	2	5
F	3	6
G	4	7

importance for the administrator. The example illustrates again the passivity of numbers. They do only what they are told to do; they do not make decisions.

What if the rankings in the six-candidate example had been fed into a computer, and all that was visible to the person who did the hiring was the final, overall, or composite ranking? The job might have gone to Bert, a candidate who all the judges ultimately agreed would not work out as well as Frances.

Ranking Procedures

As mentioned earlier in the book, an investigator cannot convert data that are placed into categories into ranks (which are more precise) without gaining more information about the ordering of things within the categories. Knowing that the "sicker" patients are kept in small rooms, while the "less sick" are on a larger ward does not tell which patient is the "sickest" of all.

Staff or therapists might be asked to rank from most to least sick three patients who are in the small rooms and four patients who are on the ward. This would create two sets of rankings, one from 1 to 3, the other from 1 to 4, with the rank of 1 being assigned to the sickest patient in each group (first data column of Table 7.2). If the "sickest" of the ward patients were obviously less sick than the "least sick" of the patients housed in small rooms, then the two sets of ranks could be combined (data column on the right). The "if" in that sentence is a big one because there certainly could be some

Table 7.3.   Illustrating Tied Ranks

Patient	Rank
A	1
B	3
C	3
D	3
E	5
F	6
G	7
Sum of Ranks	28

overlap. Surely one or two patients in the small rooms could be less sick than some who are on the ward.

For purposes of illustration, suppose that you know these patients well enough to provide dependable rankings of their overall state of health. Starting with those in the small rooms, you immediately judge that patient A is the sickest of all, so you assign patient A the rank of 1. You are not sure, however, whether patient B can really be called sicker than patient C, so you decide to give them the same rank. Do you assign both the rank of 2 because they are both tied for second place? If so, what happens to the rank of 3? You cannot give that to the next patient in line because that person is not third but fourth.

Because patients B and C share positions 2 and 3, they should be given the average of the ranks they share, which is $(2 + 3)/2$, or 2.5. Then the next person can be given the rank of 4.

When you start ranking the patients on the ward as a separate group, you notice first that patient D really seems sicker than the rest. In fact, you think this person is at least as sick as patient C. Again, you would like to assign the same rank to patient D as you did to B and C. But you cannot give patient D a 2.5 because you now have a three-way tie, not a two-way tie as you did before. Patients B, C, and D share the ranks 2, 3, and 4; the average of these is $(2 + 3 + 4)/3 = 3$, so that is the number you assign to each. In fact, the general rule is that each tied member is given the average of the ranks that would otherwise have been assigned. Assuming that you have no trouble ranking the rest of the group, the resulting set of composite ranks looks like the one in Table 7.3.

Notice that following the three-way tie among patients B, C, and D, the ranking picks up at 5. Even with the ties, patient E is fifth in order. The result is that the last rank in line is always the same as the number of things being ranked.

The general rule about assigning average ranks effectively keeps the total of all the ranks constant, no matter how many ties the series contains. In this example, the sum of the numbers 1 through 7 is 28. The sum of the ranks, including the ties shown in Table 7.3, is also 28.

Suppose you could not discriminate among any of the patients; they all looked equally sick to you. The rule says to add up all the ranks you would assign if you could discriminate and then divide by the number of ranks you have. Everybody would be given the rank of 4 (28/7) and, of course, adding 4 + 4 + 4 + 4 + 4 + 4 + 4 gives 28, so the sum is still the same. Obviously, data like these are useless because they do not discriminate—the whole purpose of ranking.

What if you really felt that the three patients in the small rooms were equally sick, that all four patients on the ward were also equally sick, and that the first group, as a group, was sicker than the second? You would assign the average of the ranks 1, 2, and 3 (that is, 2) to all patients in the small rooms, and the average of the ranks 4, 5, 6, and 7 (that is, 5.5) to all patients on the ward. (Note that the sum of three 2s and four 5.5s is still 28.) In this case you now have discontinuous data with two categories, and they would be more appropriately described with simple frequency counts than with ranks.

As stated previously, ties are usually an indication of failure to discriminate, that is, of insensitivity to differences. Because statistical computation is essentially a mathematics of differences, ties will affect the outcome of statistical tests that rely on ranked data. If the findings are strong enough and the number of ties is not great, the effect will be minimal and can be ignored. How many ties is too many is a matter for judgment: there is no single answer.

If a set of ranks contains only one pair of tied values, and if the outcome of a statistical test that uses those ranks is doubtful or of borderline significance, a simple course of action can be tried. Run the test twice more. If two persons are tied at rank 4.5, give one of them the rank of 4 and the other the rank of 5. Run the test using these ranks. Then reverse the assignment and run the test again. If both reruns produce statistical support for making the same decision of significance or nonsignificance, your problem is solved. The same logic can be extended to breaking any number of ties, but, of course, the more there are, the more reassignment must be done to cover all the possibilities. Therefore, the statistical test must be run more often, which reduces the likelihood that a clear outcome will emerge in borderline cases.

If a decision is not possible, you can do at least three things besides cheating. The first is the most empirical option. You can go back to the judges who did the ranking and see if they can find a way to break the ties. Then the statistical test can be run on better data. A more instructive alternative is to buy a good book on nonparametric statistics, such as a new edition of the classic one by Siegel (1956) or a more modern book on the same topic. Most standard textbooks on statistics also have at least some sections on nonparametrics. Look up the formulas that are used to correct for ties. The third, and most convenient, option is to call in a statistician to run the tests for you.

Testing the Difference Between Two Groups

A counseling psychologist approaches the administrator of a residential home for children, claiming that a new technique of counseling has been invented that can vastly improve children's outlook on life and self regard. The administrator agrees that the counselor should be given a chance to try the technique on a randomly selected group of six children. The group is to be counseled for four weeks and then compared with another randomly selected group of six children.

The comparison is to be made by having a neutral party come in at the end of three weeks. This person will get all 12 children together and ask each to draw a self-picture. The 12 pictures will then be ranked for the apparent optimism or happiness they express, and the ranks will be used to determine whether the group that received counseling actually seems to have a more cheerful outlook or better self-concept than the group that did not. Essentially this amounts to looking for a correlation or association between group membership and assigned ranks.

Before analysis, the data might look like those in Table 7.4. These numbers reveal nothing about the effectiveness of counseling because they do not indicate to which group each child was assigned. However, they give some idea of the task the judge faced, which was to rank 11 drawings according to the relative degree of happiness or optimism in each. Notice that in this series a rank of 1 says only that child C's picture was the happiest of the lot. It does not say how happy the picture was, or if it was happy at all. In fact, the picture

Table 7.4. Hypothetical Ranks of Children's Drawings

Child	Rank
A	6
B	2
C	1
D	11
E	7
F	5
G	Absent
H	8
I	3
J	10
K	9
L	4

may have been merely the least unhappy of a miserable group. This can sometimes be a problem when using ranks.

Once the assignments are known, the ranks may be rearranged, with the absent child (G) dropped from the analysis. The number of subjects (N) now becomes 11 (Table 7.5).

If the ranks 1 to 11 were randomly shuffled numerous times into two categories—one with 6 ranks, the other with 5—how often would the placements produce a distribution like this or more extreme than this, in terms of the overall difference between groups? Random placement should distribute high and low ranks about equally in each group most of the time. So if an unusually large number of low ranks goes to one group, they probably did not get there by chance.

The simplest eyeball test of these data is a comparison of the means of the ranks in each group. If they are the same, there is no difference between groups.

Table 7.5. Rearranged Ranks of Children's Drawings

Counseled		Not Counseled	
Child	Rank	Child	Rank
B	2	A	6
C	1	D	11
E	7	F	5
H	8	J	10
I	3	K	9
L	4		

Table 7.6.   Reversed Ranks of Children's Drawings

Counseled		Not Counseled	
Child	Rank	Child	Rank
B	10	A	6
C	11	D	1
E	5	F	7
H	4	J	2
I	9	K	3
L	8		

The mean of the ranks in the counseled group is

$$(2 + 1 + 7 + 8 + 3 + 4)/6 = 25/6 = 4.17.$$

The mean of the ranks in the other group is

$$(6 + 11 + 5 + 10 + 9)/5 = 41/5 = 8.20.$$

The difference between the means is -4.03, and it is in the "right" direction because the mean rank of the counseled group is lower, indicating that their drawings, as a group, were judged to be happier.

Now here is another interesting point about ranks: whether the rank of 1 is assigned to the best or to the poorest extreme makes no difference, as long as the rules of assignment remain consistent. The judge could have ranked the drawings from the least happy (1) up to the most happy (11)—a distribution presented in Table 7.6.

Using these ranks the mean for the counseled children is 7.83 (47/6), and for the uncounseled children it is 3.80 (19/5). The difference, which is what really interests us, is $+4.03$, and it is still in the "right" direction because the meanings of high and low ranks have been reversed.

The null hypothesis is that the true mean difference in ranks is zero. The statistical question is as follows: If the null hypothesis is true, what is the probability of obtaining a mean difference in ranks of 4.03 or greater by chance?

The U Test

The technique often used to answer this question is called the Mann-Whitney U test. Like most statistical formulas used with ranks, it is called a *nonparametric* or "distribution free" test. Basically, that means that the investigator does not have to worry about whether the raw data conform to a normal distribution or any other kind of distribution. The problem of the shape of the distribution is sidetracked by converting everything to ranks and working only with them. The *frequency distribution* of ranks is always the same: there is one item per rank, no more and no less, except for ties, which are best avoided if possible.

The following formula is used to calculate the needed value of U:

$$U = n_1 n_2 + \frac{n_1(n_1 + 1)}{2} - R_1$$

The n_1 and n_2 in this formula refer to number of ranks in each group (6 and 5, in this case). Which group is called *1* and which is called *2* does not matter as long as the labels are consistently used. The R_1 refers to the rank total for the group labeled *1*.

If the counseled group is called *1*, and if the second set of rankings (the inverted ones in Table 7.6) is used, the calculations are

$$U = (6)(5) + 6(6 + 1)/2 - (10 + 11 + 5 + 4 + 9 + 8)$$
$$= 30 + 21 - 47$$
$$= 51 - 47 = 4.$$

Consult the table in Appendix 7.A to determine whether this value is significant at the .05 level. Look across the top of the table to n_1 = 6, then down the side to n_2 = 5. Then looking down and across you will identify a cell with four numbers (5; 3; 25; 27). Under letter D (for "directional"; that is, one-tailed) are the numbers 5 and 25. This means that if U had come out anywhere between these two numbers (from 6 to 24), it would not have been significant. Since a U value of 4 lies outside this range, it is significant at the .05 level. The advantage to the investigator of using a one-tailed test in this case can easily be seen. If the test were two-tailed (nondirectional, ND in the table), the limits would be 3 and 27. Because the value of 4 lies between these numbers, the outcome would not be significant.

Once again an example shows that numbers do not make decisions, only investigators do. The decision may change, even when the numbers remain the same. In this example, the use of the one-tailed test is clearly justified, according to principles explained in a preceding chapter. In other instances, the reason for its use may not be so obvious. A handy rule is that the investigator should decide *before* running the study whether a directional or nondirectional test will be used. This decision should not be changed, even if keeping it means holding on to the null hypothesis with a two-tailed test when a one-tailed test would have permitted rejecting it.

For the sake of the exercise, see what happens if U is recalculated, calling the counseled group n_2 instead of n_1. So $n_2 = 6$; $n_1 = 5$, and $R_1 = 19$. The resulting value may be called U'.

$$U' = n_1 n_2 + \frac{n_1(n_1 + 1)}{2} - R_1$$

$$= (5)(6) + 5(6)/2 - 19$$

$$= 30 + 15 - 19 = 26.$$

This is not the same as the value obtained previously. But look at the appropriate cell in Appendix 7.A. The value of 26 is one point outside the range of 5 to 25, just as the value 4 was one point outside but in the other direction.

An easier way to get this value is

$$U' = (n_1)(n_2) - U,$$

or similarly,

$$U = (n_1)(n_2) - U'.$$

Isn't that interesting?

Now for one last challenge. Recall that the ranks used in these calculations were the second set, in which a high number represented a "happy" picture. Try going back to the first set in which a low number meant a happy picture. Recalculate U and U' to convince yourself that they still come out 4 and 26.

Incidentally, the table in Appendix 7.A covers only the .05 level of significance and group sizes of only 5 through 8. Much more elaborate tables, usually covering probability levels from .10 to .001 and sample sizes of up to 20 per group, are available in most standard textbooks on statistics.

When groups are larger than that, the value of U can be converted to a standard score (z score), the significance of which can be evaluated with a table of the properties of the normal curve. This is allowable because, when many ranks are assigned at random again and again to members of two groups, the differences between the means of the ranks for each group will tend to come out normally distributed. At least, this is what the central limit theorem says. Most differences would be near zero. Differences much greater than zero would become rarer and rarer in both directions. So a standard deviation of differences can be calculated, and a standard score can be computed for a mean rank difference of any size.

The formula by which this is done is not presented here for two reasons. First, it would take more trouble to explain than it is worth, although in reality it is not very complex, only long. Second, when group sizes are as large as 20, other statistical tests should probably be used anyway. Ranks work best with small samples.

More Than Two Groups

In the research design used for the previous example, the children being counseled were not only receiving counseling but also were receiving more attention than were the others. Therefore, the results may have been due to the extra attention and not to the counseling alone.

A third randomly selected group perhaps should have been included in the research. Children in this group would go to the same number of meetings as children in the counseled group, but they would only play games or talk. Rejection of the null hypothesis about the effectiveness of counseling would then require the counseled group to produce happier drawings than both of the other groups.

If each group contains six children, the judge's task will be harder because there will be about 18 instead of 11 or 12 pictures to rank. This design also requires a different statistical formula. Otherwise, however, the underlying logic of the approach to the problem is the same as in the two-group case.

The judge ranks the pictures without knowing to which group each child belongs. Then the code is broken, and the ranks associated with the pictures are distributed to different data columns. The mean ranks for the columns are compared to determine whether it is reasonable to say they are randomly produced, in which case the null hypothesis would not be rejected.

The correct test to use is called the *Kruskal-Wallis one-way analysis of variance for ranks*. The formula produces a single value, typically called *H*, which is checked against a special table of probability values or, if the number of groups and subjects is large, against a table of chi square. If the value is high enough, the investigator rejects the hypothesis that the true differences among the means are zero.

Rejection of this null hypothesis does not prove that counseling is effective because the same H value could arise from several different patterns of outcomes. For example, it could arise if the happiest pictures were drawn by the control group. Supplementary statistical testing would be required. Problems of inference from statistics can be quite involved when more than two groups are used in a research study.

One Group, Repeated Measures

For the most part, the analyses described in this section are used in research that calls for testing persons more than once with the same instrument. Technically, the correct term is *analyses of nonindependent data*. As noted in the preceding chapter, the investigator in this type of research must be careful not to use the wrong type of data set-up when testing changes with chi square.

Repeated-measures designs are often used in the before-after type of study, of which it is sometimes said that the subjects serve as their own controls. The usual type of question to be answered is whether the overall change in a set of scores obtained from repeated testing of the same individuals is significantly greater than zero, that is, greater than no change at all. The investigator assumes that if a certain treatment were not administered, or a certain event did not occur, persons' ranks on a particular test would not change systematically between the first and second testings. Some would go up and others would go down or stay unchanged. On the average, the amount of change would be zero, or close to it.

This type of research design can be useful when the investigator knows ahead of time that an important event is going to happen. For example, if a school or a treatment unit is about to be reorganized, tests of staff morale or of client or student satisfaction could be administered before the change and after the change. This would give two scores for each person tested. These scores could easily be converted to a single score per person by getting the difference between them. The difference can be obtained in such a way as to make an increase in morale or satisfaction come out plus, and a decrease come out minus. If the change is controversial, some may claim it will improve morale and others may claim it will make morale worse. In this case, then, a two-tailed or nondirectional test would be used.

158   FUNDAMENTALS OF RESEARCH

Table 7.7.   Example of Use of Ranks in Repeated-Measures Study

Staff Member	Before	After	d*	R
Beth	6	15	+9	7
George	16	13	−3	(2)
Mary	12	18	+6	5
Bill	8	16	+8	6
Susan	11	15	+4	3
Art	10	9	−1	(1)
Fred	13	13	0	—
Jim	14	19	+5	4

*Calculated as *After* minus *Before*, so that a plus sign indicates improvement.

Wilcoxon test. The required statistical procedure is called the *Wilcoxon matched-pairs signed-ranks test*. It may be applied to a study of morale by first setting up a table of *before* scores, *after* scores, *differences*, and *ranks* of absolute differences (Table 7.7).

When setting up this table of ranks, differences of zero are ignored because this is a test of change, and if no change occurs the data do not count. The procedure more or less pretends that Fred was not in the study at all. (Similarly, in the chi square example in Chapter 6, patients who neither improved nor became worse were dropped from the analysis.) The rank of 1 is assigned to the smallest number in the *d* column, regardless of whether the sign is plus or minus. The rank of 2 goes to the next larger number, regardless of sign, and so on until ranks have been given to all nonzero differences.

Next the *d* column is examined, and a count is made of how many pluses and minuses it contains. In this case, it contains four pluses and two minuses. The ranks of interest are the ones with the less frequently occurring sign. They have been placed in parentheses for convenience. From here on, the test is simplicity itself.

Add up the rank values of the numbers in parentheses and look up the total on a table like the one in Appendix 7.B. If the total is equal to or lower than the number in the table for the appropriate *N*, then the value is statistically significant at the .05 level. The sum of the values in parentheses is 3 (2 + 1). The table in Appendix 7.B shows that, for seven ranks, this would be just significant if the test were directional.

Recall, however, that in this case the test may not be directional because some people may claim that the change might make morale or satisfaction worse instead of better. Had that actually happened, most of the signs in Table 7.7 would have been minus instead of plus. Then the number that would have been checked out in the table would have been the sum of the ranks with plus signs. (Remember, plus and minus signs are not taken into consideration until after ranks have been assigned to absolute differences.)

To make the test truly directional, the people doing the research would have had to agree before the study was done that they would ignore any outcome suggesting that morale or satisfaction was made worse. Once more the important issue is how the investigators framed the research question. Was it a nondirectional (two-tailed) question (will the change make morale or satisfaction either significantly better or significantly worse?) or a directional (one-tailed) approach (will the change make morale or satisfaction significantly better?)? In either case, the null hypothesis is the same: the change makes no difference in morale or satisfaction. Only the alternative to the null hypothesis changes.

More generally, the Wilcoxon test may be used when subjects are so closely matched that pairs of individuals can be set up who can be treated for research purposes as being virtually the same person. This is why the test is called a test for matched pairs. The classic example is the study of twins, where one twin receives an experimental treatment while the other does not. In this situation, the differences that are of interest are taken between members of the same pairs. Ranks are assigned to these differences, and the test proceeds as before.

On the one hand, the investigator must be willing to assume that the score obtained by the nontreated member of each pair is what the treated member would have obtained if the treated member had been tested before treatment was administered. On the other hand, the investigator by using this design eliminates in advance any possible objection that the study's outcome was not valid because pretesting alerted subjects to what the investigator wanted. When justified, matching of subjects and pairing them off pays some dividends by increasing the sensitivity of research to differences, that is, by reducing the probability of committing Type II errors.

More Than One Set of Differences

Suppose one wishes to evaluate several case workers or counselors in a social agency by having clients rank the case workers' performances. (A similar design might be used in a school setting by having students rank their teachers.) Each client should be seen by

Table 7.8.   Examples of Two Levels of Agreement Among Raters

A. Low Level of Agreement

Case-Worker	Client			Sum	Mean
	A	B	C		
I	2	4	2	8	2.7
II	1	3	3	7	2.3
III	3	1	4	8	2.7
IV	4	2	1	7	2.3

B. High Level of Agreement

Case-Worker	Client			Sum	Mean
	A	B	C		
I	2	1	1	4	1.3
II	1	2	2	5	1.7
III	3	4	4	11	3.7
IV	4	3	3	10	3.3

each case worker for a specified minimum number of visits. The clients (in this case, the judges) could then rank the case workers from best to poorest. If all clients judge the same case worker to be superior, that case worker will get most of the low-number ranks. If they consistently judge another case worker to be inferior, that case worker will get most of the high-number ranks (assuming the rank of 1 means best performance). If clients cannot agree at all, ranks will essentially be randomly assigned.

These two sets of conditions will affect the overall mean ranks for each case worker quite differently. In the data in Table 7.8a for four case workers and three clients, there is little agreement among ranks, so the means for each case worker do not vary greatly. They range only from 2.3 to 2.7 (last column on the right).

In the data in Table 7.8b, the clients agree rather closely: that is, they discriminate consistently among case workers. The range of means is from 1.3 to 3.7, six times as great as in the previous example.

Notice that in this situation, the statistical approach deals with *overall variability* among means of ranks. A quick glance at the ranges does suggest that discrimination is clearer in the second set of data. Therefore, the investigator can feel fairly confident in saying that clients do see reliable differences among these case workers.

Because an eyeball test is often too crude for research purposes, an investigator may use instead the *Friedman test*. The statistical analysis in the preceding example assumes that if there were absolutely no discriminative differences between case workers, their mean ranks would be exactly equal. The variance among those means would be zero. As usual, random factors (error) are assumed to operate so that, by chance alone, the variance is always expected to deviate somewhat from zero. The Friedman test is used to establish whether an obtained measure of variation is sufficiently large to justify rejecting the null hypothesis that its true value is zero and that any deviation from zero is due to chance alone. Basically, the calculations produce a chi square. It is evaluated against a special table if the number of judges and the number of things ranked is small, but against a regular table of chi square if the number is large.

Coefficient of concordance. This type of research may also be considered a problem in correlation. If the clients all place the case workers in the same rank order, the correlation among the judges' rankings can be said to be high. The variability among mean ranks can also be used in a special formula to get a number called the *coefficient of concordance*. This number indicates the overall level of agreement among judges, considered as a whole group. It ranges from a low of zero, meaning no correlation or no variability among mean ranks, to a maximum of + 1.00, meaning perfect agreement among judges, or the greatest possible variation among mean ranks.

The coefficient of concordance never has a negative sign because it is obtained from sums and averages in which numbers are squared, and squared numbers are always plus.

Rank-Order Correlation

The correlation between pairs of ranks may be found by either of two popular methods. One is called Kendall's *tau*, named after M. G. Kendall, the person who also developed the coefficient of concordance. The other is called Spearman's *rho*. Because Spearman's *rho* is actually a special case of the Pearson product-moment correlation coefficient, it is described in Chapter 11.

A good way to explain Kendall's *tau* is to return to the earlier example of three persons who ranked six candidates for a job (Table 7.1). The problem of analysis posed by these data can be approached in either of two ways. One is to treat this as a problem of discrimination among candidates. Calculate the mean values of the ranks for each candidate. Then run a Friedman's analysis of variance to determine whether there is enough variability among these means to justify concluding that they are a nonrandom distribution of values. Another way is to turn the problem around and think of it as one of correlation among judges. Run a coefficient of concordance to determine whether there is significant agreement among the administrator, medical director, and the personnel manager.

For teaching purposes, the following discussion adopts the latter, correlational strategy, but it solves the problem a little differently. Instead of calculating a single correlation value to represent the overall agreement among all three judges, three correlations are calculated, one for each pair of judges.

First, consider the following rankings, taken from Table 7.1, by the administrator (A) and the medical director (MD):

	A	MD
Martha	1	1
Al	2	4
Frances	3	3
Bert	4	2
Charley	5	5
Ernest	6	6

Notice that the order of persons in the administrator's list is not the same as in Table 7.1. The candidates have been listed so that the rankings of the administrator are in "natural" order; that is, they go straight from 1 to 6. The outcome would be exactly the same if the medical director's ranks had been arranged in natural order instead. It is strictly a matter of convenience.

Now a value called S must be obtained. To do this, look at the ranks of the medical director as they are arranged in the preceding list. S is now just a special way of counting. Start with the top rank in the column and count how many ranks beyond it in the list are higher and how many are lower than it is. Do not add them up. Just count how many. In this case, the first rank is 1, and all the rest are higher than it. So the number above is 5, and the number below is 0.

Next move down the list one place to the rank of 4. The number of higher ranks in the rest of the list is 2 (ranks 5 and 6), and the number of lower ranks is also 2 (ranks 3 and 2). Next comes the rank of 3, with 2 above and 1 below; the rank of 2, with 2 above and none below; the rank of 5, with one above and none below; and finally the rank of 6, with none above or below, which means it can be ignored from here on.

A summary of these findings follows:

MD Ranks	Above	Below
1	5	0
4	2	2
3	2	1
2	2	0
5	1	0
6	—	—
SUM	+12	−3 = 9 = S.

As indicated, the above and below are added up, with the sum of the below values given a minus sign. These values are then added across to give the value of S, which is, in this case, 9 $(12 - 3)$.

To change S to *tau*, divide it by

$$\frac{N(N-1)}{2}$$

where N is the number of items or persons ranked, in this case 6. So, *tau* equals $+9$ divided by $6(6 - 1)/2 = 9/15 = 3/5 = .60$.

The value of 15 represents the highest S can possibly get in this example. That value would appear if the ranks of the medical director were in the same order as the ranks of the administrator. To convince yourself, arrange the numbers 1 through 6 in natural order and count up S in the way just described. Then arrange the numbers in reverse order and see if you do not obtain -15 instead of $+15$. The value $[N(N - 1)/2]$ will always give the maximum possible value for S in either direction.

The following formula expresses what was done to obtain tau:

$$tau = \frac{S}{N(N-1)/2}$$

Comparing the personnel manager's ranks in Table 7.1 with the administrator's ranks, when the administrator's ranks are arranged in natural order, produces the following arrangement:

A	PM	Above	Below
1	1	5	0
2	5	1	3
3	4	1	2
4	3	1	1
5	2	1	0
6	6	—	—
SUM		+9	−6 = 3 = S.

The denominator (15) is the same as it was before, so tau equals .20 (3/15), which shows that the administrator and the personnel manager did not agree as closely as did the administrator and the medical director.

Comparing the personnel manager's ranks in Table 7.1 with the medical director's ranks, when the medical director's ranks are in natural order, produces the following arrangement:

MD	PM	Above	Below
1	1	5	0
2	3	3	1
3	4	2	1
4	5	1	1
5	2	1	0
6	6	—	—
SUM		+12	−3 = 9 = S.

Tau equals .60 (9/15), the same as the value between the administrator and the medical director.

All three values may be placed in a small *correlation matrix* (Table 7.9). A correlation matrix is a special kind of table in which each variable is assigned one row and one column. The table as a whole represents all possible pairs of all variables, and each cell represents one pair of variables. Correlation values are inserted in appropriate cells to show the pattern of associations that are present in the data. Actually, each pair of variables appears in two cells, one in the upper right of the matrix, and one in the lower left, so it is only necessary to show one-half of the entries in the table. Also left empty are the

Table 7.9. Matrix of *Tau* Values Among Three Judges

	Administrator	Medical Director	Personnel Manager
Administrator	—	.60	.20
Medical Director		—	.60
Personnel Manager			—

diagonals of this matrix, which represent the correlation of each variable (or judge, in this case) with itself. It is not always obvious what values, if any, belong in the diagonal.

If a research study included repeated rankings of the same things or persons by the same judges, each judge's rankings could be evaluated for self-consistency. Correlations of a judge's earlier rankings with the same judge's later ones could then be entered in the diagonals of the matrix. They might be useful because an investigator might not wish to place as much confidence in the rankings of an inconsistent judge as in those of a consistent one.

The matrix in Table 7.9 shows that the lack of complete agreement among judges is due to relatively low correlation between the administrator and the personnel manager. Examination of the original sets of rankings shows that these judges disagreed mainly about Al and Charley. Al's composite rank is 4 and Charley's is 5, both of which are rather low, meaning that they are not prime candidates for the position. In an actual selection situation, this disagreement should pose no practical problem unless the first three candidates all turn down the job offer.

Statistical Significance

As with other statistics examined in this chapter, *tau* is usually evaluated for statistical significance by using a table. In this instance, the null hypothesis being tested is that *tau* is zero:

$$H_o : tau = 0.$$

Its alternative is that *tau* is greater than zero:

$$H_a : tau > 0.$$

Because only agreement among judges is of interest, the test is one-tailed. The test would be two-tailed if the alternative hypothesis that *tau* does not equal zero were stated:

$$H_a : tau \neq 0.$$

The number looked up in the table is the value of S for a given N. A partial table of probabilities appears in Appendix 7.C. It shows that, if pairs of ranks are randomly assigned to 6 items, the probability of getting a value of $S = 3$, or greater, is .360. This is hardly close enough to .05 to justify rejecting the null hypothesis. The probability of obtaining a value of $S = 9$ or greater is .068, which is almost, but not quite, significant at the .05 level. Use of one-tailed tests seems justified in this instance because significant disagreement among judges would not be of interest, even if it did occur. Notice that the failure of outcomes to be statistically significant does not necessarily reduce the practical value of the ranking procedure as a way of guiding decisions about the extreme ends of the distribution of ranks.

The most obvious way to increase the likelihood of obtaining statistically significant agreement between pairs of judges in this example would be to have more persons ranked. If 10 persons were ranked, and if the same general level of agreement held, a correlation of .20 would still not be significant, but a correlation of .60 would be. To produce this correlation value (against a denominator of 45 for rankings of 10 persons), the required value of S is 27. The table in Appendix 7.C shows that for $N = 10$ the probability associated with this value is .008, which is certainly significant at the .05 level and would be significant at the .01 level as well.

Reliability and Validity of Agreements

Everyone would probably concur that agreement among judges or raters is better for research purposes than disagreement. Bear in mind, however, that agreement is a matter of reliability not validity. Several judges may agree because all have been misled in the same way.

A common source of misjudgment is the *halo effect*, the hasty and unsupported attribution of general qualities to a person on the basis of the observation of only a few particulars. For example, several judges may agree on a single candidate for a position, yet their judgments of the candidate's overall competence may be based only on personal appearance or some especially appealing mannerism of the candidate.

Clinically, the halo effect can work both positively and negatively. Most people find it difficult to see someone who is well dressed and physically attractive as being psychologically maladjusted. At the same time, they find it difficult to be sympathetic toward someone who is disheveled or unattractive. In general, judges or raters should be used in research only if they are known to be trained and qualified to provide valid, as well as reliable, assessments.

Appendix 7.A
Abbreviated Table of the Mann-Whitney U Statistic, for Directional
(One-Tailed) and Nondirectional Test at the .05 Level

| | n_1 | | | | | | | |
| | 5 | | 6 | | 7 | | 8 | |
n_2	D	ND	D	ND	D	ND	D	ND
5	4	2	5	3	6	5	8	6
	21	23	25	27	29	30	32	34
6	5	3	7	5	8	6	10	8
	25	27	79	31	34	36	38	40
7	6	5	8	6	11	8	13	10
	29	30	34	36	38	41	43	46
8	8	6	10	8	13	10	15	13
	32	34	38	40	43	46	49	51

Appendix 7.B
Abbreviated Table of Critical Values in the Wilcoxon Matched-Pairs,
Signed-Ranks Test at the .05 Level

N	Directional	Nondirectional
6	2	0
7	3	2
8	5	3
9	8	5
10	10	8
11	13	10
12	17	13

Appendix 7.C

Partial Table of Directional Probabilities for Values of S in Kendall's *tau*

S	Number of Things Ranked (N)	
	6	10
1	.500	.500
3	.360	.431
5	.235	.364
7	.136	.300
9	.068	.242
11	.028	.190
15	.0014	.108
19		.054
23		.023
27		.008
35		.0005

—8—

CONTINUOUS DATA

Continuous and Interval Scales.

Statistical tests of data that are gathered along continuous scales are based on the same general logic that was applied to the analysis of ranks in the preceding chapter. The important difference is that, on a continuous scale, measurements may be taken to any degree of precision. A familiar continuous scale is temperature, measured in degrees. For some purposes, it is enough to say that a patient's temperature is 37 degrees Celsius. For other purposes, it may be more accurate and informative to say that it is 37.4 degrees, or even 37.452 degrees. Depending only on how sensitive the measuring instrument is, temperature may be measured to any desired level of exactness.

If temperature is thought of as an indicator of an underlying variable, such as the amount of heat that is added to or taken away from a body, then equal numbers of degrees usually represent equal amounts of heat being moved. The same amount of heat must be added to a liter of water to raise its temperature 10 degrees as must be taken out of it to lower its temperature 10 degrees. For most practical purposes, in continuous data, not only do differences in positions on a scale have meaning, but the sizes of differences have meaning as well.

Recall that the advantage of ranks over frequency counts is that ranks permit ordering individual bits of data from high to low. This is why ranks were said to be more precise than frequency counts. However, the sizes of the differences between ranks do not have any additional meaning. On a scale of ranks, the best and the next best differ by only one, whether they are actually very different or very much alike.

If three people have IQs of 130, 90, and 85, their ranks are 1, 2, and 3, respectively, even though it is plain that the first has a much higher IQ than the other two. Along a continuous scale, the difference in underlying intelligence between a person with an IQ of 110 and a person with an IQ that is 10 points lower (100) should be the same as the difference between a person with an IQ of 95 and one with an IQ of 85. Equal intervals, or differences, are presumed to have the same meaning. Therefore, a continuous scale like this one is often called an *equal interval scale* or, more simply, an *interval scale*.

Having taken IQ as an example, a little time and energy might well be spent comparing IQ to the more familiar scale of temperature. The two scales are not put together in the same way, and they do not have exactly the same properties. To measure anything along a continuum, two things are required: a place to start measuring and an agreed-upon interval size or a unit of difference. On the Celsius scale of temperature, the place to start is with ice that is just in the process of melting, that is, of being converted from the solid to a fluid state. Swedish astronomer Anders Celsius (1701–1744) proposed that the temperature of this mixture of ice and water be called *zero* degrees.

On the Celsius scale, the basic interval of measurement is the difference between the temperature of this state and the temperature of water when it is boiling, that is, just being converted from a liquid into steam. Celsius called this *100* degrees. His choice of numbers is purely arbitrary. He could have called it one degree, for instance, or 12.875 degrees, but the range of zero to 100 degrees is certainly convenient.

Note that in this case zero does not mean "nothing," which would suggest that things can never get colder (that is, have less heat) than melting ice. Clearly, that is not true. Many things, including the outdoor air in winter, get colder than that. Theoretically, the coldest anything can possibly get is about −273 degrees Celsius. This hypothetical state of absolute absence of heat is called zero or absolute zero on another scale of temperature, the Kelvin scale.

This discussion is intended to show that there is nothing sacred about a particular continuous or interval scale, including temperature and IQ. Scales are constructed by scientists for convenience. To use any scale intelligently, one must know how it was made, how its starting point and basic units, or intervals, were defined. One must also know the procedure by which scale values (measured in standard units of difference) may be determined. For most purposes, temperature can be measured by a common thermometer consisting of a calibrated glass tube that contains mercury or colored alcohol. Obviously, there are many other ways to measure temperature, just as there are many ways to estimate a person's intelligence level, or possession of some personality trait, and some ways are more precise than others.

Interval Scales in Psychosocial Research

Clinicians and investigators treat most scales that are used in psychosocial research as if they were interval scales. They therefore usually feel it is all right to analyze their data with statistical techniques that should, in principle, be performed only on equal interval scales. In many types of behavioral and health research, however, interval scales are not constructed in quite the same way as they are in chemistry or physics. Rather, the starting point for measurement is taken to be the *mean* of a distribution of scores, and the unit, or basic interval, is taken to be the *standard deviation* of the distribution.

In other words, the process of setting up a continuous scale is exactly the same as was described in the discussion of the normal curve in Chapter 5. Given a set of scores, the mean is calculated and set equal to some convenient starting point, such as zero, 50, or 100. The standard deviation, which you may recall is a special kind of average of all possible differences, is calculated and set equal to some other convenient value, such as 1, 10, or 15. This defines the scale's unit of difference. Because all such units on the same scale are assumed to have the same meaning, the resulting scores are not only continuous but also make up an equal interval scale. All kinds of numerical transformations can be done later, mostly by changing the sizes of the units and the value assigned to the mean, but the basic principle does not change.

If the mean is set equal to 100 and the standard deviation is set equal to 15, as in the statistical method of defining IQ, the assumption of equal intervals means that the same amount of difference in intelligence is represented by the difference between IQs of

85 and 100, as is represented by the differences between 105 and 120, 60 and 75, or 125 and 140. Their numerical differences are all the same (15 points). The same assumption also implies that these differences are all greater than those represented by the differences between IQs of 85 and 90, or between 115 and 120.

Most psychologists would be willing to bet that an IQ difference of 20 points represents a bigger difference in intelligence than one of 5 points. However, few would be willing to bet that a difference of 2 points represents a bigger variation in intelligence than a difference of one because all interval scales are not as precise in practice as they may seem to be in theory. For one thing, the *standard error of measurement*, which was discussed in Chapter 1, is rather large in many instruments used in behavior research. For another, questions may be raised about the assumption that equal standard score intervals represent equally large differences in the trait being measured. Few measures of mental or behavioral characteristics are as sensitive to small differences as are most familiar measures of physical quantities such as temperature, mass, or length.

Be that as it may, the task for now is to consider how continuous data, that are assumed for purposes of statistical analysis to be on equal interval scales, can be analyzed mathematically. The first illustration uses our old friend, the two-group research design.

The *F*-Test for Two Groups

Suppose that someone who works in a home for the elderly has the idea that much of the depression and confusion observed among the residents is due to the drabness and sameness of the physical setting in which they live. To test this out, a particular section of the home is remodeled to provide a more cheerful atmosphere. Walls are painted, pictures are hung, new curtains are put in the windows. A month or so after the changes are made, samples of residents in this and in another section of the home are examined. Special scales that give continuous data are administered to assess depression and confusion. The scores of the two samples are used to calculate a one-tailed test of the null hypothesis that there is no difference between the means of the groups. Some of the data from one of the tests might look like those in Table 8.1.

Basic calculations needed for the eyeball test are shown in Table 8.1. The first thing to do is inspect the means. The difference between them is 3.00 (6.00 − 3.00). If a high score on the test means greater confusion or depression, this difference is clearly in the right direc-

Table 8.1. Hypothetical Scores in a Research Study on the Effect of Altering the Institutional Environment

	Location	
	Remodeled Ward	Elsewhere
	5	9
	4	4
	1	6
	2	5
	3	5
		6
		7
SumX	15	42
SumX^2	55	268
N	5 (N_1)	7 (N_2)
$\overline{X}$	3.00 ($\overline{X}_1$)	6.00 ($\overline{X}_2$)
s^2	2.500 ($s_1{}^2$)	2.667 ($s_2{}^2$)

tion because the mean for the residents in the redecorated section is the lower of the two. It appears that further analysis is worthwhile.

This analysis follows a logic similar to that used in the analysis of ranked data. Imagine not knowing the group membership of each of the 12 persons in the study. Think of them all as being members of one large group, which is, after all, just what the null hypothesis says. If there is no difference between groups, then, as far as the research is concerned, there may as well have been only one group from the very beginning because patient location is uncorrelated with test scores. Of course, the investigator would like to prove the null hypothesis to be untenable, but, as has been mentioned several times, in the world of research the only way to do that is to start by assuming that it is correct.

If everyone belonged to one statistical group, that group would have a total N of 12 (5 + 7) members. The grand sum of the scores (ΣX, or the sum of the Xs) would be 57 (15 + 42). The grand sum of the squares of all the scores would be 323 (55 + 268). The grand mean would be

$$\frac{\text{Grand Sum}}{\text{Total N}} = \frac{57}{12} = 4.75.$$

Now the mean of the group on the remodeled ward is clearly −1.75

$(3.00 - 4.75)$ points away from the grand mean. The mean of the other is $+1.25$ $(6.00 - 4.75)$ points away from the grand mean. The mean of the second group is not quite as far above the grand mean as the mean of the first group is below the grand mean because the numbers of persons in the two groups are not equal. Equal numbers in the groups would give mean deviation scores that are the same in size but opposite in sign. As a matter of incidental interest, you might note that 5 (or N_1) times -1.75 equals -8.75, and 7 (or N_2) times $+1.25$ equals $+8.75$. The sum of these deviation scores around the grand mean is therefore still zero, even in this example.

As shown in Chapter 5, the central tendency, or mean, of each group is thought to be the best estimator of the *true score* of every person in the group. Therefore, if the experiment contained absolutely no error, and if the remodeling was effective, it may be said for purposes of analysis that every one of the five persons on the remodeled ward would have obtained a raw score of 3.0 ($\overline{X}_1$), which is the same thing as a deviation score of -1.75 from the grand mean. Similarly, every one of the seven persons in the other group would have a raw score of 6.0 ($\overline{X}_2$), or a deviation score of $+1.25$.

Between-Groups Sum of Squares

If all five "true" deviation scores of -1.75 in the first group are squared ($-1.75^2 = +3.0625$), the total is 5 times 3.0625, or 15.3125.

If all seven "true" deviation scores of $+1.25$ in the second group are squared ($+1.25^2 = 1.5625$) and summed, the total is 7 times 1.5625, or 10.9375.

The sum of *all* the squared deviation scores is therefore 26.250 (15.3125 + 10.9375). This total is called the *between-groups sum of squares* (or SS_b). Fortunately, there is an easier way to get it.

Square the SumX (raw score sum) for the first group (which is 15) and divide the result by N^1 (which is 5), the number of data points in that group. Then do the same for the next group (Sum X)^2/ N_2, or $42^2/7$). In this case,

$$\frac{15^2}{5} + \frac{42^2}{7} = \frac{225}{5} + \frac{1764}{7}$$

$$= 45.000 + 252.000 = 297.000.$$

Then, square the *grand sum* of the raw scores and divide it by the *total* N:

$$\frac{(15 + 42)^2}{12} = \frac{57^2}{12} = \frac{3249}{12} = 270.750.$$

This number will always be lower than the sum calculated first. If it does not come out that way, you have certainly made a mistake in arithmetic.

Subtract this second term (sometimes called the *adjustment for the grand mean*) from the one above. What you get is the *between-groups sum of squares* (or SS_b), the same number that was obtained before:

$$SS_b = 297 - 270.750 = 26.250.$$

This second way of calculating SS_b may seem at least as complicated as the first way, but it really is not. A little practice with several examples would probably convince you, especially if the examples contained a lot of data.

Putting all the steps together into one formula, the procedure looks like this:

$$SS_b = \frac{(\sum X_1)^2}{n_1} + \frac{(\sum X_2)^2}{n_2} - \frac{(\sum \sum X)^2}{N}$$

where $(\sum \sum X)^2$ means "the square of the grand sum" and N means "the total of all the *n*s."

Later this formula will be extended to include any number of groups. For now, two is enough. The following calculations summarize once more the translation of the preceding formulas into the numbers of this example:

$$\frac{15^2}{5} + \frac{42^2}{7} - \frac{57^2}{12} = 26.250.$$

The value obtained is not an estimate of variance, but a *sum of squares* (more accurately, a sum of squared deviation scores). To obtain an estimate of variance, this value must be divided by the appropriate number of degrees of freedom, explained later.

Within-Groups Sum of Squares

As noted earlier in this chapter and in Chapter 5, the formula for any variance (the square of a standard deviation) requires first calculating the sum of squared deviations of all scores from the mean of some appropriate group. This is done most conveniently by summing the squares of all raw scores in the group and subtracting an adjustment term. The adjustment term is the square of the sum of the scores divided by N:

$$SS = X^2 - \frac{(\sum X)^2}{N}$$

When that value is divided by an appropriate df, which is usually N minus 1, it becomes an estimate of variance (an s^2 value, a mean square, or MS).

In the present example, the SS *within* the first group is

$$55 - 15^2/5 = 55 - 225/5$$
$$55 - 45.00 = 10.00.$$

The SS within the other group is

$$268 - 42^2/7 = 268 - 1764/7$$
$$= 268 - 252 = 16.00.$$

The sum of these, or 26.00, must therefore be the *sum of squares within groups* (SS_w):

$$10.000 + 16.000 = 26.000.$$

You may well guess that this number can be obtained another way, and so it can. Furthermore, the other way is much easier than this way. But let us not get into that right now.

Summary Table and F-Test

The first column of numbers in Table 8.2 summarizes what has been done with the data so far. Ignore the rest of the columns of numbers for the moment.

Table 8.2 shows that the sum of squares between groups is 26.250, and the sum of squares within groups is 26.000. No surprises there. It also shows that these add up to 52.250, a value called the *total sum of squares* (SS_t). Remember that the within-group sums of squares

Table 8.2. Summary of Analysis of Variance (ANOVA)

Source of Variation	SS	df	MS	F
Between Groups	26.250	1	26.250	10.096**
Within Groups	26.000	10	2.600	
Total	52.250	11		

$**p < .01$

were calculated for each group separately. The between groups SS had been taken care of in the preceding set of calculations.

Total Sum of Squares

Suppose that the formula for the sum of squared deviations of raw scores from the mean had been applied to all 12 scores at once, instead of group by group as was done earlier. All scores would be made into deviations from the *grand mean*, and the result would be

$$SS_t = SumX^2 - \frac{(SumX)^2}{N}$$

$$= (55 + 268) - \frac{(15 + 42)^2}{(5 + 7)}$$

$$= 323 - \frac{57^2}{12} = 323 - \frac{3249}{12}$$

$$= 323 - 270.750 = 52.250.$$

This value, which could have been calculated first, represents the total variation of all scores around the grand mean. As has been shown in the summary table, the value has 11 *df*, or one less than the total number of data points.

Partitioning

The total sum of squares (52.250) has actually been broken down (or partitioned or analyzed) into two parts, *sources* as they are called in the summary table. One part, the between-groups sum of squares (SS_b), is based on the squared differences between group means and the grand mean. The other is based on the squared differences between individual scores and the means of their own groups (SS_w, or the within-groups sum of squares).

The first, SS_b, represents variation that is presumably due to the fact that all persons in the group of five people were on a remodeled ward, while the persons in the other group of seven were not. The second, SS_w, represents variations of individuals within their own groups and is regarded as *error*. It is not due to room location and must therefore be due to other uncontrolled or (we think) random factors.

Of the total degrees of freedom available (11), only one can belong to the SS_b because, once the grand mean has been fixed as the zero point for deviation scores, only one of the two group means is free to vary. As soon as one group mean gets any value at all, the other can be calculated exactly: it must be the difference (weighted, if necessary, for differences in *n*s) between the known mean and the fixed grand mean. An extension of the same logic applies when data are analyzed from more than two groups. That is why, in the analysis of variance, the *df* between groups is always one less than the number of groups.

The rest of the *df* are within groups. Each group has one *df* less than the number of data points within it. That amounts to 4 in the group of five subjects and 6 in the group of seven subjects, or the total of 10 shown in the table.

Both sums of squares and *df* values, between and within groups, must add up to the correct total sum of squares and *df*. Therefore, when calculating the SS values, one can start with the total SS, then calculate either the between-groups or the within-groups SS and obtain the third term by subtraction:

$$SS_t = SS_b + SS_w \; ; \text{ or}$$

$$SS_b = SS_t - SS_w \; ; \text{ or}$$

$$SS_w = SS_t - SS_b \; .$$

That will be done in a subsequent example.

Mean Squares

Having the sums of squared deviation scores and degrees of freedom well in hand, estimates of variance can now be calculated by simple division:

$$MS = \frac{SS}{df}$$

$$MS_b = \frac{26.250}{1} = 26.250$$

$$MS_w = \frac{26.000}{10} = 2.600.$$

A total MS is not needed. It is not used in the F-test.

The value of F. The next step is also simple. To obtain the value of F, divide the mean square between groups by the mean square within groups. If MS_b is less than MS_w, do not waste your time. F will then be less than 1.00, which means that the estimate of random variation (MS_w) is greater than controlled experimental variation (MS_b), so the outcome cannot possibly be statistically significant. In this research the value is much greater than 1.00:

$$F = \frac{MS_b}{MS_w} = \frac{26.250}{2.600} = 10.096.$$

Significance of F. The best estimate of variance based on differences in ward location alone (MS_b) is 10.096 times as large as the best estimate of variance based on random factors (MS_w). That seems pretty high, but is it significant? A table of F values tells the story (Appendix 8.A).

To read this table, look across the top for the number of df between cells (1), and look down the left side for the number of df within cells (10). Tracing down and across from these points reveals the critical values of 4.96 at the .05 level and 10.04 at the .01 level of confidence. The obtained value of 10.096 is greater than 10.04 (although not by much), so the null hypothesis may be rejected at the .005 level of confidence. That level of confidence is half of .01 because it was decided before the test was run that it would be one tailed, and the obtained difference between groups is in the hoped-for direction.

The size of this F-ratio would have been exactly the same if the direction of the difference had been reversed, but that result would have been meaningless as far as this research question is concerned.

Therefore, it is permissible to divide the probability value by two when establishing the level of statistical significance.

The *t*-Test

For testing the difference between the means of two independent groups, most textbooks recommend using the *t*-test rather than the *F*-test. The easiest way to calculate *t* can be explained very quickly. First, run the type of analysis of variance that was described earlier. Then take the square root of *F*. For most purposes, that is all there is to it. The square root of 10.096 is 3.177, the value of *t* in this example.

Significance of t

To evaluate *t* for statistical significance without using the table of *F* values, use a table like the one in Appendix 8.B. This table is not read in exactly the same way as is the table of *F*. In this table, look down the column on the left for the *df* within groups. As in the analysis of variance, *df* is equal to

$$(N_1 - 1) + (N_2 - 1), \text{ or}$$

$$(N_1 + N_2 - 2).$$

In the present case, $(5 + 7 - 2) = 10$. The obtained value of *t* (3.18, rounded to two places) is just barely greater than the value of 3.17, required for significance at the .01 level, two-tailed, or the .005 level, one-tailed, when $df = 10$.

Another Formula for t

The formula that is usually given for calculating *t* looks like this:

$$t = \frac{\overline{X}_1 - \overline{X}_2}{\sqrt{\dfrac{\sum X_1^2 - \dfrac{(\sum X_1)^2}{N_1} + \sum X_2^2 - \dfrac{(\sum X_2)^2}{N_2}}{N_1 + N_2 - 2} \left(\dfrac{N_1 + N_2}{N_1 N_2}\right)}}.$$

Although this calculation is lengthy and has probably frightened off many a student, it is far from impossible. Substitute the proper means, sums, and values for N in this formula, where the subscripts 1 and 2 stand for the two groups being compared. Calculate the result, and the value of t will be exactly the same as the square root of F, calculated by the method described earlier.

The conclusions drawn from an F-test can never conflict with those drawn from a t-test because all the values in the first column of an F table, for numerators with 1 df, are simply the squares of the values in the table of critical values of t. Thus, for example, the critical value of t at the .05 level, for a test with $df = 15$ within groups, is 2.13. When squared, this becomes 4.54, the same as the tabled value for an F ratio based on 1 and 15 degrees of freedom.

Too many t-tests. In some studies, especially in exploratory research, investigators rely heavily on the t statistic. Even though only two groups are assessed, several scores may be available for each. The investigator may therefore run a series of t-tests, one for each available score, and report a whole list of values of t and their associated probability levels. Both investigator and reader may easily forget that when statistical tests are carried out at a decision level of .05, about 5 percent of them will be significant by "chance" alone. The probability of committing a Type I error is, in fact, set exactly by the *alpha* level that is selected for use in data analysis. A certain number of such errors is unavoidable, even under the best of conditions.

One way to reduce the likelihood of committing Type I errors is to set a stricter decision level for all tests of the null hypothesis. The *Bonferroni inequality* has been proposed as a way of deciding what level to set (Grove and Andreason 1982). The name of the procedure sounds impressive, but it is actually rather simple to use. If all decisions are equally important, just divide the decision level by the number of statistical tests being run. Then use that level for each individual test.

For example, if the overall *alpha* level (α) is set at .05, and six t-tests are being run, then each should be evaluated at the .00825 (.05/6) level rather than at the .05 level. When this procedure is used, the overall *alpha* for the research remains .05, although each specific test is judged by stricter standards.

Besides its simplicity, a particular advantage of this approach is that it may be used for any statistic that is used many times in the same research, not just for t-tests. A disadvantage is that, while reducing the likelihood of committing Type I errors, any tightening of the *alpha* level increases the likelihood of committing errors of

Table 8.3.   Results of a Hypothetical Study of a Smoking Reduction Program

| Person | Average Cigarettes Per Day | | | |
	Before	After	Total	$\overline{X}$
A	20	5	25	12.5
B	15	20	35	17.5
C	10	10	20	10.0
D	35	20	55	27.5
E	18	10	28	14.0
Sum	98	65	163	
$\overline{X}$	19.6	13.0	16.3 (Grand Mean)	

the second type. In other words, it makes a research study less sensitive to real differences between groups. Generally, when many null hypotheses must be tested in a single study, it is better to base statistical decisions on analysis of variance or other multivariate procedures that are specially designed to estimate probabilities in such cases.

The *F*-Test for Repeated Measures

The logic of the F- and t-tests described above is similar to the logic of the Mann–Whitney U-test for ranks. All these tests are appropriate when each group contains different persons, and every person is tested only once. But what happens when the same persons are tested twice? This situation is similar to the rank order situation in which the matched-pairs, signed-ranks test was used to evaluate change.

The classical example of this type of research is the before-after study. Suppose that five people who enter a smoking reduction program are asked to count the number of cigarettes they smoke per day for a week before the program starts. This establishes a *baseline* for later evaluations of program effectiveness. Then, six weeks after the program is over, they repeat the count, with the results shown in Table 8.3.

The mean for the group decreased from 19.6 cigarettes per day to 13.0, and an examination of the changes shows that only one person (B) was smoking more after the program than before. The statistical test of the overall change can be one-tailed because the opposite outcome, however great, would not cause the investigator to reject the null hypothesis that the treatment does not work (that is, to conclude that it does.) Be careful of those multiple negatives.

The problem may also be approached with analysis of variance (ANOVA), but the procedure is somewhat more complicated than in the preceding example. In the analysis of variance for this problem, two terms are called *main effects*, and one is called their *interaction*. A main effect is an estimate of variance (mean square) based on differences among the means of either the rows or columns in the data table. Therefore, one source of variation is the main effect due to overall differences between persons A through E, regardless of treatment results. Clearly, person D, who smoked an overall average of 27.5 cigarettes per day, is generally a heavier smoker than person C, who smoked an overall average of 10.0. Because there are five persons in the study, the number of degrees of freedom for this source of variation is 4 $(N-1)$.

Another source of variation is the main effect due to differences between group means before and after treatment. This will have only one degree of freedom, but it is the one that is of main concern to the investigator.

So far, 5 *df* have been accounted for (4 between persons and 1 between test periods). But the data table contains 10 numbers, so the total *df* is 9. That leaves 4 *df* unaccounted for. These are due to the interaction of persons and treatment. The interaction is made up of differences between persons in how much they changed from before treatment to after treatment. Notice, for example, that person A dropped from 20 to 5 cigarettes per day (a change of -15), while person C did not change at all, and person B's consumption actually increased. These differences in responsiveness from person to person constitute *error* in the experiment. The logic is that if the treatment were absolutely perfect, differences in effectiveness would not be found; every person would have been affected by the treatment in exactly the same way and to exactly the same degree. Obviously, this is not what happened in this study. But interactions are not always error terms. Sometimes they are interesting in their own right, as Chapter 9 will point out.

The *df* for any interaction is always the product of the *df*s of the main effects that it contains. In this case, *df* equals 4 (4 × 1). The summary table for this analysis is shown in Table 8.4. Although the variation among persons and the variation among test periods are both more than twice as large as the interaction term, neither is statistically significant. The table in Appendix 8.A does not show the critical values for the .10 level (two-tailed), which are needed

Table 8.4. Summary of Analysis of Variance

Source of Variation	SS	df	MS	F
Persons (P)	372.600	4	93.150	2.320 NS
Test Periods (T)	108.900	1	108.900	2.712 NS
Interaction: (P × T)	160.600	4	40.150	
Total	642.100	9		

to determine significance at the .05 level (one-tailed). The values actually required, however, are almost twice as large as those obtained. Therefore, despite the apparently favorable outcome, based on an inspection or eyeball test of the before and after means, the null hypothesis cannot be regarded as untenable.

Calculations

In case you are interested, here is how the numerical values in the summary values were obtained. First, the total SS was calculated using the sum of all squared scores, the squared sum of all the scores, and the total N:

$$SS_t = SumX^2 - \frac{(SumX)^2}{N}$$

$$(20^2 + 15^2 + 10^2 + 35^2 + 18^2 + 5^2 + 20^2 + 10^2 + 20^2 + 10^2) - \frac{(163)^2}{10}$$

$$= 3299 - \frac{(26,569)}{10} = 3299 - 2,656.900 = 642.100.$$

The SS between persons was then calculated. Each person's total was squared and divided by 2 (because that is the number of data points making up the total for each person). The results were added up, and the same adjustment term $(SumX)^2/N$ was subtracted:

$$SS_p = \frac{(SumX_{p1})^2}{2} + \frac{(SumX_{p2})^2}{2} + \frac{(SumX_{p3})^2}{2} + \frac{(SumX_{p4})^2}{2}$$

$$+ \frac{(SumX_{p5})^2}{2} - \frac{(SumX)^2}{10}$$

$$= \frac{25^2}{2} + \frac{35^2}{2} + \frac{20^2}{2} + \frac{55^2}{2} + \frac{28^2}{2} - \frac{163^2}{10}$$

$$= \frac{625}{2} + \frac{1225}{2} + \frac{400}{2} + \frac{3025}{2} + \frac{784}{2} - \frac{26569}{10}$$

$$= \frac{(625 + 1225 + 400 + 3025 + 784)}{2} - \frac{26569}{10}$$

$$= \frac{6059}{2} - 2569.0$$

$$= 3029.5 - 2656.90$$

$$= 372.6.$$

Next the sum of squares for test periods was calculated:

$$SS_{tp} = \frac{(SumX_{tp1})^2}{5} + \frac{(SumX_{tp2})^2}{5} - \frac{(SumX)^2}{10}$$

$$= \frac{98^2}{5} + \frac{65^2}{5} - \frac{26569}{10}$$

$$= \frac{(98^2 + 65^2)}{5} - 2656.90$$

$$= 2765.80 - 2656.90$$

$$= 108.90.$$

Do you see where the values in the preceding calculations come from? The outcomes values were entered into the first numerical column in the summary table. Then the sums of squares for the main effects were subtracted, one after the other, from the total SS to get the SS for the interaction. Next all SS values were divided by the appropriate *df*s. Finally, the resulting MS values for each main effect were divided by the MS of the interaction to produce the *F*-ratios. Follow this step-by-step description slowly and carefully, and the calculations will not seem as complicated as they probably appeared at first sight.

Interpretation

The main effect MS for test periods is the matter of major concern. If it were significant, the treatment could be judged to be effective.

The main effect MS for persons was not of any special research interest. Had it been significant, the persons in the study would have been found to differ significantly from each other in overall smoking frequency. In certain types of research, such *individual differences* are important, but not in this particular study.

The *t*-Test for Repeated Measures in One Sample

The same test could have been run a bit more simply as a *t*-test. As in the matched-pairs, signed-ranks test, this procedure would be performed, not on the raw data, but on the differences between before and after scores, taken from Table 8.3. These are shown below:

Person		d
A		15
B		-5
C		0
D		15
E		8
	SumX	33
	SumX^2	539
	s^2	80.300
	$\overline{X}$	6.600

The mean ($\overline{X}$) in this case is the mean of the set of differences. It therefore has the same importance as the main effect between *test periods* in the analysis of variance.

For this type of *t*-test, the null hypothesis is that the true mean difference is zero and the obtained mean of 6.60 is a random deviation from that value. The hypothesized value of zero is what would appear if there had been no overall changes in smoking frequency. The calculated value of s^2 (80.300) can be used to obtain an estimate of how much random variation can be expected around the hypothetical value of zero. However, it represents the variance of the difference scores on a person-by-person basis, not the variance (or standard error) of the mean of the whole group.

The square root of s^2 (± 8.96) tells how much variation in treatment effectiveness is to be expected among persons who take the treatment, but it does not tell how much variation can be expected for the group mean. What is needed is an estimate of the *standard error of the mean of the differences*, that is, the variation that could be expected among means of difference scores if a very large number of similar groups of persons were given the same treatment.

This value should be a smaller number than the *sd* of the scores for individuals because each mean represents a combination of difference scores from five persons. Each should therefore be a more dependable figure than the score from a single individual. To estimate the standard deviation of a set of means like this, divide the *sd* of the sample by the square root of N (N being the size of the sample) and take the square root:

$$s_{\bar{x}} = \frac{s}{\sqrt{N}}.$$

In this example, the standard error of the mean is

$$s_{\bar{x}} = \frac{8.96}{\sqrt{5}} = 4.007.$$

The value of t is, then, just a standard score, but with $s_{\bar{x}}$ in the denominator:

$$t = \frac{\bar{X}_d - 0}{s_{\bar{x}}} = \frac{6.600}{4.007} = 1.647.$$

The value 0 is included in the numerator of this formula to show that it is not the mean difference alone that is being tested. What is being tested is the variation of the obtained mean difference from its expected value, according to the null hypothesis, which is 0.

The number of degrees of freedom in this test is one less than the number of difference scores $(5 - 1) = 1$. According to the table of t, a value of 2.13 is required at the .10 level of significance, two tailed, or the .05 level, one tailed. The result of this study is therefore not statistically significant—the same conclusion reached by the analysis of variance. As was pointed out before, this is no accident, for F still equals t. The square of 1.647 is 2.712, the same value as was obtained in the F-test, for the variance between test periods.

One-Way Analysis of Variance for More Than Two Independent Groups, No Repeated Measures

A one-way ANOVA is one that contains no interactions. It provides only an overall test of the null hypothesis that the true differences among the means of two or more groups are all zero. The null hypothesis implies that whatever differences are actually found are no greater than could be found if all groups were samples drawn at random from the same statistical universe. When more than two groups are involved, the calculations are an extension of those used in the two-group situation.

Going back to the first example in this chapter (Table 8.1), imagine that two additional groups were included in the design testing the effectiveness of remodeling on the level of confusion of the residents of a home for the elderly. The additional groups might be ones in which different types of activities were introduced to occupy residents' time. For convenience, the four groups are called R (remodeling), A1 (Activity 1), A2 (Activity 2), and E (residents from elsewhere in the home). The data table, along with some preliminary calculations, is presented in Table 8.5. The data for groups R and E are the same as before.

As before, first calculate the total sum of squares, disregarding groups.

The grand sum of scores is

$$(15 + 42 + 17 + 40) = 114.$$

The grand sum of squared scores is

$$(55 + 268 + 105 + 406) = 834.$$

The total N is $(5 + 7 + 3 + 4) = 19$.

$$SS_t = \sum X^2 - \frac{(\sum X)^2}{N}$$

$$= 834 - \frac{114^2}{19} = 834 - \frac{12996}{19}$$

$$= 834 - 684.000 = 150.000$$

Table 8.5. An Expansion of the Research on Environment Modification

	R	E	A1	A2
	5	9	8	8
	4	4	4	10
	1	6	5	11
	2	5		11
	3	5		
		6		
		7		
N	5	7	3	4
SumX	15	42	17	40
SumX^2	55	268	105	406
$\overline{X}$	3.0	6.0	5.7	10.0
Total N	19			
Grand SumX	114			
Grand SumX^2	834			
Grand Mean	6.00			

The next thing to calculate is the sum of squares between the four groups. Square the sum of each group and divide it by the number of scores in the group. After adding all these values together, subtract the same adjustment term, $(\Sigma X)^2/N$:

$$\mathrm{SS_b} = \frac{(\sum X_R)^2}{N_R} + \frac{(\sum X_E)^2}{N_E} + \frac{(\sum X_{A1})^2}{N_{A1}} + \frac{(\sum X_{A2})^2}{N_{A2}} - \frac{(\sum X)^2}{N}$$

$$= \frac{15^2}{5} + \frac{42^2}{7} + \frac{17^2}{3} + \frac{40^2}{4} - 684.00$$

$$= \frac{225}{5} + \frac{1764}{7} + \frac{289}{3} + \frac{1600}{4} - 684.00$$

$$= 45.00 + 252.00 + 96.33 + 400.00 - 684.00$$

$$= 793.33 - 684.00$$

$$= 109.33.$$

Subtracting $\mathrm{SS_w}$ from $\mathrm{SS_t}$ gives the sum of squares between groups:

Table 8.6.   Summary Table of One-Way ANOVA for Four Groups

Source	SS	df	MS	F
Between Groups	109.33	3	36.443	13.442**
Within Groups	40.67	15	2.711	
Total	150.00	18		

$**p < .01$

$$SS_b = SS_t - SS_w$$
$$= 150.00 - 109.33$$
$$= 40.67.$$

These numerical values are now entered into the first column of numbers in a summary table (Table 8.6). Degrees of freedom are also calculated.

The total df is $(N - 1) = (19 - 1) = 18$.

The df between groups is one less than the number of groups $(4 - 1) = 3$.

The df within groups can be calculated in three ways: as the total df minus the df between groups $(18 - 3) = 15$; as the total N minus the number of groups $(19 - 4) = 15$, as the sum of the degrees of freedom within each group separately (4 for group R, plus 6 for group E, plus 2 for group A1, plus 3 for group A2 equals 15). Each way achieves the same answer.

As before, the needed mean squares are obtained by dividing sums of squares by their appropriate dfs. F is obtained by dividing the MS between groups by the MS within groups. The table in Appendix 8.A shows that, with 3 df in the numerator and 15 df in the denominator, the value of 5.42 would be significant at the .01 level. The obtained F of 13.442 is clearly much larger than this. The investigator may feel justified in concluding that it is unreasonable to argue that the four groups have equal "true" means or that they come from samples belonging to a single statistical universe.

Interpretation

What, in particular, makes this argument unreasonable? An eye-ball test suggests that the mean for group R is lower than the rest, while the mean for group A2 is higher than the rest. If that is the case, then Activity 2 has actually increased patients' confusion rather than decreased it. Probably this interpretation is correct, but these results alone are not sufficient to establish its validity beyond doubt.

If that outcome had been thought of ahead of time as a possibility, an additional set of *planned comparisons* could have been run next. Those might have consisted of another analysis of variance comparing group A2 with the other three groups combined into a single group (*df* between groups = 1; within groups = 17). Or another ANOVA might be used to test A2 against E and A1 combined (*df* between groups = 1; within groups = 12). Then, in still another ANOVA, R (the lowest) could be tested against E and A1 combined (*df* between groups = 1; within groups = 13).

Notice that when more than two groups are involved, the question of whether a one-tailed or two-tailed test is being run does not arise. The overall *F* test is not sensitive to direction in such situations. It may be sensitive to direction only in supplementary analyses where only two groups are tested against each other.

Whenever more than two groups are involved and supplementary tests are conducted the danger of capitalizing on chance also arises. Many ways of avoiding this danger have been devised, among them Scheffe's test, Duncan's multiple range test, Neuman-Kuel's test, Dunnett's test for comparisons with a control group, at least two varieties of Tukey's tests (A and B), and an approach called the *method of orthogonal comparisons* (Winer 1971). Because of the lack of agreement as to which of these tests is best and because different approaches are suited to different types of research situations, the serious student of statistics is usually required to learn them all. Now you know what to expect if you become a serious student of statistics.

More Than Two Measurement Periods

Repeated Assessments of the Same Group

As is true for simple one-way analysis of variance, *F* tests may be performed to analyze experiments in which a single group of individuals is tested more than once. This type of research, often called *time series research,* can be useful in treatment studies if changes are expected to take place over a long period of time and several follow-up testings are required to evaluate them. It is also useful in studying processes, such as learning, to establish rates of improvement at different stages in training. Statistical analysis of time series data can become very complex if the number of repetitions is large, say greater than 8 or 10.

No specific examples of repeated-measures analysis of variance are worked out in this book. All you probably need to know is that the sources of variance are the same as in the simple before-after design. One main effect term represents the overall individual differences among participants, regardless of test period. Its df is one less than the number of participants. Another main effect term represents overall differences among test periods. Its df is one less than the number of test periods. The interaction term serves as the estimate of error. Its df is the product of the dfs of the two main effects.

In time series research, difficulties in interpretation arise because the analysis of variance procedure in general is based on the assumption that data points are independent; that is, that the value of one data point is not influenced by the value of another. When the same person is tested more than once, the assumption of independence becomes questionable because factors such as differences in individual skill levels, practice, boredom, or recall of previous responses may begin to exert an influence on scores in later testings. A degree of dependence is therefore introduced into the data, and a corresponding degree of uncertainty arises about how to interpret outcomes. As suggested earlier, time series analyses (usually of a type that employs what is called the *Box-Jenkins approach*) take dependencies among a series of means into account and may be used if the series is long enough. However, no agreed-upon solution has been found to the problem of repeated-measures designs that use fewer than about 30 retests.

Assessing Different Groups at Each Period

Testing different groups of subjects along a time series eliminates dependencies due to within-subject factors, but it may not eliminate the possibility of bias entirely. Suppose an investigator examines levels of usage of alcohol among teenagers by testing a different randomly selected group of tenth graders every week for a school year. The mean level of usage may still be affected by seasonal factors or by events that take place in the community, such as a one-month police crackdown on drunken drivers. The long-range effectiveness of any attempt to experimentally change teenagers' alcohol use must take such factors into account. Again, a special form of time series analysis may be used to evaluate the effectiveness of such a program if enough data points are collected over a long enough period of time.

Shorter term studies may also be conducted in which independent groups are tested at regular intervals on the same variable. In a study of this type, the investigator may wish to know whether the effects of a particular drug on behavior, such as lever pressing in a Skinner box, diminish regularly over time. Different groups of rats could be given the same dose of the substance. Then one group would be tested after 30 minutes, another after 1 hour, another after 90 minutes, and so on.

The analysis of variance would produce a main effect for time periods and an estimate of error variance that is based on variations between organisms within their own groups. The investigator would rely upon random assignment of organisms to ensure that groups were equivalent in all other respects because there is no way to test their equivalence before the experiment is run. To test the animals in advance on the lever-pressing apparatus, or to test a single group of animals many times instead of just once, would introduce dependency—due to repeated assessment of the same organisms—into the data.

This does not mean that the data could not be analyzed by the usual statistical techniques, which are based on assumed independence of data. Remember the passivity of numbers. But it does mean that statistically sophisticated colleagues who tend to be sensitive to dependencies in data would probably criticize such analyses.

To return to the example, if the effect for time periods were significant, the investigator would reject the null hypothesis that the true means for the groups, tested at different time periods, are equal. In this type of research, however, the investigator usually wants to know more than just that the array as a whole is nonrandom or even which particular test periods are significantly different from the others. The investigator would probably like to know whether performance (lever pressing) increases (or decreases) steadily from interval to interval, or whether change in performance comes rapidly at first and then tapers off. In other words, the shape of the curve that traces changes in the dependent variable over time is of considerable interest as well. Special supplementary statistical tests can be run to determine whether these changes over time trace a straight line, or a curve with one hump (which can be described by a *quadratic* equation), or even more humps than that. Obviously, the possibilities are more numerous than can be explored in this chapter.

Appendix 8.A
Abbreviated Table of Critical Values of F at the 5% and 1% Levels
for use in ANOVA (1% Level Underlined)

df for Denominator	df for Numerator						
	1	2	3	4	5	10	20
1	161	200	216	225	230	242	248
	4052	4999	5403	5625	5764	6056	6208
2	18.51	19.00	19.16	19.25	19.30	19.39	19.44
	98.49	99.00	99.17	99.25	99.30	99.40	99.45
3	10.13	9.55	9.28	9.12	9.10	8.78	8.66
	34.12	30.82	29.46	28.71	28.24	27.23	26.69
4	7.71	6.94	6.59	6.39	6.26	5.96	5.80
	21.20	18.00	16.69	15.98	15.52	14.54	14.02
5	6.61	5.79	5.41	5.19	5.05	4.74	4.54
	16.26	13.27	12.06	11.39	10.97	10.05	9.55
10	4.96	4.10	3.71	3.48	3.33	2.97	2.77
	10.04	7.56	6.55	5.99	5.64	4.85	4.41
15	4.54	3.68	3.29	3.06	2.90	2.55	2.33
	8.68	6.36	5.42	4.89	4.56	3.80	3.36
100	3.94	3.09	2.70	2.46	2.30	1.92	1.68
	6.90	4.82	3.98	3.51	3.20	2.51	2.06
infinity	3.84	2.99	2.60	2.37	2.21	1.83	1.57
	6.64	4.60	3.78	3.32	3.02	2.32	1.87

Appendix 8.B
Some Critical Values of t for Two-Tailed Tests

	Significance Level			
df	.10	.05	.02	.01
1	6.31	12.71	31.82	63.66
2	2.92	4.30	6.96	9.92
3	2.35	3.18	4.54	5.84
4	2.13	2.78	3.75	4.60
5	2.02	2.57	3.36	4.03
6	1.94	2.45	3.14	3.71
7	1.90	2.36	3.00	3.50
8	1.86	2.31	2.90	3.36
9	1.83	2.26	2.82	3.25
10	1.81	2.23	2.76	3.17
15	1.75	2.13	2.60	2.95
20	1.72	2.09	2.53	2.85
infinity	1.65	1.96	2.33	2.58

—9—

MORE COMPLICATED ANALYSES

Preliminaries: Statistical Analysis and Research Design

Research is a way of asking and answering questions about nature. Statistical analysis is not the essence of research, but it does provide a set of useful tools that help investigators decide which of several possible answers to a research question is most likely to be correct.

Chapter 3 examined the agreed-upon way of writing up scientific reports. First, the research question is posed. Next, the subjects, procedures, and methods of data collection are described. A discussion of the statistical tests that have been used to analyze the results and an interpretation of the outcome follow. But research projects are not usually carried out in this rather straightforward, step-by-step way. This process is the ideal rather than the real state of affairs in most instances, especially in the behavior and health sciences and in applied settings.

One Extreme

At one extreme of poor research planning is the situation in which an agency that delivers services to clients collects information helter-skelter over a period of years. Eventually someone calls in a statistician or methodologist to consult about how the resulting supply of data should be analyzed for research purposes. Undoubtedly exceptions occur, but as a rule such attempts to design research or analyze data after they have been collected in an unplanned way do not work out well.

Granted, no investigator can foresee every turn of events that might take place, especially when planning an exploratory or purely descriptive research study. Nevertheless, before any study is begun, a conscientious investigator should have good reason to believe that needed data can be collected and analyzed. The investigator should also have some ideas about how the analysis of those data will proceed. As indicated in Chapter 1, not all data need be treated mathematically. However, all data should be treated systematically and with procedures that make them, and the conclusions they support, as dependable as possible.

The Other Extreme

Total failure to plan in advance for the collection and analysis of data is one extreme. The other extreme is for the investigator to succumb to the temptation to design only research that suits a particular type of statistical analysis. An investigator at this extreme might develop enthusiasm for carrying out a certain study only because some well-known or newly developed procedure for data collection or statistical analysis makes the project interesting. Whether the question that the project answers is of any practical value would not be important. All that would matter is that the research design be "state of the art," that it use the most complicated and technically advanced techniques available through contemporary technology.

Advancing technology has hypnotic appeal, and scientists are strongly inclined to use it, even on occasions when it may be less than appropriate. For example, in determining whether a treatment program affects patients' quality of life, a descriptive approach may be more useful and valid than one that attempts to test hypotheses with numbers. Yet some might be tempted to feel that a study that is built around multivariate research design, with data that are subjected to causal analysis, is certain to be better because it treats the problem in a mathematically complicated way.

The following sections describe some of the complications of elaborate analysis of variance procedures and the research designs that are associated with them. Remember that more elaborate, complicated, or technical research is not necessarily better than simple research. Good research design requires the art of matching research questions appropriately to procedural strategies and techniques of data analysis. All the components are equally important.

The Purpose of Analysis of Variance: A Quick Review

Basically, the mathematical procedure called *analysis of variance* does just what its name implies. The overall variation (sum of squares) within a large group of scores is broken down (analyzed) into two parts. One part is variation associated with controls or limits that the investigator has put on research conditions. The other part is uncontrolled. Each of the two sources of variation is divided by its appropriate *df* to produce mean squares. Every mean square is thought of as being an estimate of the variance of some universe or population.

The variance estimate produced by a controlled source is compared with the estimate produced by an uncontrolled source by dividing the former by the latter. The *F*-ratio that results is then evaluated to determine whether it is significantly larger than 1.00, which is the value that would appear if the two estimates were exactly equal. If *F* equaled 1.00, or nearly 1.00, both numbers could be considered estimates of the same parameter, or universe value. Only if *F* is greater than 1.00 do the rules of conventional scientific practice allow an investigator to check further to see whether the research outcome might be statistically significant.

One-Way Analysis of Variance

The simplest form of research design that uses analysis of variance has already been described. It is the independent multiple-group design in which several groups of subjects are tested, each under a different set of conditions. Data from research conducted with this design are processed as a one-way analysis of variance. If only two groups are involved, the *F*-ratio is equal to the square of *t*, and the test may be treated as one tailed or two tailed, depending on the type of hypothesis that has been formulated. If more than two groups are used, the *F*-ratio can only be used to suggest whether the differences among the set of group means as a whole significantly deviate from zero. If they do, supplementary tests must be used to locate specific sources of nonrandomness.

Comparing variances within groups. In all *F*-ratios that are used to test hypotheses in experiments, one term represents *con-*

trolled variation and the other term is called *error*. The error term is sometimes also called a *residual* (or the *remainder*) because it is often obtained from the sum of squares that remains after all controlled variation has been removed from the total. To test the hypothesis that the true values of the two terms are equal, the error term is always placed in the denominator of the F-ratio, never in the numerator. In the usual F-test of experimental data, if the SS between controlled conditions is less than the SS within them, the F-ratio is not even calculated. In other words, estimates based on controlled variation must be larger than estimates based on uncontrolled variation, or there is no logical point in running the test.

Sometimes an F-test of the ratio between two variances is carried out differently, with the only condition being that the larger of two estimates goes in the numerator. The main research use for this procedure is to test whether the variances within two groups (not between them) are estimates of the same parameter. This is called a test for *homogeneity of variances*. The larger within-group variance is divided by the smaller, and the result is evaluated on a table of critical values of F. Because, in this case, the term that goes into the numerator is not selected before data are collected, the probability listed in the table of F must be doubled.

This F-test reveals whether the two separate estimates of random variation (one within each group) are estimates of the same parameter. If the F-ratio is not significantly large, the investigator presumes that the variances are homogeneous and proceeds with the data analysis.

If this F-ratio is sufficiently large, the investigator is expected not to use the analysis of variance or the usual t-test to evaluate the difference between means of the two groups. This is because proper use of the analysis of variance requires that the variances within groups be, for all practical purposes, equivalent. If only two groups are tested, and a t-test is being run, a special formula may be used instead of the usual one to overcome this difficulty. No such direct way is available to deal with the calculation of F when within-groups variances are not estimates of the same parameter.

Often, however, data may be transformed to meet statistical requirements. For example, transformation might involve analyzing the square roots or logarithms of obtained scores, instead of analyzing the scores themselves. Because the selection of an appropriate transformation requires considerable knowledge of statistics, such procedures should be undertaken only with the guidance of an appropriately trained person.

Strictly speaking, the requirement of homogeneity of estimates of error variance applies to more complicated research designs as well as to simple ones, such as the two-group design (Wike 1971). Numerous tests have been devised to evaluate homogeneity of variance in complicated research designs, but none is completely satisfactory. There has been some tendency in recent times to ignore the problem because nonhomogeneity seems to have little effect on the outcomes of most analyses. Nevertheless, many computer programs that are used to run such complicated analyses provide both tests of and adjustments for lack of homogeneity of variance. If a multiple-group design is used, it is a good idea to have the data analyzed by a statistician who knows how to interpret such tests and adjustments.

Examples of More Complicated Designs

Investigators have invented a number of complicated research designs, all of which lend themselves to statistical treatment of data by analysis of variance. Each design contains both sources of controlled variability and sources of variability that are assumed to be random. For example, the one-way, independent multiple-group research design that has already been described can be considered a more complicated version of the two-group design.

In the multiple-group design, the investigator tests several groups of subjects. The estimate of variance based on the sum of squares between (or among) group means is said to be controlled because the investigator has applied different treatments to each group. The variance estimate based on the pooled (that is, combined) sums of squares within groups is said to be random and is the estimate of error.

This between-group type of research can be made more elaborate by building into it a feature called a *factorial structure*. In a factorial structure, each level of every independent variable appears at every level of every other independent variable as will be explained more fully later.

Start with a simple two-group research plan in which a treatment is administered to one group of persons but not to the other. Suppose that the treatment is expected to be more effective with one type of patient than with another. For example, it might be more effective with younger patients than with older patients, or more effective when administered one way than another, or less effective when used alone than when administered in combination with some other form of treatment. A psychotropic drug, for instance, might work

Table 9.1.   A 2 × 2 Factorial Design, with Independent Groups

	Treatment	No Treatment	
Older	$n_{ot} = 30$	$n_{on} = 30$	$N_o = 60$
Younger	$n_{yt} = 30$	$n_{yn} = 30$	$N_y = 60$
	$N_t = 60$	$N_n = 60$	$N = 120$

best in younger persons, when the drug is administered four times a day instead of just once, and when it is used in conjunction with psychological counseling. All these factors can be built into a single research project, but, as seems only natural, the project would be quite complicated. The following discussion begins with a much simpler example.

A 2 × 2 Factorial Design

Think about the possibility of dividing the subjects in both groups of a two-group study into subgroups—older and younger—which would give four groups altogether. This could be done by breaking the large group into older and younger halves after testing everyone on the outcome measure but before analyzing the data. This procedure is the so-called *median split*. The median referred to is the median of the distribution of ages.

A better way to accomplish the same thing is by preplanned selection of subjects. Subjects could be chosen in advance so that half of them are between 35 and 45 years of age (the "older" group) and half are between 20 and 30 years of age (the "younger group"). Suppose a grand total of 120 persons was planned for in advance. To keep the numbers in the subgroups equal, 60 subjects would be chosen in each subgroup. They would be randomly assigned to the treatment or no-treatment condition, so that 30 older and 30 younger persons received treatment and 30 older and 30 younger persons did not.

As usual, the reason for assigning people to these conditions at random is to try to ensure that the subgroups do not differ in ways other than those intended by the investigator. Another reason is to attempt to ensure that there is *homogeneity of within-groups variances*. The research structure is a 2 × 2 factorial design, with independent (or, more accurately, randomized) groups (Table 9.1).

In this table, those lowercase *n*s that are not parts of subscripts refer to the number of persons who are assigned at random to conditions in each cell. The upper case Ns refer to the total number of persons who are assigned to conditions in each row or column, disregarding cells.

Variations in this design. The factorial approach is not limited to two groups along each dimension. If two treatments plus a no-treatment condition were used, the design would be called a 3 × 2 (or 2 × 3) factorial design, with independent (or randomized) groups. If three levels of age had also been included, instead of two, it would be called a 3 × 3 factorial design, with independent groups.

Suppose the investigator chose not to allow other variables (such as whether subjects are men or women) to vary randomly, but instead deliberately treated them as sources of "controlled" variability. This could be done, but it would require adding a third dimension to the table. If the original design was 2 × 2, the revised design would be 2 × 2 × 2 (treatment, age, sex) and would contain eight cells instead of only four (older male, treatment; older male, no treatment; older female, treatment; older female, no treatment, etc.). If the total N remained at 120, and if the investigator wanted to keep equal ns in each cell, the number of subjects per cell would have to be reduced by half, to 15 instead of 30.

Main effects. Before adding other dimensions to the research design think about what can be learned by applying analysis of variance to data collected in the relatively simple 2 × 2 factorial structure. Table 9.2 shows hypothetical data from a small study with only four persons in each cell.

No attempt is made here to demonstrate how to perform the actual analysis of these data, although the procedures are straightforward extensions of those already described in Chapter 8. A look at the means and the resulting summary table should be enough to show what can be done with the data.

Note at the far right of Table 9.2 that the mean for the older persons on the outcome measure is 2.5, while the mean for the younger persons is 3.0. If high scores mean more symptoms then it appears that younger patients, with or without treatment, experienced more symptoms than did older patients.

The mean for younger patients is 0.25 above the grand mean of 2.75. The mean for older patients is 0.25 below the grand mean. The differences between the means of the two groups and the grand mean are equal because the numbers of younger and older patients are the same. These differences are the basis of the main effect for age.

Table 9.2. Data for a 2 × 2 Factorial Design, with Independent Groups

	NT		T		
	4		3		
Older	3		1		
	2		1		
	3		3		
(Subtotals)	12		8	$\sum X_o$	20
$\overline{X}_{on}$	3.0	$\overline{X}_{ot}$	2.0	$\overline{X}_o$	2.5
	6		0		
Younger	5		1		
	4		2		
	5		1		
(Subtotals)	20		4	$\sum X_y$	24
$\overline{X}_{yn}$	5.0	$\overline{X}_{yt}$	1.0	$\overline{X}_y$	3.0
$\sum X_{NT}$	32	$\sum X_T$	12	$\sum\sum X$	44
$\overline{X}_{NT}$	4.0	$\overline{X}_T$	1.5	Grand $\overline{X}$	2.75

Because there are two levels of age (two groups), this main effect has 1 *df*.

Across the bottom of the table, note that the mean for all persons not receiving treatment is 4.0, which is 1.25 above the grand mean. The mean for all those receiving treatment is 1.50, which is 1.25 below the grand mean. These differences are the basis of the main effect for treatment. The *df* is again one less than the number of levels of treatment, or 1. If a variance estimate based on these differences were found to be significant, the investigator would conclude that treatment has reduced symptoms, whether patients are relatively older or younger.

Interaction. A significant main effect may not tell the whole story. A glance at the two means for the younger persons shows that these differ by 4.0 points (5.0 − 1.0). The means for the older patients, however, differ by only 1.0 points (3.0 − 2.0). The difference between the differences (the *second-order difference*) is 3.0 points (4.0 − 1.0). If significant, this second-order difference implies that younger persons benefited much more from treatment than did older patients, that is, there was an interaction between treatment effects and age.

Figure 9.1 presents one way of graphing this interaction. One line shows the sharp drop in the mean for younger patients. The other

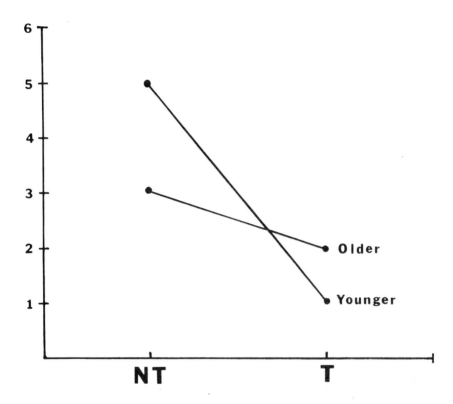

Figure 9.1.   Interaction of treatment effects and age of subjects.

line shows the much less pronounced decrease for the older ones. The figure also suggests that one reason older patients showed less benefit is that their scores are relatively low without care. Perhaps older persons only seem to benefit less because they are generally less in need of treatment.

The word interaction was used in the preceding chapter in the description of a research study using a single group, repeated-measures design (the before-after test). In that research, only one main effect was of interest: the main effect due to treatment. The other main effect, due to differences among the means of the total scores for persons, was not important to the research. The interaction of persons by testings served as the estimate of error for testing treatment effectiveness.

The before-after difference for any one person in that study could be thought of as providing a single test of treatment effectiveness. Variations among the before-after differences from person to person

Table 9.3.   Summary Table of Analysis of Variance for 2 × 2 Design

Source	SS	df	MS	F
Ages (A)	1.000	1	1.000	1.200 NS
Treatment Conditions (C)	25.000	1	25.000	30.012 **
Interaction: A × C	9.000	1	9.000	10.804 **
Within Cells	10.000	12	.833	—
Total	45.000	15		

$**p < .01$

made up a set of second-order differences. In the same way, variations in treatment effectiveness between older and younger persons make up a pair of second-order differences in the 2 × 2 design just described.

In this 2 × 2 factorial design that uses independent groups rather than repeated testings of the same persons, the interaction MS can also be used as the denominator of an F-test for the effectiveness of treatment. Suppose the investigator already knows that both the treatment and the interaction terms are significant when tested against the random error term (within-cells MS). If another F-test of the treatment term, this time against the interaction, turned out to be significant, it would show that the treatment is generally effective for all persons even though the interaction shows that it is also more effective for one group than the other.

If the test of the treatment term against the interaction were not significant, the outcome would imply that the overall treatment effect may not be completely reliable. The treatment was actually effective for only one group. Its influence on that one group was so powerful that it made the overall treatment mean look significant, even though it was not.

Summary table. Table 9.3 shows how the hypothetical results in Table 9.2 would be summarized. Notice that, as usual, the total *df* is one less than the total number of values in the data table. The *df* for ages is 1. The *df* for the interaction is the product of the *df* for the terms it contains (1 × 1). The rest of the *df* [(15 − 1 − 1 − 1) = 12] is assigned to the error term (pooled within-cells sum of squares). This also equals the sum of the 3 degrees of freedom (3 + 3 + 3 + 3), that are present in each of the four groups.

Table 9.3 shows that the F-test of the overall main effect for age is scarcely greater than 1.00 and is clearly not significant. The overall effect for treatment is significant at the .01 level, and the inter-action is also significant at the .01 level.

As indicated earlier, when main effects and interactions are both significant, the significant main effect should be tested against the interaction. A glance back at Figure 9.1 shows that the treatment appears to be much more effective for younger than for older persons. A supplementary test against the interaction gives an F-ratio of

$$\frac{25.000}{9.00} = 2.778,$$

for 1 against 1 df. This value is nowhere near being significant. Therefore, the hunch was correct. Although the interaction is sig-nificant, the main effect is not significantly greater than the inter-action. Supplementary statistical tests can be used to determine whether, as seems likely, the treatment effect is significant for youn-ger persons alone.

Unequal ns. In this example, the number of subjects in each subgroup or cell of the factorial design was the same. In actual research, they need not be equal. If they are not, however, the process of calculation becomes somewhat complicated. Before the advent of computers, calculation by hand posed quite a problem, but now in-vestigators rarely give much thought to such matters. Their greatest difficulty is to select the computer programs that will perform the analysis of variance in the most appropriate way, or provide the most convenient form of printout, or the most useful types of sup-plementary statistical tests of complicated interactions.

Unequal ns do not change the number of df for main effects or interactions. The total df remains one less than the total number of values in the data table. The df within cells is still the total of the dfs for all the groups. What is affected is the way in which sums of squares are figured.

More about degrees of freedom. Just for practice, examine the breakdown of degrees of freedom for a more involved two factor design. In this example, suppose there are three treatment groups, four levels of age, and different numbers of persons in each cell. In other words, this will be a 3×4 factorial design with independent, randomized groups and unequal ns. The design is shown in Table 9.4. The values in the cells are the numbers of persons in each subgroup.

Table 9.4. Numbers of Subjects Assigned to Cells of a 3 × 4 Design, with Unequal n's

Age Levels	Treatment Levels			
	I	II	III	*n*
I	3	4	4	11
II	5	3	4	12
III	6	2	3	11
IV	6	4	2	12
n	20	13	13	(N) 46

The total *df* is 45 (46 − 1).
The *df* for treatment levels is 2 (3 − 1).
The *df* for age levels is 3 (4 − 1).
The *df* for the interaction is 6 (2 × 3).
The *df* within cells may be calculated as the total minus all the main effects and interactions:

$$45 - 2 - 3 - 6 = 34.$$

Or it may be calculated as the sum of the *df*s for all 12 cells:

$$(2 + 3 + 3 + 4 + 2 + 3 + 5 + 1 + 2 + 5 + 3 + 1) = 34.$$

As a rule, it is not wise to have any cell contain fewer than two data values. There can be no variance within a cell that has only one value. Its *df* would be zero. Therefore, that cell cannot contribute meaningfully to a total estimate of error. For similar reasons, no cell should be empty, for that destroys the essential balance of the overall study. The research would no longer have a factorial design. Modern statistical methods for computers offer ways of getting around the problems posed by such incomplete or unbalanced designs but it is probably best to avoid introducing such problems if possible.

A Three-Factor Factorial Design

The type of research in the examples just described may be extended by adding a third, fourth, or any number of independent variables, provided that each is fully crossed with the rest. For example, two modes of treatment administration (I and II) might be included in the design (or two different psychotherapists, in a study of counseling), along with several levels of treatment and subject age. Then, for each category of treatment, there must be groups of persons in every age group who are subjected to each mode of administration.

Again, for simplicity, suppose that there are two levels of treatment (some [T] and none [N]), two levels of age (older [O] and younger [Y]), and two modes of administration of treatment (I and II). This, then, is a 2 × 2 × 2 factorial design. Assuming once more a total of 120 subjects, then one-half will receive treatment, one-half will not. One-half will be older, one-half will be younger. One-half will be administered the treatment by mode I, the other half by mode II.

These calculations seem to account for a total of six halves, which is three times more than is mathematically possible—one of the beauties of this research design. The investigator can, in effect, perform three studies of 120 persons each, using only a total of 120 persons. Not only that, but the investigator can test interactions as well.

To represent this type of design requires a three-dimensional figure, one dimension for each factor (Figure 9.2). The figure contains eight cells (2 × 2 × 2), one for each logically required combination of levels of the three independent variables. It shows the research design as three views of a cube: top, front, and side. The top view appears to set up impossible conditions: those under which no treatment is administered in two different ways. If that were the case, these cells could contain no data. The design would be unbalanced, and special statistical procedures would be required to analyze the results. However, the conditions needed to maintain balance could be met if *no treatment* really meant *placebo*, for a placebo can be administered in more than one way.

Main effects. In this research, a comparison can be made between all the older and younger subjects by combining data from appropriate cells in the front and side views of Figure 9.2. Combining the four cells in the upper layer gives the mean for all older subjects as a group. Combining all four cells in the lower layer gives the mean for all younger subjects as a group. The comparison is not biased because each combined group contains equal numbers of persons who received treatment or placebo and who were administered the substance by mode I and mode II.

Similar procedures, using other combinations of cells, give tests of the main effect of treatment and the main effect of mode of ad-

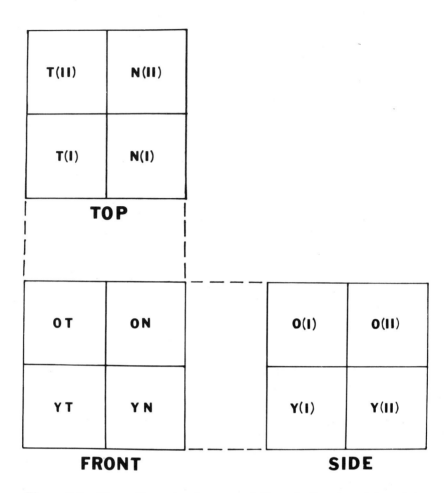

Figure 9.2. Three-dimensional representation of a 2 × 2 × 2 factorial research design.

ministration. So far so good, but the interaction structure gets a little complicated. Age may interact with treatment level, regardless of mode of administration. To evaluate this interaction, the mean outcome for each age group at each treatment level regardless of mode of administration must be obtained. This is done by collapsing the figure so that only the front view of Figure 9.2 remains. That puts 30 persons in each cell of the resulting four-cell square. The faces on this square are labeled OT, ON, YT, and YN (older, with treatment; older, no treatment; younger, with treatment; younger, no treatment). Variations among the means for each of the cells are

Table 9.5. Degrees of Freedom for Main Effects and Interactions in a
2 × 2 × 2 Factorial ANOVA

Source	df
Treatment (T)	1
Subject Age (A)	1
Mode of Administration (M)	1
TA	1
TM	1
AM	1
TAM	1
Pooled within cells variation	112
Total	119

the basis for the age (A) × treatment (T) interaction mean square. It has 1 *df* because 1 times 1 is still 1.

Now, by collapsing the figure sideways so that only the side view remains, subjects can be combined across the two levels of treatment. This leaves a different four-cell square of $n = 30$ per cell. The faces on this square are labeled O(I), O(II), Y(I), and Y(II) because treatment levels (T) are now being ignored. The means in this square provide the basis for calculating the age (A) by mode of administration (M) interaction. Finding that this interaction is significant might imply that people at one age level respond more favorably to a particular way of giving treatment, whether the treatment contains any active ingredient or not.

Another two-way interaction table can be set up by squashing the box down so that its upper and lower levels are combined, leaving only the top view of Figure 9.2 remaining. The cells of the resulting four-cell square are labeled T(I), N(I), T(II), and N(II). The means of these cells provide the basis for calculating the T × M interaction. This interaction would be significant if, for example, the treatment was effective when administered by one technique (or one therapist) but not the other, regardless of the age of the person treated.

Finally, the three-way interaction A × T × M would reveal whether one or two specific combinations of age, treatment, and mode of administration were particularly effective or particularly ineffective. For example, significance might appear if the active therapeutic agent produced particularly bad effects when administered by injection to older persons. Table 9.5 summarizes all sources of variance and their associated degrees of freedom.

The information contained in the three-way interaction is highly specific and may not be of particular interest. Higher order interactions are sometimes ignored even when the interactions are statistically significant because they can be very difficult to interpret. In fact, as suggested earlier, investigators sometimes use them as error terms, or estimates of random variation, against which lower order interactions or main effects can be tested.

An investigator who is willing to treat higher order interactions as estimates of error variance can get away with using only one subject per cell of the research design. In the present example, that would mean running the entire study with only eight subjects. It would also mean that the test of each main effect would be based on two subjects per cell. Finally, it would mean that if the three-way interaction were significant, there would be no way of knowing it because there would be no error term against which to test it. Such a skeleton-type research design may be highly efficient in its data collection, but it is not very powerful or sensitive. It is likely to produce Type II errors, errors an investigator makes by failing to reject the null hypothesis when it should be rejected, when a genuine effect is missed.

For purposes of preliminary investigation, certain sacrifices in information and power may be acceptable. Notice, however, that no matter how many or few subjects are used, the df for the three-way interaction is only one, because the dfs for the main terms that make it up are all 1, and $1 \times 1 \times 1$ is still 1. Glance at the table of F requirements for significance when there is 1 df in the denominator. The table shows that the MS in the numerator must be at least 161 times as large as the MS in the denominator for the F-ratio to reach the .05 level of statistical significance. Under those conditions, the likelihood of committing a Type II error is high.

Extensions of the design. A factorial design may be extended two ways: by increasing the number of levels for one or more factors to more than two and by increasing the number of factors. The rules for determining df remain the same, but if factors are added, the number of interactions increases dramatically. Two-way interactions must include all possible pairs of factors; three-way interactions must include all possible triplets, and so on.

Just for fun, the breakdown of interactions and degrees of freedom for a $2 \times 3 \times 4 \times 2$ factorial analysis of variance is presented in Table 9.6. For simplicity, the main effects are labeled A, B, C, and D, and it is assumed that data from three subjects are in each cell.

Table 9.6. Degrees of Freedom for Main Effects and Interactions in a 2 × 3 × 4 × 2 Factorial ANOVA with three Subjects Per Cell

Main Effects	df
A	1
B	2
C	3
D	1
Two-Way Interactions	
AB	2 = (1 × 2)
AC	3 = (1 × 3)
AD	1 = (1 × 1)
BC	6 = (2 × 3)
BD	2 = (2 × 1)
CD	3 = (3 × 1)
Three-Way Interactions	
ABC	6 = (1 × 2 × 3)
ABD	2 = (1 × 2 × 1)
ACD	3 = (1 × 3 × 1)
BCD	6 = (2 × 3 × 1)
Four-Way Interactions	
ABCD	6 = (1 × 2 × 3 × 1)
Residual (Within Cells)	96 = (2 × 48)
Total	143

Since the total number of cells is 48 (2 × 3 × 4 × 2), that implies 144 (3 × 48) subjects altogether, or a total of 143 (144 − 1) degrees of freedom.

Each cell has 2 df, so the residual or within-cells term contains 96 df (2 × 48). In most cases, this term can serve as the error term for all the terms above it. In some instances, however, one or more main effects will be defined as *random variables* by the investigator. This introduces additional complications into the data analysis. Some of these are discussed briefly in the section on the so-called *mixed-model analysis of variance*, which follows.

Mixed Designs

Sometimes it seems that investigators never pass up a chance to make things more complicated. Actually, most of the more complicated research designs they have developed serve very useful purposes. For example, the mixed-model designs described here provide efficient approximations to multivariate analyses, but they can be carried out with far fewer subjects. If you care to learn more about this type of research design, a book by Winer (1971, pp. 514–603) is a good place to look.

Recall that a repeated-measures design is one in which the same subjects are tested more than once, usually under different experimental conditions. As has already been pointed out, the simple, one-group, before-after type of study is a basic form of repeated-measures research. To produce a mixed-model design, a one-way, multiple-group design is combined with a repeated-measures research study. All persons in several groups are tested more than once.

For example, one group may be given Treatment A, another Treatment B, and a third Treatment C. One of these groups could be in a placebo or no-treatment condition. All subjects could be tested three times: just before treatment, immediately after treatment, and six months after treatment for follow-up evaluation. This produces a 3×3 mixed-model design. If four persons were in each group, there would be 12 persons in the study but a total of 36 observations ($3 \times 3 \times 4$), or 35 df to be accounted for. A hypothetical set of data is shown in Table 9.7.

The means across the bottom of Table 9.7 show an overall increase from test period I to test period III, with the greater increase occurring between period I and period II—exactly what might be expected in a successful study of this type. The means for the treatment conditions (down the second column from the right) suggest that Treatment A is best. Treatment C is next best, although it is rather far behind A; the means differ by 1.08 (6.25 − 5.17) points. Treatment B is least effective, although it is not as different from C—with a difference of 0.59 (5.17 − 4.58) points—as C is from A.

At the pretest period, the means for the three groups are fairly close, but groups A and C improve across test periods, while the means for group B actually decrease slightly. This suggests the possibility of a treatment by test period interaction.

Finally, there is the question of differences among subjects, regardless of treatments and test periods. The last column on the right shows the mean for each person. If this were a simple one-way analysis of variance with three independent groups of four persons each, and a single testing with no repeated testings, there could be no interaction of subjects or treatments with test periods. The sums of squares among subjects, within treatment groups, would be pooled

Table 9.7. Hypothetical Data for a Mixed-Model ANOVA Design

Treatment Group	Test Period I	Test Period II	Test Period III	Sum	Subject $\overline{X}$
A	6	8	7	21	7.0
	2	3	4	9	3.0
	4	6	8	18	6.0
	8	10	9	27	9.0
SumX	20	27	28	75	
$\overline{X}$	5.0	6.75	7.0	6.25	
B	7	6	5	18	6.0
	3	2	1	6	2.0
	9	7	6	22	7.3
	1	3	5	9	3.0
SumX	20	18	17	55	
$\overline{X}$	5.0	4.5	4.25	4.58	
C	8	5	6	19	6.3
	2	3	4	9	3.0
	5	6	11	22	7.3
	4	7	1	12	4.0
SumX	19	21	22	62	
$\overline{X}$	4.75	5.25	5.50	5.17	
Sum(SumX)	59	66	67		
$\overline{X}$	4.92	5.50	5.58		

to make up an error term for the test of treatment differences. It would have only 9 *df* (3×3).

Something similar happens in this mixed-model design, but there is an additional consideration: due to repeated testings, subjects interact with test periods. Despite the general tendency in group A for people to improve across all test periods, the fourth person's scores decrease between period II and period III. Similarly, in group B, the fourth person goes against the subgroup trend by improving steadily. These variations can also be regarded as a form of exper-imental error, and they will appear in a pooled interaction term called the *interaction of persons and test periods, within groups*. It contains the interaction of persons and test periods in group A (*df* $= 3 \times 2 = 6$), plus similar interactions in groups B and C, for a total of 18 *df*.

The outcome of the actual analysis of variance of these data is

Table 9.8. Analysis of Variance of 3 × 3 Mixed-Model Study

Source	df	MS	F
Treatment (T)	2	8.583	<1.000 NS
Subjects (S) within T*	9	16.537	—
Test Periods (P)	2	1.583	<1.000 NS
T × P	4	2.167	<1.000 NS
S × P, within T*	18	3.565	—
Total	35		

*Error terms (see text).

summarized in Table 9.8. The most obvious thing about this table is that none of the F-ratios is greater than 1.00. Therefore, none can be statistically significant.

As indicated by the preceding discussion, this analysis contains two separate error terms, which is appropriate since the research combines two separate types of research design. The error term for the first design is made up of variations between subjects within treatment groups. The other error term is the pooled interactions of subjects and test periods. Other, still more complicated mixed-model designs contain more than two error terms.

The first error term, *subjects within treatment groups*, is the same within-groups term that would be used if the investigator had obtained only one outcome score per person instead of three. It is used to test for overall differences among treatment groups (the main effect for T). In this mixed-model research, failure of significance for this main effect alone would not necessarily imply that the treatments were not differentially effective. Some rather large differences between treatment groups that might appear at test period II (immediately after treatment) could be covered up, or "washed out," in the totals if the differences between groups at test period I (pretreatment) and test period III (six-month follow-up) were not great.

The main effect for test periods is the repeated-measures factor. It is based on overall changes in outcome measures, regardless of treatment group. In this particular research, failure of this term to reach significance is not necessarily of great concern to the investigator either. Significance, of course, would indicate a general trend that is independent of types of treatment administered. However, marked changes by one treatment group could be masked by lack of change, or by changes in the opposite direction by other groups.

Both the main effect for test periods and the interaction of test periods by treatment groups are tested against the pooled interactions of subjects by test periods, within treatment groups. As in the simpler before-after design, this term measures individual differences in score changes from test period to test period.

The interaction of treatment groups and test periods (T × P) is the term of primary interest and concern. The fact that this term is not significant means that there is no reason to believe there were systematically different shifts in outcome measures between the groups over time. Consequently, there is no basis for arguing that any specific treatment brought about greater change than any other. In other words, even though the eyeball tests looked promising, the experiment was not powerful enough to allow the investigator to place any confidence in them.

Probably what is needed is to repeat the experiment with more persons in each treatment group. Perhaps some adjustments could also be made in treatment strengths. Another possibility would be to use a more sensitive test of outcome, if one is available. This would increase the sensitivity of the study to the changes that actually do occur. Finally, attention might be paid to the possibility of increasing the homogeneity among subjects. For example, if the 12 persons in this preliminary study ranged in age from 18 to 75 years, limits might be placed on the age ranges in the next set of samples.

The reason for increasing homogeneity among persons is to reduce individual differences in responsiveness to treatment conditions. This should cut down the size of the error terms somewhat. Of course, it would also limit the generalizability of the findings—a price that often must be paid to decrease the likelihood of committing a Type II error.

A final word about the T × P interaction term in this research example. Although the investigator would like it to be significant, if it had been, that alone would not have proved that any treatment was effective. Significance could just as easily appear if two groups had stayed the same and one got markedly worse. A graphic display of the interaction and supplementary tests could be used to tease out what caused the overall F-ratio to be high.

Further Complexities

Mixed-model designs can include more than one grouping factor and more than one set of subject factors. For example, the research design here could have included a *mode of administration* (M) factor in addition to the *treatment type* (T). Different subjects would then be randomly assigned to each factorial combination of treatment mode and treatment type. All would be tested three times, as in the original example. This would add to the summary table a main effect for M and interactions of M-by-T, of M-by-subjects, and the three-way interaction of M-by-T-by-subjects.

The basic cell of this research would be a single M-by-T condition. Therefore, every term that involves subjects would be calculated as a pooled variance within modes and treatments. Because subjects are presumably a random factor, each term that involves subjects would be an error term for something else that does not include subjects.

An investigator might also wish to add subject variables to the design. The research might then include, for example, three sets of older men given Treatment A administered by Mode X. The design could also contain younger males, older females, and younger females. The basic cell would therefore be a single sex-by-age-by-treatment-by-mode condition, and the analysis would be correspondingly more elaborate.

Finally, there is no reason for all within-groups factors to be persons. An attitude scale might measure several categories of attitudes, such as attitudes toward physical environment, attitudes toward health care, attitudes toward administrative procedures. On the attitude scale, each category might contain several items. A main effect for *categories* could be tested against an error term based on variations among *items within categories*.

Similarly, suppose one is testing three types of drugs that are generically different from each other but are all advertised as treatments for the same condition. Samples of each substance could be tested for effectiveness. A main effect for drugs could be tested against an error term based on (presumably homogeneous) variations among samples within generically different drugs.

The possibilities may seem endless. Indeed, they are.

Analysis of Variance as Information Processing

As the preceding examples have shown, research based on analysis of variance models can sometimes tell an investigator more about a particular problem than anyone cares to know. Analysis of variance can become so complicated and technical that an investigator or student may forget that one of its most valuable features is its remarkable efficiency at organizing information. Quite aside from the tests of significance it produces, analysis of variance imposes upon the entire research process a degree of rigor that forces the investigator to think every research problem through carefully and to consider every possible logical implication of all research procedures (Hays 1973).

A real problem is posed by the fact that complicated ANOVAs produce many F-tests, which raises again the possibility of being misled or of capitalizing on chance when interpreting research results. In general, the best way to avoid such difficulties is to plan research carefully and to concentrate attention upon those terms that were expected in advance to provide the crucial tests of significance.

PRODUCT-MOMENT CORRELATION

Variation, Covariation, and Differences: A Summary

Research is a process of systematically observing differences or variations. This includes not merely differences but associated differences, not merely variation but covariation. In short, research is nearly always a search for correlations. Correlation coefficients and their uses have been mentioned wherever they seemed appropriate, but they have not been explained in detail. Therefore, a good way to begin this chapter, which describes how to calculate the Pearson product-moment correlation coefficient, is by integrating the various ideas about correlation in general that have been presented so far.

An obvious way to look for a correlation is to measure two variables and see whether changes or differences in one go along with changes or differences in the other. In a rehabilitation agency for persons with physical disabilities, both intelligence and success in learning activities of daily living (ADL) must be measured, if one wishes to find out whether intelligence is related to patients' success in a program teaching ADL. The data may then be examined with statistics such as the *product-moment correlation coefficient*, one of the two *rank-order correlation coefficients* (see Chapter 7), or the *phi coefficient* or *contingency coefficient* (see Chapter 6).

If intelligence is positively related to success in the program (that is, if more intelligent patients do better than less intelligent patients), then the number that represents the correlation will be positive. If, for some reason, more intelligent patients are systematically less successful than less intelligent patients, the number will usually be negative. Whether positive or negative, the closer the number is to 1.00, the stronger the relationship. As has been noted, in some cases, indexes of correlation range only between 0.00 and + 1.00, never having negative values. However, in all instances, a value of exactly zero means that the relationship is essentially random, which is the same as saying that there is no relationship at all.

Correlation indexes or coefficients are often called *predictors*. In this example, they would be predictors of success in ADL training. Any correlation, positive or negative, that indicates nonrandom co-variation and does not change much over time can be used in prediction, which is the basis for actuarial research. However, actuarial research is mainly practical or economic. It is not usually used to test theories, although observed correlations can sometimes start people thinking about why things happen as they do or about how to bring about changes that will affect a correlation coefficient.

Given that the correlation in our example is positive, arrangements could be made for therapists to spend more time working with patients who get lower scores on an intelligence test, and relatively less time with patients who get higher scores. If that program were successful, later testing should show that the correlation dropped closer to zero because steps were taken to counteract it. Ideally, of course, there should be at least two groups: one in which training makes allowance for intelligence test scores and one in which training goes on as usual. If all assignments are random and all other conditions remain constant, the correlation should be unaffected in the second group. But anyone who works in an institutional setting knows that random assignment and constancy of conditions are not the rule in such places.

All indexes of correlation are calculated between lists containing pairs of scores. In a research on persons, each person must have two scores, one for each variable being measured. Anyone who has a score on only one variable cannot be included in the calculations.

If three variables are measured, correlations must still be between pairs of variables. Therefore, three variables give three indexes, four variables give six indexes, etc. The results can be represented as a *matrix* of correlations, like the one used in Chapter 7 with three variables or the one shown in Table 10.1 that contains eight fictional variables. Notice in Table 10.1 that the diagonal once again is empty. In this example, it might be said to represent the correlation of each

Table 10.1. A Matrix of Correlation Coefficients for Eight Variables

Variable	Variable							
	I	II	III	IV	V	VI	VII	VIII
I	—	42	21	37	65	82	16	21
II	42	—	19	18	43	06	27	32
III	21	19	—	11	12	70	41	16
IV	37	18	11	—	57	28	39	34
V	65	43	12	57	—	41	72	23
VI	82	06	70	28	41	—	27	33
VII	16	27	41	39	72	27	—	27
VIII	21	32	16	34	23	33	27	—

Note. Table entries omit decimal point.

test with itself. Sometimes this correlation is assumed to be 1.00. More often, it is a figure less than 1.00, called a *communality*. This figure is usually computed during the process of factor analysis by a complex procedure that need not be described here.

Notice that the matrix in Table 10.1, like the smaller one in Chapter 7, is symmetrical about the diagonal. In other words, all the numbers in the upper right of the matrix are the same as those in the lower left. In this instance, all numbers on both sides of the diagonal have been included, but, as mentioned in Chapter 7, investigators commonly publish only half of the matrix. The reader can easily fill in the blanks.

Note also that the number of entries in each half of the table is 28, the number of different paired comparisons that can be made for eight things. The formula for obtaining this number should look familiar. It is the same one that was used in the denominator of the formula for Kendall's *tau*:

$$\frac{N(N-1)}{2}.$$

In this case,

$$\frac{8(7)}{2} = 28.$$

Finally, a word about the numbers themselves. As mentioned before, a correlation coefficient is not a percentage. A value of .40 does not mean that two variables have 40 percent common variance, or that predictions of one variable from the other will be 40 percent accurate. What the numbers mean will become more apparent when the methods for calculating them are explained.

Certain kinds of correlation coefficients lend themselves to mathematical manipulation by procedures such as *factor analysis* and *multiple regression*. Factor analysis squeezes the redundancies out of a matrix and is often used to reduce the number of tests or measures by combining variables that are closely correlated with each other. For example, if three tests measuring aspects of psychological adjustment correlate highly with each other (make up a single factor), they may either be combined into a single test, or one or two of them may be dropped from future investigations.

The purpose of multiple regression is usually prediction. Suppose variable I in Table 10.1 measures treatment outcome. It is what the investigator would like to be able to predict, the criterion. A glance at its correlations with other variables suggests that only variables V and VI could be used successfully as predictors because they are the only ones that appear to correlate substantially with variable I. Suppose, however, that variable VIII is the criterion. A good predictor of this variable is not so easy to find. Multiple regression enables the investigator to select the best combination of predictors of a criterion by taking into account all the information in the correlation matrix.

Not-So-Obvious Examples

Some types of research, such as our old friend the two-group research design, appear not to lend themselves to correlational analyses. For example, one set of persons is given treatment A, and the other is given treatment B (which could be no treatment). After a period of time, the investigator compares the means of the two groups on some measure of outcome. This looks like a situation calling for a straightforward test of a single difference between two means, not one that involves a correlation coefficient.

Indeed, to someone who had not read the preceding chapters, the situation might look like one in which a correlation coefficient could not even be obtained. As stated earlier, to calculate a correlation value, two scores are needed for each person. But in this study, the investigator has only one number for each person: the single score on the measure of outcome. Therefore, it seems impossible to correlate one set of values with another. Appearances can be deceiving, however, for this study is also correlational because the investigator is really searching for an association between two variables.

What makes it difficult to see that this research is correlational is that one of the two variables is imaginary. Furthermore, it uses only two numbers: membership in group A (which could arbitrarily be given the numerical value 1, to indicate the presence of the treatment of interest) or membership in group B (which could be given the value 0, to indicate the absence of the treatment of interest).

Now everyone in the study can be given a pair of numbers. The first, more imaginary, one is either a 1 or a 0; the second is the outcome score. The fact that everyone in the same group gets the same score on the arbitrary variable does not matter. If an index of correlation is calculated that relates the two numbers, one representing each person's group membership and one representing that person's outcome, the index will still be zero if the means of the groups are identical. It will approach either plus or minus 1.00 as the difference between means increases. Whether it has a plus or minus sign depends on which group is called 1 and which is called 0.

The purpose of this example is to show that the research basis for all scientifically interesting statements is the detection of correlations. As the next chapter will make clear, all statistics used for analytical purposes in research can be thought of as expressing some form of correlation. Some of the actual calculations required to demonstrate this are described in subsequent sections.

Product-Moment Correlation Coefficient

The product-moment correlation coefficient was developed as a measure of association by Karl Pearson (1857-1936). Pearson was an English mathematician and professor of eugenics at the University of London. In his honor, the coefficient is still referred to as the Pearson product-moment correlation coefficient, or Pearson r. Just after its introduction, enthusiasm ran high for this particular statistic because it seemed to offer a way to express mathematically the degree of association between two underlying variables. That in turn seemed to hold out the promise of eliminating intuition and guesswork from scientific research. For example, many theorists had speculated that personality or intelligence was associated with various features of the human physique. The development of quantitative psychological tests in the early twentieth century seemed to suggest that relationships between mind and body could at last be reduced by mathematical analysis to a single number or index, the correlation coefficient.

Limitations

For three main reasons, the correlation coefficient accomplished less than had been expected. The first reason is that measures of the variables being correlated must be quite precise. Few if any psychological tests of intelligence or anything else are accurate enough to allow precise statements to be made about, say, the relationship between race and intelligence. For that matter, the same is true about anthropological measurements of race.

The second reason is that the product-moment correlation coefficient alone is *bivariate*. It can manage only two variables at a time. Few relationships of interest to behavior and health scientists are that simple. As noted in a preceding section of this chapter, factor analysis is applied to bivariate correlation coefficients and has been devised as one way of handling multivariate problems. However, a limitation of factor analysis is that a single analysis can produce an unlimited number of ways of reducing a large matrix to a simpler structure. No one knows which reduction is correct, or if any is.

Furthermore, the outcomes of multivariate techniques (including those called by such names as path analysis, structural equations, analysis of covariance, causal modeling, canonical correlation, discriminant function analysis, multiple regression, and multivariate analysis of variance) can never be any better than the measures of the variables used to obtain the bivariate rs that make up the primary correlation matrix. Uneven quality of measures can be as bad as having all the measures equally poor or equally good. At least when all measures are of about the same quality, the investigator may hope to make up for the difficulty by using large samples of subjects.

The third reason that the product-moment correlation coefficient did not prove to be the magical solution to all scientific problems in psychology and related fields is that it only applies to straight-line relationships between variables. Suppose, as an unlikely example, that a state such as anxiety tends to increase steadily with increases in physical or psychological stress or strain. The usual product-moment correlation coefficient would then be a good indicator of the relationship between anxiety and stress because as one variable increases the other increases; as one decreases the other decreases also. No one expects the observed relationship to be perfect, even if both variables were measured without error. The question is not whether increases in stress produce perfectly predictable increases in anxiety. All the investigator probably wants to know is the strength of the general tendency. Product-moment correlation will serve the purpose as long as the tendency is adequately represented by a straight line in two-dimensional space.

In many circumstances, however, the relationship between anxiety and stress appears to be curvilinear rather than a straight line. It might be more like an upside-down U (Figure 10.1b). Anxiety increases as stress increases, but only up to a point. This point might represent the place at which internal turmoil is replaced by outwardly directed action. When one decides to do something about a stressful situation, anxiety may disappear, even though the stress continues to increase. Or the peak might represent a point of fatigue or collapse. At this limit, anxiety gives way to resignation.

In Figure 10.1a, horizontal and vertical projections (dashed arrows) from point 1 show clearly that a low score on Y is associated with a low score on X. At point 2, a higher score on Y is also obviously associated with a higher score on X. In Figure 10.1b, matters are not so simple. Horizontal and vertical projections from point 1 show that higher scores on Y (anxiety, perhaps) are associated with only midrange scores on X (physical stress). In fact, up to the top of the curve, a straight line might approximate fairly well the functional relationship between X and Y. So far so good. But lower scores on Y at point 2 on the horizontal projection are associated with either lower or higher scores on X.

This curve might also describe, among other things, problems in psychological adjustment (Y) in relation to a condition like hearing loss (X). At low levels of loss, few problems may exist, and adjustment may pose few difficulties because the loss does not interfere much with daily activities. At high levels of loss, problems may also not be severe because the person accepts the hearing loss and learns ways to live with it or overcome it. The most serious problems of adjustment tend to be in intermediate ranges. In this range, the loss is serious enough to cause problems but not severe enough to induce the person to accept the reality of being deaf. Not being sure is often more troublesome than knowing the worst. Complex associations like those just described can be managed statistically, but the techniques for doing so are best reserved for discussions of curvilinear correlation in more advanced texts.

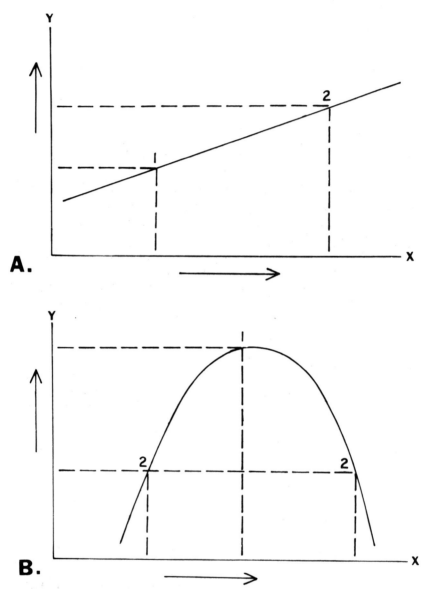

Figure 10.1. Two possible types of bivariate relationships.

Regression

The straight lines that are drawn to serve as guides for predicting the value of one variable from the value of another are usually referred to as *regression lines*. The mathematical formulas that describe them are called *regression equations*. The process of getting the values needed to set up regression lines and regression equations is called *regression analysis*. When more than two variables enter the picture, the process is called *multiple regression analysis*. Most of us ordinary mortals find multiple regression analysis to be more complicated than can be managed conveniently, so it will not be covered in detail here.

The dictionary definition of the word *regression* refers to the general idea of falling back to origins—seemingly a strange way to describe a situation that involves prediction of values on one variable from a knowledge of values on another. However, remember that in statistics the "origin of all things" is the mean of a distribution, so regression implies moving toward the mean, or something like the mean. Given that the mean stays the same, individuals with extreme scores on the first testing can generally be expected on repeated testings to obtain scores that are closer to the mean.

The usual normal curve is a frequency distribution that is supposed to represent random variation around a mean. The random factors that caused certain scores to come out extremely high or extremely low on the first testing are most likely to operate differently the next time around. Therefore, on a second testing they will probably not make the score even more extreme than it was. More probably, they will bring it closer to the average. If Dr. M's median golf score is in the midnineties, he may still score in the low eighties on a particular day when everything comes together just right. But unless his game has actually improved (in which case the deviation is not random but systematic), the next few times out he will likely score in the midnineties again. This is an example of regression to the mean, and in the long run it is expected by statisticians, even if it is not by Dr. M.

The same is true in prediction to a regression line. Look back at the top of Figure 10.1a, which displays a straight-line regression of Y (the dependent variable) on X (the independent variable). This regression line is really a kind of average. The complete picture of the data showing the observed relationship between Y and X looks more like Figure 10.2.

Another Scattergram

As in the first scattergram shown in Chapter 3, each point in Figure 10.2 stands for a pair of scores. There are 15 Xs but 30 values,

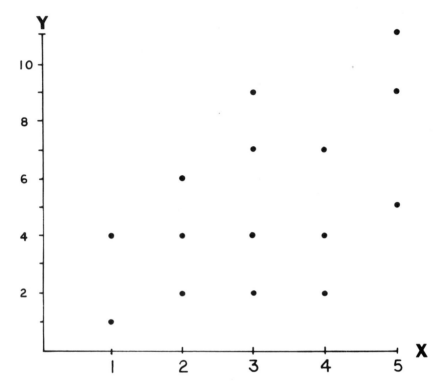

Figure 10.2.   A scattergram of 15 data points.

15 on the abscissa and 15 on the ordinate. Moving from left to right along the X axis and counting upward shows that there are two scores of 1, three scores of 2, four scores of 3, and so on. Moving up the Y axis and then across shows that there is one score of 1, three scores of 2, none of 3, four of 4, and so on. The first two pairs on the left have the coordinates $X = 1$, $Y = 1$; $X = 1$, $Y = 4$. The last three pairs on the right have the coordinates $X = 5$, $Y = 5$; $X = 5$, $Y = 9$; $X = 5$, $Y = 11$.

Looked at without the solid regression line, Figure 10.2 shows only a general tendency for higher values of Y to be associated with higher values of X. Knowing that a person has a score of 4 on the variable X, one would still be hard put to know what score to predict that person has (or will get) on Y. It is probably somewhere between 2 and 7, but where?

The regression line represents a compromise, a simplification or summarization of the best guesses that can be made about scores on Y if one is given a set of scores on X. It is a kind of average, but it is based on the squared deviations of scores around the regression line rather than on simple differences. The equation that describes this line is calculated in such a way that the sum of the squared deviations of the observed values around the line is as low as it can possibly be. The line is therefore called the *least squares regression line*. The equation for it can be set up directly from knowing the value of the product-moment correlation coefficient between X and Y and the standard deviations of X and Y.

Variations on the theme. This particular example involves only two variables, but least squares regression analysis can technically be carried out for relationships among several variables. If the example had three variables instead of two, a Z axis could be added. Imagine it running straight through the paper, at the zero point, where X and Y meet, and at right angles to both the X and Y axes, which are already at right angles. The three variables would then be *orthogonal* to each other. The scattergram would be three dimensional, and the regression would be represented not by a line but by a surface. Regression surfaces can be extended to four or more dimensions.

Whatever its size or shape, a regression line or surface of any number of dimensions does not describe all the information the data contain. Only a scattergram does that. The regression line represents a set of best guesses. Suppose that a straight regression line like the one in our example is used to predict that a person with a score of 5 on variable X will in the future get a score of 8 on variable Y. If variable X measures a condition, such as severity of a patient's hallucinatory activity at the time of admission to a hospital, and variable Y is an indicator of success in treatment after three weeks of care, this prediction would be useful indeed. It would be based on a correlation that indicates that, in general, the more severely ill patients tend to fare best in this particular institution.

To expect that the prediction of a score of 8 on variable Y will be exactly correct would be unreasonable. The person may actually get a 10 or a 5 or a 4. This is where the idea of regression comes in. The statistician presumes that if one guess is pretty far off, due to random factors alone, others will not be. Differences between predicted and obtained values should tend in the long run to balance out. Some will be a bit too high and some a bit too low, but the average of the differences around the regression line, curve, or surface should approach zero. A simpler way of putting this is to say that the statistician is not ready to alter the regression line just because a few predictions based on it are wrong.

At this point, it may be hard not to think in terms of the well-known "gambler's fallacy." According to the gambler's fallacy, a series of losses must be followed by a series of wins to preserve the law of averages. As a type of logic, however, statistics does not allow one to think in terms of the next three tosses of the dice, but only of a series of an infinite number of tosses. Therefore, the occurrence of even a long run of improbable events cannot be used to predict the forthcoming occurrence of an equally long and equally improbable run of events of the opposite kind.

City planners or public health officials like to think about drainage systems in terms of what they call the "ten-year flood" or the "hundred-year flood." The gambler's fallacy might lead citizens to assume that if a city has a hundred-year flood in 1987, it is not going to have one in 1988. Statisticians make no such assumption. The statistical guess applies to periods of time measured in millennia, not years. Furthermore, it assumes no change in underlying meteorological conditions, that is, no changes in the conditions under which randomness was estimated. Finally, it speaks only about overall trends, not specific events.

The idea of prediction will come up again. The most important thing to do at this point is to consider how the Pearson product-moment correlation coefficient is calculated.

Calculations

The first thing to understand about the correlation coefficient is that it is a *ratio*, a fraction simplified to a decimal value by dividing the numerator by the denominator. No one should be surprised to learn that both terms in this particular fraction involve the calculation of sums of squared deviations from means and of terms that are very much like the sums of squared deviations from means.

Numerator

The number that goes into the numerator of the ratio for determining r is not actually a sum of squares but a sum of *cross-products*. A cross-product is not the result of multiplication performed in anger. It is simply what appears when one number in a pair of scores is multiplied by the other. Table 10.2 presents a short list of paired raw scores and their cross products.

Table 10.2.   Data for Calculating a Product-Moment Correlation Coefficient

| | Variable | | Cross-Product |
	X	Y	(XY)
	1	4	4
	2	3	6
	3	9	27
	6	7	42
	8	7	56
Sum	20	30	135
$\overline{X}$	4.0	6.0	(Not Needed)
SumX^2	114	204	(Not Needed)

The sum of the cross products of every X and its paired Y (lower right) does not equal the product of the sums of X and Y.

$$\text{Sum}XY \neq (\text{Sum}X)(\text{Sum}Y); \text{ or}$$

$$\sum XY \neq (\sum X)(\sum Y).$$

In this case, the product of SumX and SumY is 600 (20 × 30). The fact that these numbers are not the same is not a matter of immediate concern because neither one goes into the numerator for calculating r by this particular method. But the difference will become important later on.

What is needed for the numerator is the sum of the cross-products of the *deviation scores* for X and Y. Table 10.3 shows every score on X as a difference (deviation) from its mean of 4.00, and every score

Table 10.3.   Deviation Scores and Cross-Products of Data in Table 10.2

| | Deviation Scores | | Cross-Products |
	x	y	(xy)
	−3	−2	+6
	−2	−3	+6
	−1	+3	−3
	+2	+1	+2
	+4	+1	+4
Sum	0	0	+15

on Y as a difference from its mean of 6.00. In this table the xs and ys are lowercase to show that they are deviation scores and also to distinguish them from raw scores, for which uppercase letters are usually used. The table also shows the cross products of these deviation scores and their sum.

As usual, the sum of the deviations of individual scores about the means of their own groups is zero. Notice, however, that cross-products can be negative as well as positive. In that respect, they are not like squared deviation scores, which can only have positive signs. The sum of a set of cross-products of deviation scores need not be zero. If their sum is positive, the resulting r will be positive. If the sum of the xys is negative, the resulting r will be negative. If it is zero, the resulting r will be zero.

The term needed for the numerator of the fraction is the sum of these cross-products. As is shown in the table, it is 15.0.

An easier way to get this value is to go back to the raw scores. Find the sum of the XYs (135). Multiply SumX (20) by SumY (30) and divide by N (5). This comes to 120 (600/5). Subtract this "adjustment term" from the sum of the XYs to get 15 (135 – 120). Just the number we needed.

This procedure resembles the one used in preceding chapters to get sums of squared deviation scores. Expressed as a formula, the procedure for obtaining the sum of cross-products of deviation scores from raw scores is

$$(\textstyle\sum XY) - \frac{\sum X \sum Y}{N}.$$

A little algebraic manipulation (trust me, if you can't figure it out) gives the following alternative:

$$\frac{N(\sum XY) - \sum X \sum Y}{N}$$

Recalculating with this formula gives

$$\text{SUMxy} = \frac{5(135) - 20(30)}{5} = \frac{675 - 600}{5}$$

$$= \frac{75}{5} = 15.00.$$

When doing this sort of calculation, remember to keep track of plus and minus signs because the total can come out negative. So much for the numerator, at least for now.

Denominator

The denominator of the fraction needed for calculating r is obtained from the product of the separately calculated sums of squared deviation scores for X and Y. The sum of the raw X^2 is 114 (1 + 4 + 9 + 36 + 64). The sum of the raw Y^2 is 204 (16 + 9 + 81 + 49 + 49). The sum of the squared deviation scores (SS, in analysis of variance) is

$$SS_X = Sum(X^2) - \frac{(SumX)^2}{N} = 114 - \frac{20^2}{5}$$

$$= 114 - \frac{400}{5} = 114 - 80 = 34.00.$$

The sum of squared deviation scores for Y (SS_y) is

$$204 - \frac{30^2}{5} = 204 - \frac{900}{5} = 24.00$$

The product of these sums of squares is

$$(34.00)(24.00) = 816.$$

That is almost, but not quite, the number needed. To obtain the denominator, it is necessary to take the square root of 816, which is approximately 28.566. Now, at last, everything is ready.

Ratio

This is the big moment. It is in fact the product moment. The desired correlation coefficient is now obtained merely by dividing the numerator (+15) by the denominator (28.566). The denominator always has a plus sign:

$$r = \frac{15}{28.566} = .525.$$

The formula that describes what was just done is called the *deviation score formula*, and even though it is complicated to use, it looks very simple:

$$r = \frac{xy}{\sqrt{(SS_x)(SS_y)}}.$$

Raw Score Formula

No one can ever go wrong calculating r by the procedure just described, but at least one other way to do it is easier when calculations are being done by hand. The formula may look frightening, but it is not hard to use if you can keep track of all the numbers along the way. It accomplishes exactly what was accomplished by the procedure described earlier, but it condenses some of the steps. As a result, no means or sums of squares are produced during the calculations.

The best way to use this formula is to begin by examining the raw scores and listing six values from the data: SumX, (SumX²), SumY, (SumY²), Sum XY, and N (meaning the number of *pairs*). For this example they are

$$\text{Sum}X = 20 \qquad \text{Sum}Y = 30 \qquad \text{Sum}XY = 135$$

$$(\text{Sum}X^2) = 114 \qquad (\text{Sum}Y^2) = 204 \qquad N = 5.$$

These values are then plugged into the following awesome looking formula:

$$r = \frac{N(\text{Sum}XY) - (\text{Sum}X)(\text{Sum}Y)}{\sqrt{N(\text{Sum}X^2) - (\text{Sum}X)^2} \sqrt{N(\text{Sum}Y^2) - (\text{Sum}Y)^2}}$$

or

$$r = \frac{N(\sum XY) - (\sum X)(\sum Y)}{\sqrt{N(\sum X^2) - (\sum X)^2} \sqrt{N(\sum Y^2) - (\sum Y)^2}}.$$

Here is the first step. Be sure you see why each number is where it is. (SumX²) can easily be confused with (SumX)² or Sum XY with (SumX)(SumY).

$$r = \frac{5(135) - (20)(30)}{\sqrt{5(114) - 20^2} \ \sqrt{5(204) - 30^2}}$$

Here is the next step:

$$r = \frac{675 - 600}{\sqrt{570 - 400} \ \sqrt{1020 - 900}}$$

$$= \frac{75}{\sqrt{170} \ \sqrt{120}} = \frac{75}{(13.038)(10.954)}$$

$$= \frac{75}{142.829} = .525.$$

The correlation coefficient has just been calculated by means of something called the *raw score formula*. Direct calculation of deviation scores was not required, which may not seem like much of a gain in convenience when working with only five pairs of scores, but it is of considerable help as N gets larger.

One More Example

Table 10.4 lists the 15 pairs of scores shown in the scattergram of Figure 10.2, along with their cross-products.

First method. Obtain Sum_{xy} (sum of cross-products of deviation scores):

$$Sum_{xy} = \frac{N(\sum XY) - (\sum X)(\sum Y)}{N} = \frac{15(272) - 47(77)}{15}$$

$$= \frac{(4080 - 3619)}{15} = \frac{461}{15} = 30.733.$$

This is the numerator. Save it someplace.

Then obtain SS_x and SS_y, each is the sum of squared scores minus an adjustment term, consisting of the squared sum of scores divided by N:

$$SS_x = 173 - \frac{47^2}{15} = 25.733$$

$$SS_y = 519 - \frac{77^2}{15} = 123.733.$$

Table 10.4. Raw Scores Shown in Figure 10.2 and Their Cross-Products

	Variable	
X	Y	(XY)
1	1	1
1	4	4
2	2	4
2	4	8
2	6	12
3	2	6
3	4	12
3	7	21
3	9	27
4	2	8
4	4	16
4	7	28
5	5	25
5	9	45
5	11	55
SumX	47	77	272
SumX^2	173	519	—

Now take your choice. Either find the square roots of each SS (5.073 and 11.124, respectively) and multiply them to get 56.428. (Allow for differences due to rounding errors.) Or multiply the two SS values first,

$$(25.733)(123.733) = 3184.0213,$$

and then take the square root (56.427).

This is the denominator. Recall the numerator and do the necessary division:

$$\frac{30.733}{56.427} = .545.$$

Second method. The six needed values are

$$SumX = 47 \quad SumY = 77 \quad SumXY = 272$$

$$SumX^2 = 173 \quad SumY^2 = 519 \quad N = 15.$$

The formula is

$$r = \frac{N(\sum XY) - (\sum X)(\sum Y)}{\sqrt{N(\sum X^2) - (\sum X)^2} \; \sqrt{N(\sum Y^2) - (\sum Y)^2}}.$$

Plug in the values:

$$r = \frac{15(272) - (47)(77)}{\sqrt{15(173) - 47^2} \; \sqrt{15(519) - 77^2}}.$$

Multiply everything out and do the necessary subtractions:

$$\frac{4080 - 3619}{\sqrt{2595 - 2209} \; \sqrt{7785 - 5929}} = \frac{461}{\sqrt{386} \; \sqrt{1856}}.$$

Take square roots in the denominator and multiply it out. Or multiply first and then take the square root. Divide numerator by denominator:

$$\frac{461}{(19.647)(43.081)} = \frac{461}{846.412} = .545.$$

Statistical Significance

The simplest way to find whether a correlation coefficient differs significantly from zero is to look it up on a special table. An abbreviated version of such a table is provided in Appendix 10.A. The values in the table are for two-tailed tests, which means the probabilities can be divided by 2 if the test is based on a directional prediction. In this situation, a directional prediction is one that states in advance whether r will be positive or negative in sign. The df is the number of data pairs minus 2 because two means had to be fixed to get deviation scores on both X and Y. For 13 df, an r of .545 exceeds that required at the .05 level but not that required at the .01 level.

Prediction

Adjusting for Unit Sizes

The investigator may wish to use these data to set up a regression line that could serve as a guide for predicting values on Y from

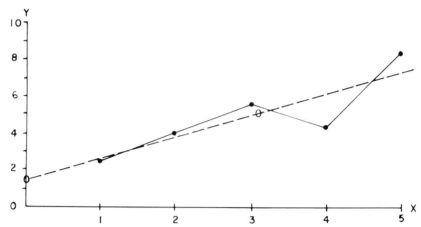

Figure 10.3.   A plot of mean Y values for each value of X in Figure 10.2 (solid line) and of the least squares regression line (broken line).

known values of X. Look back at Figure 10.2 and focus attention on the first column of data points, just above $X = 1$ on the abscissa. Then find the mean of the two data points directly above $X = 1$. That mean would be $Y = (4 + 1)/2 = 2.5$. A mark could be placed at $X = 1$, $Y = 2.5$. The same thing could be done at $X = 2$, (mean $Y + 4.0$), and so on down the line. A series of short straight lines could be drawn to connect these average points. The result would look like the solid line in Figure 10.3. Ignore the two little circles and the dashed line for now. This graph makes sense, but the mathematically inclined researcher wants a more "elegant" solution. A single straight line would do the job. The question is how to plot it.

Go back to the top graph in Figure 10.1 and notice the rising straight regression line, which indicates that the correlation between X and Y is positive. The line shows that as the values on X increase, the values on Y increase also. We need to know by how much. The answer lies in finding a number that relates the rate of increase of scores on Y to the rate of increase of scores on X. When the data are in standard scores, that number just happens to be the Pearson product-moment correlation coefficient.

The kicker in that sentence is the term *standard scores*. Standard scores are based on the same unit of measurement in both X and Y, the standard deviation. To use a correlation coefficient to determine regression, units on X and Y must nearly always be made equal in size. Allowance must be made for the fact that the raw score units of measurement on scale X are not the same as the raw score units of measurement on scale Y. The best way to make them mathematically equal is to transform them into standard deviation units. Do this by assuming that the meaning of all standard deviations is the same from scale to scale, even if the meaning of the raw scores is not. In other words, assume that as far as the sds are concerned, $1 = 1$.

The standard deviation of X is the square root of (SS /df), or (using values calculated earlier):

$$s_x = \sqrt{\frac{25.733}{14}} = 1.36 \text{ (rounded)}.$$

The standard deviation of Y is

$$s_y = \sqrt{\frac{123.733}{14}} = 2.97 \text{ (rounded)}.$$

The sd of Y is (2.97/1.36) or 2.18 times as large (in raw score points) as the sd of X (also in raw score points). Put another way, every raw score unit on X is equivalent to 2.18 raw score units of Y.

The correlation coefficient itself indicates that every sd unit increase in X is associated with .545 sd units increase in Y. Therefore, each increase of one raw score point in X goes along with an increase of (.545)(2.18) or 1.19 (rounded) raw score points for Y. This value (1.19) is typically called b, or the *raw score regression weight*.

For predicting Y from X, the formula for b is

$$b_{y.x} = r \frac{s_y}{s_x} = .545 \frac{2.97}{1.36} = 1.19.$$

In predicting raw score values, b will practically never be the same for the regression of Y on X ($Y.X$) as for the regression of X on Y ($X.Y$). This is because the ratio of standard deviations must be reversed in the two cases. Every raw score unit on X is equivalent to 2.18 units on Y, but every raw score unit of Y is equivalent to only 1.36/2.97 or .46 units of X. Therefore, b for $X.Y$ equals

$$b_{x.y} = r \frac{s_x}{s_y} = .545 \frac{1.36}{2.97} = 0.25 \text{ (rounded)},$$

instead of the 1.19 for the *b* of *Y. X*. For our purposes, only the regression of *Y* on *X* need be of concern. The logic is the same, whichever way the prediction goes.

Fixing Two Points

To draw any straight line requires fixing two points. Any two will do. To draw a regression, the first point is easily found. It is where the *statistical zero points* of *X* and *Y* come together, that is, where the mean of *X* and the mean of *Y* cross. The mean of *X* is (47/15) or 3.1. The mean of *Y* is (77/15) or 5.1. Go to the right 3.1 units of *X* in Figure 10.3, then come up 5.1 units. The circle there indicates where the two means come together. This point can be fixed so easily because, no matter how high or low a correlation is, a score at the mean of one variable always predicts a score at the mean of the other.

One way to get the second point for the straight line is to find the value that would be predicted for *Y* if *X* were zero. This value of *Y* can be marked on the ordinate itself, and it is called the *Y intercept*. We know the mean of *X* is 3.1 raw score units to the right of zero. We know that every change in a raw score unit of *X* is worth a change of 1.19 raw score units in *Y*. A drop of 3.1 raw score units on *X* (from the mean down to zero) is therefore worth a drop of (3.1)(1.19) or 3.7 raw score units on *Y*.

A drop from what? Why, from the mean of *Y*, the starting point for all statistical measurement. Therefore, the *Y* intercept equals (5.1 − 3.7) or 1.4. Inserting that as a point of the *Y* axis gives us what is needed to draw the regression line. It is shown as the dashed line in Figure 10.3. It is also called the *best-fit line* or the *least squares best-fit line*.

To express this line as an equation, call the *Y* intercept *a*. Insert it and the *b* weight into the following general formula that can be used to describe any straight line:

$$Y' = bX + a.$$

So,

$$Y' = 1.19X + 1.4.$$

If *X* = 5, then

$$Y' = 1.19(5) + 1.4 = 7.4.$$

Check that out on the graph and see if it doesn't look right. Then try inserting the mean of X and predicting the mean of Y.

There are other ways of setting up straight line regression equations. The main concern here is with what they mean, not with the technicalities of the various procedures for deriving them.

Common Variance

With a little stretch of the imagination, the ratio expressed in the deviation score formula for calculating the product-moment correlation coefficient could remind one of the F-ratio in the analysis of variance. The numerator is the sum of cross products of deviation scores. If high scores on X are paired with high scores on Y, this number will be high. If high scores on X are paired with low scores on Y, it will be low; in fact, the sum of deviation scores will be negative. So, the more extreme the numerator is in either direction, the stronger the association is between variables. For the moment, think of it as *variability* (not *variance*) in one factor that is accounted for by *variability* in the other. It is something like a between-groups term in an analysis of variance.

The denominator contains the two sums of squared deviation scores within groups. So, when the numerator is divided by the denominator, the result is a ratio of shared variability to unshared variability. But it still cannot be called an index of common variance.

Remember that the SS values in the denominator were converted to square roots before r was calculated. They are therefore more like standard deviations than like variances. A standard deviation may be converted to a variance by squaring it. Similarly, squaring r tells how much variance X and Y have in common. An r of .545 is equivalent to about .30, or 30 percent, common variance. An r of .80 is equivalent to about .64, or 64 percent, common variance. An r of $-.30$ is equivalent to about .09, or 9 percent, common variance.

The meaning of the term *common variance* is not easy to grasp at first. One helpful way to think about it is to recall the idea behind the scattergram and then relate it to a restatement of the basic ideas behind the F-test. A scattergram shows all the points used in calculating a correlation coefficient. The regression line that may be drawn on a scattergram shows the straight line that provides the best-fitting estimate of the underlying relationship between the two variables being correlated. Think of the variance among the points along that regression line as being variance that is due to regression. It is the variance that could be accounted for or explained by the regression of one variable on the other. Therefore, it represents what the two variables, X and Y, have in common.

Divide the sum of squares due to this regression by the sum of squares of the total variation for the factor being explained or "predicted." The result is the proportion of variance in the explained variable that can be accounted for by the regression line. It is, in fact, r^2.

With a little more imagination, this basic idea can be stretched to include regression situations in which the relationship between variables is not a straight line but a more complex curve. Again, the variation of points along the curve is hypothesized to be common variance. The usual name for a value like this is eta^2, rather than r^2. This discussion concerns only r^2, though it is well to keep in mind that many principles can be extended to apply to the general curvilinear case as well.

Error

Since r^2 measures the proportion of variance two variables have in common, and since 1.00 represents all the variance there is, then $(1.00 - r^2)$ represents the variance in one variable that is not associated with variance in the other. It is an indicator of error.

One way to use this error term is in the following formula for testing the significance of r without using the special table:

$$F = \frac{r^2(df)}{1 - r^2}$$

The terms in this formula are familiar: r^2 is the proportion of common variance, df is the degrees of freedom, and $(1 - r^2)$ is the proportion of variance unaccounted for. In the present example,

$$F = \frac{.545^2(13)}{1 - .545^2} = \frac{.297(13)}{1 - .297} = \frac{3.861}{.7030} = 5.492.$$

Evaluated against a table of F, for 1/13 df, this value is again found to be significant at the .05, but not at the .01 level.

Most textbooks give the preceding formula as a formula for t. It looks like this:

$$t = \frac{r\sqrt{n-2}}{\sqrt{1-r^2}}.$$

Calculation in this example gives

$$t = \frac{.545\sqrt{13}}{\sqrt{1-.545^2}} = \frac{1.9650}{\sqrt{1-.297}} = \frac{1.9650}{\sqrt{.703}} = \frac{1.9650}{.8385} = 2.3435.$$

This may be looked up in a table of t for $df = 13$. Or it may be squared to produce 5.492, and evaluated as F for $df = 1/13$, as was done earlier. Personally, I have always found that quite interesting.

Multiple Correlation

When more than two variables are correlated, the result is a matrix of bivariate rs (that is, of correlations among pairs of variables), just as in factor analysis. As noted earlier in the chapter, when one of these variables is picked as a *criterion* (sometimes called a *dependent variable*), the others become *predictors* (or *independent variables*).

A procedure called *multiple regression* can be used to produce a formula that has the same purposes as the simple regression-line formula used in this chapter but is more complicated. The procedure also produces a correlation coefficient, called the *multiple correlation coefficient*. It is usually designated by the uppercase letter R to distinguish it from its bivariate little brother.

The formula for testing the significance of multiple R is as follows:

$$F = \left(\frac{R^2}{1-R^2}\right)\left(\frac{N-K}{K-1}\right)$$

In this F-ratio, N stands for the number of subjects upon which the various correlations are based, and K stands for the number of variables. The formula is similar to the F-test for bivariate r. The only difference, really, is that the df term in the bivariate formula has been replaced. The ratio produced by this formula cannot be converted to a t value because the t-test can be used only in the bivariate situation.

This F-ratio is tested by referring to an F-table, using $(K-1)$ as the number of degrees of freedom in the numerator and $(N-K)$ as the number of degrees of freedom in the denominator.

Never fear. This book delves no further into the complexities of multiple regression. In the final analysis, multiple regression is merely an extension and elaboration of the two-variable case.

Appendix 10.A

Critical Values of Product-Moment Correlation Coefficients

df	Level of Significance for Two-Tailed Test			
	.10	.05	.02	.01
2	.900	.950	.980	.990
4	.729	.811	.882	.917
6	.622	.707	.789	.834
8	.549	.632	.716	.765
10	.497	.576	.658	.708
11	.476	.553	.634	.684
12	.458	.532	.612	.661
13	.441	.514	.592	.641
14	.426	.497	.574	.623
15	.412	.482	.558	.606
20	.360	.423	.492	.537
25	.323	.381	.445	.487
30	.296	.349	.409	.449
40	.257	.304	.358	.393
80	.183	.217	.257	.283
100	.164	.195	.230	.254

—11—

CORRELATION: A FUNDAMENTAL IDEA

The General Concept of Association

The basic task of scientific investigation is to observe, record, and interpret objective and dependable associations between events that are carefully measured or systematically controlled. The preceding chapter showed how to calculate the best-known and most important coefficient of association: the product-moment correlation ratio. This chapter shows how the concept of correlation underlies a number of other statistics that have already been examined, including chi square, the t-test, and the F-test. The chapter also introduces the Spearman rank-order correlation coefficient, which could have been described in Chapter 7 on ranks, but has deliberately been held until now, and it covers other basic ideas about correlation and the analysis of variance.

This chapter's emphasis on the fundamental importance of correlation is not meant to suggest that other statistical tests should all be replaced by correlation coefficients. From a strictly mathematical point of view, however, many of them could at least be supplemented by some type of correlation index. For example, some complicated designs in analysis of variance may just as well be treated as problems in multiple regression (or multiple correlation, which is basically the same thing).

251

Strength of Association

The usual argument in favor of relating a variety of statistical tests of differences among means to the correlation coefficient is not that the correlation coefficient is better than other tests but that it tells something most other tests do not. Pearson's r shows not only whether a difference or relationship is statistically significant but also how strong the relationship is.

The strength of a relationship is not the same thing as its statistical significance. This idea can be tricky to understand at first. After all, statistical significance is a measure of association, and surely a more significant outcome has more strength than a less significant one. In any given research, a t value of 4.00 obviously indicates a stronger association (correlation) between group membership and scores on the dependent variable than does a t value of 2.00. Yes, it does, but the catch lies in the phrase *in any given research*. What if two different studies are being compared? In one of them, a t of 4.00 may result from a weaker correlation than does a t of 2.00 in the other research. The next section tells how that can happen.

Degrees of freedom. The most important factor that makes for differences in strength of association is that old familiar companion, *degrees of freedom.* Suppose a study with 10 *df* gives a t value of 3.20. That value is significant at the .01 level. Suppose another study with 5 *df* produces exactly the same value of t. A glance at a table of critical values of t shows that 3.20 is not significant at the .01 level. If, to obtain indexes of the strengths of the relationships or associations, correlation coefficients were calculated between experimental conditions and the difference between group means, they would not be the same, even though the values of t are identical.

The strength of a relationship between two variables is not measured by how unlikely the relationship is to happen by chance. Strength is measured by *common variance*: the proportion of variance in one condition that is associated with the other. The preceding chapter said that r^2 tells what proportion of variance two variables have in common, just as $(1 - r^2)$ tells how much they do not share. Two variables with 50 percent common variance are more closely (more strongly) associated than two variables with 25 percent common variance. Two variables with 100 percent common variance are not even two variables. They are the same variable.

A high proportion of common variance indicates a strong association, whether it is based on 5 or 500 degrees of freedom. Of course, a strong relationship is more likely to appear at random if the number of cases observed is small. Therefore, as the table of critical values of r shows, if df is small, relationships must be very strong (r must be very high) to be significantly different from zero. Lower rs are significant if df is large.

In summary, two studies with different numbers of observations, and therefore different numbers of degrees of freedom, can produce equally significant results based on different strengths of association between variables. Similarly, two studies with different numbers of observations can demonstrate the same strength of association between variables, but the results of one study may be statistically significant, while the results of the other may not be. Significance is a matter of probability. Strength of association is a matter of common variance or, as it is sometimes called, *variance accounted for in one variable by variance in the other.*

Investigators who look for differences among groups are often strongly encouraged by statisticians to report not only the level of statistical significance of their results but also some indication of the strength of the associations that have been observed. Few investigators seem to do so, but when they do, the correlation coefficient or some near equivalent is usually used for the purpose.

Frequency Data: Chi Square and the *Phi* (Fourfold-Point) Coefficient

Chapter 10 showed that the product-moment correlation coefficient is designed for use with data on continuous scales. Chapter 6 showed that chi square is used when the data are frequency counts within categories. Offhand, the two do not appear to be very similar. One way of seeing similarities between them was described in Chapter 6, where the *phi* coefficient was presented as a measure of association that is obtained directly from chi square. That chapter also suggested that *phi* is really a special case of r. Indeed, this is in fact the case.

The hypothetical problem that will be examined is of a type that might be of considerable interest in some service delivery settings. It is the problem of using a pretest measure of some sort to select individuals for treatment who are most likely to benefit from it. A variation of this problem is how to use some kind of pretest to assign individuals to the particular form of care that is most likely to help them when several different possibilities are available. The investigator's job is to find out whether the pretest is effective in selecting

Table 11.1. Hypothetical Results of a Study of Preassignment to Treatment

		Successful	Unsuccessful	Total
Assigned by Pretest	o	70	30	100
	(e)	(55)	(45)	(100)
Randomly Assigned	o	40	60	100
	(e)	(55)	(45)	(100)
Totals	o	110	90	200
	(e)	(110)	(90)	(200)

persons for different types of treatment. In terms of probability, the task is to find out whether assignment of treatments by pretesting produces a greater proportion of successful treatment outcomes than does assignment of treatments at random.

In the simplest case, research of this type requires using two groups of subjects. These subjects should be selected at random from a larger group, or population. Ideally, the larger group would be the entire population of those who are admitted for care. Members of one group would be assigned to treatment conditions by some systematic method, or test. Members of the other group would be assigned to treatment conditions at random. (The ethical problems that might be raised by assigning people randomly to treatment conditions were discussed in a preceding chapter, and we must presume in this example that the investigator has found a satisfactory solution to them.)

After a period of time, the success of all persons in the study would be evaluated and success rates would be totaled for the two groups (Table 11.1).

In this table, the calculated values of expected frequencies have been included for convenience. They were obtained from the marginal totals. For example, the value of 55 in the upper left results from multiplying the row total (100) by the column total (110) and dividing by the grand total N (200). An eyeball test suggests that assignment by pretest is effective. Out of 100 assignments by pretest, 70 produced successful outcomes. Out of 100 assignments at random, only 40 were successful.

Test of Significance

To evaluate the statistical significance of this outcome, chi square should be run in the usual way, with the correction for discontinuity.

Notice that because this is a 2 × 2 table with only 1 *df*, and because equal numbers of persons were tested in the two assignment conditions, values of (o − e) are equal in all cells. Chi square in this example is calculated as follows:

$$\chi^2 \ (\text{corrected}) \ = \ \text{Sum} \left[\frac{(|o-e| \ - \ .5)^2}{e} \right]$$

$$= \frac{(|70-55|) \ - \ .5)^2}{55} \ + \ \frac{(|30-45| \ - \ .5)^2}{45}$$

$$+ \ \frac{(|40-55| \ - \ .5)^2}{55} \ + \ \frac{(|60-45) \ - \ .5)^2}{45}$$

$$= \frac{14.5^2}{55} \ + \ \frac{14.5^2}{45} \ + \ \frac{14.5^2}{55} \ + \ \frac{14.5^2}{45} \ = \ 16.990.$$

For 1 *df*, this value is clearly significant. So there does appear to be a relationship between outcome and type of procedure used to assign patients. But how strong is that relationship? Based on chi square alone, it seems to be rather strong, but chi square is not enough.

As indicated in Chapter 6, one way to find out what the correlation is in this situation is to run a *phi* coefficient. Calculation is quite easy: simply divide chi square by N and take the square root. But remember that in Chapter 6 *phi* was calculated from the *uncorrected* chi square. This is because *phi* is not itself a test of statistical significance but a description of the degree of relationship between two variables.

In this example, the (o − e) value for an uncorrected chi square is 15.0 in each cell, instead of the 14.5 that was used to get the corrected chi square. Otherwise, the calculations are the same, and the result is a chi square value of 18.182. Figure that one out for yourself; it is good practice. The *phi* coefficient is, then

$$phi \ = \ \sqrt{\frac{\chi^2}{N}} \ = \ \sqrt{\frac{18.182}{200}} \ = \ \sqrt{.091} \ = \ .302.$$

This is perhaps not as impressive as the chi square value may have led you to hope. As will be shown, however, it is a genuine product-moment correlation coefficient, just like the ones calculated in Chapter 10.

Phi *and* r

It has been noted several times in preceding chapters that each set of factors that define this type of chi square table can be called a variable and given numerical values. For example, every person with a successful outcome may be given a numerical value of 1 on the outcome variable; every person with an unsuccessful outcome may be given a value of 0 on that variable. Every person assigned to treatment by pretest may be given a value of 1 on the pretest variable; every person assigned at random may be given a value of 0 on that variable.

A look at the data table shows there are 110 persons with a score of 1 (successful) on outcome and 90 persons with a score of 0 on outcome. Calling the outcome variable X, then SumX is 110 and $SumX^2$ is 110 because the square of every score of 1 is 1 and of every score of 0 is 0.

The pretest was used to assign 100 of the total of 200 persons, so SumY is 100 and $SumY^2$ is 100.

The total number of persons who are assigned by test and randomly is 200, so that takes care of five of the six terms needed for calculating a correlation coefficient. The sixth term is the sum of cross-products.

The way the variables have been set up, people who were assigned by the test and were successful in treatment have scores of 1 on both variables. Therefore, the cross-product for each of them is 1. Everybody else in the study either has one score of 1 and one score of 0 (cross-product equals 0) or two scores of 0 (cross-product also equals 0). So the sum of cross-products equals the number of persons in the upper left cell of the 2 × 2 chi square table, or 70.

Putting it all together:

$$SumX = 110 \qquad SumY = 100 \qquad SumXY = 70$$

$$SumX^2 = 110 \qquad SumY^2 = 100 \qquad N = 200.$$

Plug these into the raw score formula for *r*:

$$r = \frac{N(\sum XY) - (\sum X)(\sum Y)}{\sqrt{N(\sum X^2) - (\sum X)^2} \ \sqrt{N(\sum Y^2) - (\sum Y)^2}}$$

$$= \frac{200(70) - (110)(100)}{\sqrt{200(110) - (110)^2} \ \sqrt{200(100) - (100)^2}}$$

$$= \frac{14000 - 11000}{(99.499)(100)} = \frac{3000}{9949.87} = .302.$$

Under some conditions *phi*, like *r*, may have a maximum value of plus or minus 1.00. Try reversing the assignment of scores of 1 and 0 on the outcome or pretest variable and recalculating *phi*. It will come out negative.

In other words, when the data can be summarized in a 2 × 2 table, the formula for the *phi* coefficient is just a short-cut formula for the product-moment correlation coefficient. As indicated in the main title of this section, *phi* is also called the *fourfold-point correlation coefficient*. It should be run only on 2 × 2 (fourfold) tables where data consist of frequency counts, and the factor of interest is essentially only "present" or "absent," as points in each of the cells.

When chi square tables are larger than 2 × 2, *phi* should not be used. In some instances, numerical values can still be assigned to levels of each dimension, and product-moment *r*s can be run on the data, but they must be calculated directly, using the regular formula for a Pearson *r*. There are no short-cut formulas as there is for *phi*.

Phi *and the Contingency Coefficient*

The contingency coefficient C is a measure of association that can be used with chi squares based on any number of cells. It is also easy to calculate but, as was noted in Chapter 6, it has its drawbacks. The main one is that it is not a product-moment correlation coefficient and can therefore be somewhat difficult to interpret at times. The maximum value the contingency coefficient can reach is not 1.00. It is never greater than 1.00, but the maximum does vary depending on the number of cells in the table. This means that contingency coefficients can be compared with each other only if the chi square tables they are based on are the same size.

The formula for the contingency coefficient is

$$C = \sqrt{\frac{\chi^2}{\chi^2 + N}}.$$

In this example, $C = .289$, a value somewhat lower than that obtained for *phi*. This outcome is logical because the formula for C contains one more term in the denominator than does the formula for *phi*.

A Family of Statistics

One reason chi square can be directly related to the product-moment correlation coefficient is that chi square belongs to the same general family of statistical procedures as do r, the F-ratio, and the t-test. As Chapter 9 showed, when the means of two groups are being tested against each other, $F = t^2$. Under certain specific conditions, chi square, F, and t are not only closely related, they are practically the same thing. In fact, with a minor qualification, any chi square can be converted to an F-ratio by dividing the chi square by its own df; that is,

$$F = \frac{\chi^2}{df}, \quad \text{or} \quad \chi^2 = F(df).$$

The minor qualification is that this F value is looked up on the table of critical values of F as if it had a denominator with an infinitely large df. This is usually the bottom horizontal line in the table.

Check it out. Find the chi square required for significance at the .01 level for any df. For $df = 10$, that value is 23.21. Look up the .01 level value for a df ratio with 10 df in the numerator and infinity in the denominator. Lo and behold! It is 2.32, which is one-tenth of the required chi square.

So if you are ever carrying out research in a jungle and termites eat up everything except your table of critical F values, you can still run statistical tests of many kinds. As shown in Chapter 9, you can evaluate a t-test by squaring it and looking up the value in the first column of the F table (for $df = 1$ in the numerator). As shown in Chapter 10, you can test the significance of r by calculating t, which can then be squared and looked up in the F table. Now it has been revealed to you that you can look up chi square on the bottom row of the F table just by dividing the chi square value by its df. It seems these wonders never cease.

Nonparametric Statistics

The statistics just discussed are called *parametric statistics* because they make specific assumptions about the shape of the statistical universe from which data are drawn. They are held together by a common set of assumptions about the normal curve.

The word *parametric* is derived from the word *parameter*, a defining characteristic of some mathematical entity. The radius is a parameter of a circle. The mean and standard deviation are parameters of the normal curve and are the main numerical entities around which normal curve statistics are built.

As has been noted before, numerous alternate techniques have been developed called *nonparametric* or *distribution-free statistics*. These names seem to imply that the investigator must make no assumptions at all about statistical universes, but that is not exactly true. What some of these procedures do is sacrifice statistical power or sensitivity to gain "robustness." For example, chi square is sometimes called a nonparametric statistic mainly because it is typically used with data that are too crude or insensitive to justify the use of more powerful statistical tests.

Rank-order statistics work by requiring the investigator to convert all data into a *rectangular distribution* in which every score occurs equally frequently. In this case, every rank occurs just once. However, most statistics based on ranks then assume that the means of a series of random selections of ranks will not be rectangular but will be normally distributed.

Recall that in the Mann-Whitney U-test all scores were first combined into a single group and ranked. Then these ranks were distributed back into original groups, and the means or totals of these ranks were used for carrying out statistical comparisons. No assumptions were made about the underlying distribution of the scores that were ranked in the first place. Therefore, the test is nonparametric in that respect. But the tests performed on the rank totals are parametric. When the number of data points is large, nonparametric tests may even require the calculation of standard scores and the direct use of a table of normal curve properties to evaluate the statistical significance of an outcome.

Central Limit Theorem

The explanation for this is to be found in the central limit theorem, mentioned in Chapter 7. According to this theorem, the frequency distribution of means, and other statistics that are derived from different distributions, even non-normal ones, tends to become normal as the number of samples increases. Suppose you have a large set of different rankings of 30 items, with no ties. If you count the

Table 11.2. Hypothetical Scores, Ranks, Differences, and Cross
Products in a Study of Benefit from Care

Patient	Pretreatment Score	Pretreatment Rank	Benefit Score	Benefit Rank	Rank Differences d	Rank Differences d²	Cross-Products of Ranks
William	23	8	6.8	5	3	9	40
Mary	14	4	5.1	1	3	9	4
Susan	6	1	10.2	8	−7	49	8
Robert	19	6	6.1	4	2	4	24
Ed	21	7	5.4	2	5	25	14
Joan	15	5	6.0	3	2	4	15
Carl	8	2	8.3	7	−5	25	14
John	10	3	7.0	6	−3	9	18
Sum						134	137

number of ranks of 5, 8, 12, or 19, etc., in 50 sets of these rankings,
there must be exactly 50 of each rank, which is not a normal distribution. No ranks are normally distributed. Yet, if you randomly
sample 5 ranks out of each of the sets, then calculate the mean of
each set of 5, and plot the frequency distribution of the 50 means,
the result will look something like a normal curve—maybe not exactly, but more like one than does the distribution of ranks themselves. Many nonparametric tests take advantage of this theorem,
thereby bypassing the need to assume normality in the raw data.
The relationship between nonparametric and parametric statistics
becomes apparent in the calculation of a rank-order correlation coefficient called Spearman's *rho.*

Spearman's *rho.* Chapter 7 described Kendall's *tau*, a statistic
that measures the strength of relationship between two sets of paired
ranks. Kendall's *tau* is not a product-moment coefficient because it
is actually more closely related to chi square than to *r.* Remember
that *tau* was based on frequency counts of a special kind. But Spearman's *rho* is different. It is, in fact, nothing more than another
shorthand formula for the product-moment correlation coefficient
when it is used with ranks.

This is more easily demonstrated than discussed. Table 11.2 shows
some hypothetical data in which patients' status at the time of entrance to treatment is compared with their estimated benefit from
treatment when it is over. The investigator may be interested in

seeing whether those in the best health before treatment seemed to benefit most from it. A positive correlation would indicate that patients who are in the best health upon entrance to treatment benefit most. A negative correlation would indicate that most benefit is gained by those in the poorest health at the beginning.

As was done when calculating *tau*, scores on both variables are separately ranked. For Spearman's *rho*, however, differences between ranks are calculated, squared, and summed. (For the moment, ignore the last column in Table 11.2.) The resulting value, in this instance, is 134. This value is multiplied by 6, the result is divided by $N(N^2 - 1)$, and the result of that is subtracted from 1.

The formula and calculations for *rho* are

$$rho = 1 - \frac{6(\text{Sum } d^2)}{N(N^2 - 1)} = 1 - \frac{6(134)}{8(64 - 1)}$$

$$= 1 - \frac{804}{504} = 1 - 1.595 = -.595.$$

Apparently, patients in the poorest condition at the start of treatment gain most from care. This seems a reasonable outcome.

All that needs to be done now is to show that the formula for the product-moment correlation coefficient yields the same result. Notice, however, that it will do so only when it is applied to the ranks, not to the original scores. The ranks on both variables run from 1 to 8, so both variables have the same sum and the same sum of squares. These are merely the sum of all the numbers from 1 to 8 and the sum of their squares.

The sum of cross products is:

$$(8 \times 5) + (4 \times 1) + (1 \times 8), \text{ etc. } = 137.$$

This figure can be found in the last column on the right in Table 11.2. The six required terms are, therefore,

$$\text{Sum} X = 36 \qquad \text{Sum} Y = 36 \qquad \text{Sum} XY = 137$$

$$\text{Sum} X^2 = 204 \qquad \text{Sum} Y^2 = 204 \qquad N = 8.$$

The correlation coefficient is

$$r = \frac{N(\sum XY) - (\sum X)(\sum Y)}{\sqrt{N(\sum X^2) - (\sum X)^2} \sqrt{N(\sum Y^2) - (\sum Y)^2}}$$

$$= \frac{8(137) - (36)(36)}{\sqrt{8(204) - 36^2} \sqrt{8(204) - 36^2}}$$

$$= \frac{1096 - 1296}{\sqrt{1632 - 1296} \sqrt{1632 - 1296}}$$

$$= \frac{-200}{\sqrt{336} \sqrt{336}} = \frac{-200}{336} = -.595.$$

This value exactly equals the one calculated by the simpler formula. Furthermore, it will come out that way every time because when the data consist of ranks, the formula for *rho* can be derived directly from the formula for *r*.

One thing you might wish to do is calculate *r* from the original scores to compare it with *rho*. You should get $r = -.70$, a value that indicates a somewhat stronger relationship than does *rho*. This does not always happen.

Significance of rho. In the preceding chapter, a formula was presented for testing *r* by calculating a value for *t*. Strictly speaking, this approach should not be used to test *rho*. The reason is that the usual way of testing *r* makes some assumptions about normality of distributions that *rho* does not. As has already been noted, when scores are ranked, normality of distributions is deliberately destroyed. Consequently, a different type of test of statistical significance may seem to be required, and so it is.

It is probably a tribute to the robustness of normal curve statistics that the table of critical values for *r* provides a good approximation of critical values for Spearman's *rho* if the number of pairs of scores is more than 10. Below that limit, a special table for *rho* is required. The range between 10 pairs and 30 pairs is a bit doubtful, so if a special table of significance levels for *rho* is readily available, it is probably best to use it, particularly in cases of borderline significance.

Product-Moment Correlation and the *t*-Test

The preceding chapter presented the following formula for obtaining a *t* value that can be used to test the significance of a product-moment correlation coefficient:

Table 11.3.   A Hypothetical Study of Side Effects

	Group	
	T	O
	8	2
	9	0
	3	2
	4	0
	7	5
		6
SumX	31	15
SumX^2	219	69
$\overline{X}$	6.20	2.50

$$t = r \sqrt{\frac{df}{1 - r^2}}.$$

A little algebraic manipulation turns this around to give this formula for r:

$$r = \frac{t}{\sqrt{df + t^2}}.$$

This shows that in a test of the mean difference between groups, the value of t can be made into a correlation coefficient.

As a sort of review before trying out the formula, a t-test will first be run on scores from two independent groups. The calculations will use the analysis of variance approach in which $t^2 = F$ to help show that analysis of variance itself can also be thought of as being a special case of product-moment correlation.

Suppose a therapist observes that a certain form of treatment seems to bring about an undesirable set of side effects that other treatments do not. The side effects consist of a number of specific symptoms that can be listed on a series of rating scales. A group of patients receiving the suspected form of treatment (T) and a group of patients receiving other forms of treatment (O) rate themselves to indicate whether or how strongly they experience each symptom. Their scores are the totals of their ratings. There are five persons in group T and six in group O. Table 11.3 presents the results.

The difference between means is quite large and will probably be

Table 11.4. Summary Table of Analysis of Variance

Source	SS	df	MS	F
Between Groups	37.336	1	37.336	5.764*
Within Groups	58.300	9	6.478	
Total	95.636			

*$p < .05$

significant. In fact, the difference is so large that one wonders why
the investigator would bother to run a t-test at all. Every score in
group T is higher than every score in group O. Nevertheless, investigators should take nothing for granted and, anyway, calculating the statistics is good practice. First, the total sum of squares:

$$SS_T = SumX^2 - \frac{(SumX)^2}{N}$$

$$= (219 + 69) - \frac{(31 + 15)^2}{(5 + 6)} = 288 - \frac{46^2}{11}$$

$$= 288 - \frac{2116}{11} = 288 - 192.364 = 95.636.$$

The term $(46)^2/11$ has been called the *adjustment term*. To get the
between-group sum of squares, this term is subtracted from a total,
obtained by squaring each group sum, dividing that by the number
of scores in the group, and adding up the results:

$$SS_B = \frac{(SumX_T)^2}{n_T} + \frac{(SumX_O)^2}{n_O} - \frac{(Grand\ SumX)^2}{N}$$

$$= \frac{31^2}{5} + \frac{15^2}{6} - \frac{46^2}{11}$$

$$= 192.20 + 37.50 - 192.364 = 37.3192.364 = 37.336.$$

The summary table is shown in Table 11.4.

In this table, the sum of squares within groups was obtained by
subtracting SS_B from the total. As usual, mean squares were obtained by dividing appropriate sums of squares by df, and F is the
ratio of SS_B to SS_W. Despite the large difference between obtained

means, F is significant at only the .05 level (two-tailed). This is the price the investigator pays for using small samples.

Since $F = 5.764$, and t is the square root of F, in this example, $t = 2.401$. This value may be plugged into the formula for r to indicate the strength of the relationship (or association) between the occurrence of side effects and the type of treatment used:

$$r = \frac{t}{\sqrt{df + t^2}} = \frac{2.401}{\sqrt{9 + 2.401^2}} = \frac{2.401}{\sqrt{9 + 5.765}}$$

$$= \frac{2.401}{3.843} = 0.625.$$

A check of significance of this value of r, using a table of critical values for r, with $df = 9$, shows that it, too, is significant at the .05 level. In this instance, however, the absolute size of the correlation value shows that the relationship between treatment and side effects is fairly strong, even though the t-test is statistically significant at only the .05 level.

Common Variance

In the preceding example, squaring the value of r gives .39 as the proportion of shared or common variance. But it may not be obvious what two variables share this variance. It is "shared" by the variation between treatment conditions and the variation among scores on side effects. Usually the investigator would say that treatment differences "account for" .39, or 39 percent, of the variance in side effects.

To say that one variable accounts for another is to suggest a causal connection rather than just an observed association. Causation is an inference, and not something that is proven absolutely by data, but the usage is so common that few investigators in the behavioral and social sciences would argue the point strongly.

Another way to obtain the value of the common variance is to run a product-moment correlation coefficient directly from the data. As has been demonstrated before, this is accomplished by assigning another score to each person in the study. That means creating a new variable that might be called *kind of treatment*. Variables of this general type are "dummy" variables because they are artificial. They are not measured from observations but are created by the investigator only for purposes of statistical analysis.

Table 11.5. Use of a Dummy Variable in a Two-Group Study

Group	Type of Treatment*	Side-effect Score	Product
T	1	8	8
T	1	9	9
T	1	3	3
T	1	4	4
T	1	7	7
0	0	2	0
0	0	0	0
0	0	2	0
0	0	0	0
0	0	5	0
0	0	6	0
Sum	5	46	31
SumX^2	5	288	—

*This is the dummy variable.

All persons in group T are given the score of 1, and all persons in group O are given a score of 0 on this new variable. The data are presented in Table 11.5.

The six values needed to calculate the correlation coefficient are

Sum (Type) = 5; Sum (Side Effects) = 46; Sum (Cross products) = 31

Sum (Type)^2 = 5; Sum (Side Effects^2) = 288; N = 11.

Again the formula for r is

$$r = \frac{N(\text{Sum}XY) - (\text{Sum}X)(\text{Sum}Y)}{\sqrt{N(\text{Sum}X^2) - (\text{Sum}X)^2} \ \sqrt{N(\text{Sum}Y^2) - (\text{Sum}Y)^2}}.$$

Here, X is type of treatment, and Y is side-effect scores. So, the calculation of r is as follows:

$$r = \frac{11(31) - (5)(46)}{\sqrt{11(5) - 5^2} \ \sqrt{11(288) - 46^2}}$$

$$= \frac{341 - 230}{\sqrt{55 - 25} \ \sqrt{3168 - 2116}} = \frac{111}{\sqrt{(30)} \ \sqrt{(1052)}}$$

$$= \frac{111}{(5.477)(32.435)} = \frac{111}{177.646} = .625.$$

The circle now seems complete. The original value of $t = 2.401$ can be restored by placing this value back into the formula

$$t = r \sqrt{\frac{df}{1 - r^2}}$$

(Allow for rounding in the third decimal place.)

This type of correlation index is sometimes called a *point biserial coefficient*, which is merely a special case of the product-moment coefficient in which one variable is continuous and the other is dichotomous (consists of only two possible values).

Product-moment correlation and the F-test. The same results could have been obtained from the F-ratio. Since

$$r = \frac{t}{\sqrt{df + t^2}}$$

then,

$$r^2 = \frac{t^2}{df + t^2}.$$

And since $F = t^2$, then F may be substituted wherever t^2 appears:

$$r^2 = \frac{F}{df + F}.$$

This approach gives the "proportion of variance accounted for" directly:

$$r^2 = \frac{5.764}{9 + 5.764} = .390.$$

So, although F and t are equivalent, the F-test is a bit handier, even when only two groups are involved. (By the way, if you look closely, you may see a resemblance between this formula and the one for the contingency coefficient, C. The similarity may become more apparent if you take the square root of both sides of the preceding equation.)

More Than Two Groups

William L. Hays (1973, pp. 484–488) proposed a more general formula that can be used in one-way analysis of variance for any number of groups. This formula produces a value called *omega squared*. It can also be interpreted as an estimate of the strength of a statistical relation. The formula is

$$\text{est. } omega^2 = \frac{SS_B - (k - 1)MS_W}{SS_T + MS_W}.$$

The terms have their usual meanings:

SS_B: sum of squares between groups;

k: number of groups;

MS_W: mean square within groups;

SS_T: total sum of squares.

Applying this to the preceding example gives

$$\text{est. } omega^2 = \frac{37.336 - (1)(6.478)}{95.636 + 6.478}$$

$$= \frac{37.336 - 6.478}{102.114} = \frac{30.858}{102.114} = .302.$$

This figure is not very different from the value of .39 obtained from the previous formula for *r*. *Omega* squared is not a product-moment correlation coefficient, but it is interpretable in somewhat the same way, and it does have the advantage of being usable no matter how many groups are involved in the research design. Remember, the use of *r* is limited to bivariate situations.

Similar formulas have been developed for estimating the strengths of association in more complicated analysis of variance designs. These require calculating several estimates of variance accounted for, one for each main effect and one for each interaction.

A General Principle

In all experiments that use the analysis of variance, or related approaches, several ways can usually be found to analyze a variance into one part that is accounted for and another that is not. This is all that is needed to calculate a number that means something very much like what a correlation coefficient means. Many values of this type are called *intraclass coefficients*, or in some particular cases, *eta*^{2}.

Intraclass Correlation

In general, a correlation value can be calculated any time a variance can be broken down into one part that is accounted for and another that is not. The correlation value is obtained by finding the ratio of the variance accounted for to the total relevant variance (the sum of variance accounted for plus error). As indicated earlier, this type of correlation is called *intraclass correlation*, and the index that results is called an *intraclass correlation coefficient*.

Sometimes the calculation of an intraclass coefficient is not quite as simple as this discussion makes it seem. One might suppose that in a simple one-way analysis of variance, variation between groups goes in the numerator, while the total variance goes in the denominator. Remember, however, that in statistics everything is an estimate. Even the between-groups variance is not precise or absolute. It, too, usually contains some randomness. Therefore, adjustments must be made in the mean square between cells to remove the part that is due to random variation. (Check back to see how this was done in the numerator of the formula for *omega*^{2}.) This adjustment is itself an estimate because it comes from the variance within cells, which is also not precise. How these adjustments are made depends in large part upon the types of assumptions the investigator makes about the factors included in the research design. The general problem is one of *components of variance*.

Components of Variance

When an experiment containing independent groups includes many subjects, the subjects are usually thought of as being a sample. Differences among them constitute a *random factor* in the research. So, any estimate of variance based on these differences within groups is thought of as being randomly determined and can be used as an error term for testing appropriate controlled sources of variance.

But differences between *treatment conditions* may or may not be assumed to be random. If four treatments are compared in a simple one-way research design, the investigator may choose to think of them in either of two ways. On the one hand, the investigator may prefer to consider them to be the only four treatments that are of interest. In that case, treatments are not sampled but *fixed*. The investigator has no plans to generalize beyond the four specific treatments studied. Differences among them are not random.

On the other hand, the very same treatments may be assumed to be representative of the various treatments that could be administered. This assumption might be appropriate in a study that evaluates the overall effectiveness of a program that includes many different forms, or levels, of therapy, but in which only a few of the components are selected for close examination. In this case, results will be generalized from the four treatments studied to the program as a whole. The treatment effect contains a random component because the treatments are thought of as being a sample, rather than the entire statistical universe.

Naturally, any experimental factor that contains randomness contains error. Therefore, any estimates of variance it produces will include more than just "variance accounted for." Adjustments must be made in these mean squares to remove the estimated effects of random variation on the mean square between treatments. Although correlation estimates, which are based on analysis of variance, are measures of association, they are not identical to product-moment coefficients. Like everything else in statistics (for that matter, in all of research), their value is determined to some degree by the assumptions the investigator makes ahead of time. In large measure, statistical analysis serves researchers as well as it does because investigators have reached a fairly high level of agreement about what assumptions may and may not be made under different sets of circumstances.

CRITICAL REVIEWS OF TWO RESEARCH REPORTS

Many of the ideas and procedures that have been described in the preceding chapters may be illustrated by examining two selected research reports that appear in Appendixes 12.A and 12.B. The first article is reprinted there in its entirety, just as it appeared originally in the *Journal of Clinical Psychology*. The second article is slightly abridged; one elaborate table describing characteristics of the persons tested has been deleted because it contains more detail than is needed for purposes of this book.

A special advantage of using these particular articles is that both draw upon the same pool of data. Despite that similarity, however, each article treats those data quite differently. The first article provides a straightforward statistical test of a rather clearly stated theory. The research is *quasi-experimental*. Although its independent variable (personal commitment to long-term use of a specific drug) is examined at several levels, the variable was not deliberately manipulated by the investigators (nor could it possibly have been manipulated by them). Instead, the various "settings" of this variable were achieved by selecting persons with appropriate personal backgrounds for examination.

The second article frames its purposes in the form of research questions rather than as hypotheses. Its approach is correlational, and the investigators are more attentive to patterns of persons' scores on a number of tests than to differences between the means of groups as wholes.

Both articles are by the same pair of investigators, and both use statistical procedures that have been described in this book. The articles are fairly brief compared with many reports of research in the behavior and health sciences. In this chapter, the reports are analyzed somewhat differently. The first is examined section by section. In the second, more attention is paid to its quantitative operations.

The First Article

Title

The title of the first article (Appendix 12.A), "Drugs and Personality: Extraversion-Introversion", is fairly clear, considering its brevity, yet it does not indicate whether drugs are intended to be the independent variable and personality the dependent variable, or the reverse. On the one hand, the title could mean that the research attempts to show that using certain drugs makes people either introverted or extraverted. On the other hand, it could mean that the research looks at how being extraverted or introverted causes a person to use drugs or to prefer a particular kind of drug over others. Even though cause-effect relations are clearly implied by the theory being tested, the data from this research cannot be cited in direct support of any statements about cause and effect. The only thing this study does is relate drug preference and personality traits to each other in persons who had already been using drugs for a long period of time.

The statements of authorship indicate that both of the investigators are associated with institutions in the midwestern United States: the Greater Kansas City Mental Health Foundation, which seems to be a community-centered organization, and the University of Kansas. A footnote to the title indicates that the data for this research were collected under the auspices of a federal agency, the National Institute on Drug Abuse. Thus, it appears that this project is the result of efforts to combine the resources of the academic world and a community-based agency to obtain grant money for research.

As a supplement to examining the statements of authorship, a glance ahead at the list of references shows that these two investigators have published several other articles and books on the topics of research methodology and drug abuse. They therefore appear to be qualified to write on the subject of drug use and personality. At least, this seems to have been the opinion of those in their profession who evaluated their work for publication.

Abstract

The abstract of the article alludes first to a theory that is attributed by the authors to a well-known psychologist, Hans Eysenck. The abstract notes that this theory leads to expectations that are the opposite of what common sense might lead one to suppose. Another way of saying this is that the expectations that the theory generates are "counter intuitive." Theories with counter intuitive implications are thought to be particularly useful in research, especially in the behavior and social sciences, which are often accused of wasting a good deal of time and effort proving the obvious.

In effect, the abstract poses this question: Which is correct, common sense or the theory proposed by Eysenck? The abstract then summarizes the results of the authors' study, which was carried out with matched groups of chronic, heavy drug users. These results apparently supported neither Eysenck's views nor those of "common sense."

This abstract, less than 110 words long, tells most of what a reader would probably like to know, but it does leave out some information that might be helpful, such as the number of persons in each group that was examined, and the fact that all the participants were adult men. Although it mentions that two other instruments, in addition to the questionnaire developed by Eysenck, were used to assess extraversion, it does not name them. They were the *Si* scale of the *MMPI* and an extraversion score that can be obtained from the *Sixteen Personality Factors Questionnaire*.

Introduction

In the body of the article, the first paragraph of the introductory section notes that a test of Eysenck's theory can be carried out relatively simply because Eysenck himself developed a questionnaire to measure the critical variable: extraversion-introversion. The next paragraph lays some groundwork for the reader by summarizing the appropriate definitions of extraversion and introversion. Clear definitions are especially important in this study because these words are used in many different ways by many different authorities and knowing just what Eysenck and the investigators had in mind can be helpful. The third paragraph summarizes Eysenck's rationale for arguing that stimulants promote introversion while depressants promote extraversion. The rest of this paragraph presents the logic of the research itself. If Eysenck's theory is correct, then people who have taken appropriate substances in large enough quantities for long periods of time should show the effects on their personalities that the theory predicts.

The fourth paragraph briefly mentions which questionnaires were administered to the persons studied and the types of research questions that were to be answered by the analysis of research data. Subsequent paragraphs (*Research Context*) mention that the data were obtained as part of a larger program of research. This is worth noting because data that are collected in the context of a large-scale research program may not yield the same results or conclusions as data collected in a project where only one or two tests are administered in isolation.

Method

The authors reveal in the section on method how the men who were examined were recruited and selected for the research. This section indicates that five series of nine men each were examined. The first series consisted of men who had used cocaine (a stimulant). The second series consisted of men who used amphetamine and related substances (another class of stimulants). The third consisted of men who used opiates (mainly heroin). Opiates, of course, are "downers," sedatives, or narcotics. The fourth series consisted of men who used barbiturates and sedative-hypnotics. The fifth series contained comparable men who did not use hard drugs.

The variables on which the groups were matched are then described, and basic descriptive information is provided about the various groups. Because detailed data about the persons examined had already been published, this article refers to another report where additional information may be obtained. A reader who wants to know more about these people right away might find this slightly annoying, but reference to information in work already published is common in scientific reports. When several reports are derived from the same program of investigations, the practice is almost essential for the sake of brevity.

A careful and critical reader might detect the fact that the data for this project were not collected from persons in all groups simultaneously, but consecutively, from persons in one group at a time.

The article does not indicate how long the entire data collection process took, but a check of other material published by these investigators would show that the complete research program lasted almost 10 years—a long time between the testing of members of the first group (the cocaine users) and the last (the nonusers). Therefore, results of the study might be affected by changes in the community or in general social attitudes and beliefs that took place during the course of the investigation. At this point, the critical reader who wonders about that possibility might make a mental note to find out whether the article takes up this matter in its discussion section.

The paragraph on measures is brief and to the point. It tells what tests were used, and it explains why 2 of the 45 men selected for study were not administered the *Eysenck Personality Inventory*. It also indicates that the participants were tested individually. This is worth knowing because data collected from persons tested individually may not be quite the same as data collected when people are tested in large groups, as in classrooms.

Results

The results section of this article reports mainly F-tests, means, and standard deviations. The first result is most important, which is probably why it is presented first. It is the one-way analysis of variance of raw scores on the Extraversion Scale of the *Eysenck Personality Inventory*. The degrees of freedom for this test are reported immediately after the letter F, as is customary in reports of psychological research. Being based on five group means, the df for the numerator is 4. The df for the denominator is the number of persons who were tested minus 5 (the number of groups). Had all men selected for study taken the test, this value would be 40 ($45 - 5$), but, as noted in the article, one died and another absconded, so it is only 38. The resulting F-ratio of 6.172 is significant at the .01 level.

F-ratios, calculated for the other two scales on the *Eysenck Personality Inventory*, have the same number of df (4, 38), but they are not statistically significant.

In a one-way analysis of variance with more than two groups, the F-test tells only whether the null hypothesis can be rejected in regard to differences among all the means in an entire array. Therefore, supplementary statistical tests must be carried out to determine which specific means account for statistical significance when it appears. A special technique for the purpose, *Duncan's Multiple-*

Range Test, was applied to the means of the Extraversion scores. This procedure is designed to reduce the likelihood of capitalizing on chance when testing the elements of an array that consists of more than two means. If the means are placed in order, from lowest to highest, this procedure applies more strict standards of significance to tests of differences between means that are far apart in the series than it does to tests of differences between means that are closer together. The procedure permits grouping means into statistically defensible clusters. In this case, the procedure showed that the means for cocaine users and opiates users did not differ from each other and that the means of these two groups were lower than the means for the other three groups, which also did not differ from each other.

The article also reports another type of comparison: test-score means against test norms. Compared with "industrial norms," the mean of the group made up of the combined cocaine users and opiates users falls at the 35th percentile. The mean of the combined group of all other persons tested falls at the 84th percentile. The authors made this comparison in anticipation of possible questions about whether any persons who were examined were really extraverted or introverted. Significant differences might conceivably have been found between groups even if all subjects in the study scored above or below the expected mean of the population as a whole. This comparison shows that, on the average, the combined opiates and cocaine users do, indeed, fall on the introverted side of the mean of the normative group, while the rest of the persons fall on the extraverted side.

The suitability of using "industrial" norms based on a sample of British men may be a matter of minor concern. The article offers no explanation for the use of these norms rather than others that might have been selected. On the face of the matter, the choice does not seem unreasonable. Industrial norms are probably more appropriate than norms based on college sophomores. Nevertheless, the report leaves it to the potential critic to look up these and other alternatives to find whether norm selection would make any difference in the interpretation. Notice that norm selection does not affect decisions about the significance of differences between groups because these differences were obtained from the analysis of raw scores.

Someone who is really picky might criticize the authors for not reporting the values of the standard deviations for the combined groups. Means, *sd*s, and *n*s are reported for all subgroups, so the authors might reply that enough information is included elsewhere in the article for a concerned reader to calculate these, if they are needed. An interesting exercise might be to figure out how that could be done.

The next set of analyses that is described was carried out to test more directly the proposition that stimulant users would score lower on extraversion than would users of depressants or, presumably, than would nonusers of drugs. To accomplish this, the data were reorganized by combining scores from appropriate subgroups of testees. No significant differences were found, so the analysis did not support the proposition; that is, it did not permit rejection of the null hypothesis of no differences between groups.

Because of the lack of demonstrable differences among groups on several tests, some norm-related interpretations are cited that describe the entire group of persons studied. They appear to be slightly above average on both Extraversion and Neuroticism (a little more than 1 *sd* above the normative mean) and a bit below average on the *L* Scale, which is presumed to measure falsification of responses. Of course, the citation of a value on the Extraversion Scale for the group as a whole is not completely appropriate because other analyses have already shown that the group means on scores from this test are not homogeneous.

The report pays relatively less attention to the analyses of data from the *Si* Scale of the *MMPI* and the extraversion score derived from the *Sixteen Personality Factors Questionnaire*. The findings show no differences between stimulant users and users of depressants. Apparently, they also did not show cocaine and opiates users to score differently from the rest of the groups, as had analyses of Extraversion scores from the Eysenck scale. The data did suggest that nonusers scored lower on Introversion (on the *Si* Scale) and higher on Extraversion (on the *16PF*). Note that the only specific statistical test value cited in this paragraph of the report is the one that is significant. The authors doubtless felt that readers would not be interested in all the details of the rest of the calculations.

Discussion and Conclusions

The discussion section of the report begins by contrasting again common-sense expectations and those asserted in the theory proposed by Eysenck. In this way, the discussion section, like the abstract, leads one to expect that a so-called *critical* or *crucial experiment* has been conducted.

At one time in the history of science, researchers thought that

Truth (with a capital T) could be arrived at by experimentation alone. A crucial experiment was therefore said to be one in which two theories are placed into direct competition. The idea was that the outcome of such an experiment would reveal in a clear-cut way which theory is True and which False.

Generally, a crucial experiment was intended to compare two theories that produced clearly testable, but contradictory, hypotheses about the outcome of a single experiment. Of course, there is no logical reason why one of these theories could not say that statement X is true, while the other says that statement X is false. Many experiments that were intended to be crucial turned out later not to be. In any case, the idea that truth can be gained by examining the outcome of a single experiment has been generally abandoned.

One currently popular view is that of the philosopher Karl Popper, who claimed that while data alone can never prove an hypothesis to be true, they can disprove (or falsify) it in a properly designed experiment. Another view, more like the one adopted here, is that data alone can neither prove nor disprove anything absolutely, no . matter how carefully collected and analyzed the data may be. Certainly, data can add a considerable weight of credibility to one alternative or another. Still, no matter how any experiment turns out, some explanation, other than the ones that are proposed by the experimenter, is always possible.

An interesting historical case in point is the famous Michelson-Morley experiment, which allegedly disproved the theory that space is occupied by a substance called ether. Common sense, which is consistent with the theory that asserts the existence of ether, says that when an observer measuring the speed of light is moving in the same direction as the measured light, the observer's motion will reduce the apparent speed of the light to that observer. When the observer is moving against the light, however, the speed of the observer's motion will be added to the apparent speed of the light, thus increasing its measured velocity. The experiment, which was carried out in 1887, demonstrated that the measured speed of light is constant, whether it is determined while the observer is moving in the same direction as the light or while the observer is moving in the opposite direction from the light.

The data produced by the experiment are not in doubt. Thus, it seems to disprove conclusively the theory of ether. However, as Kneller (1978, p. 92) pointed out, certain other scientists quickly countered the now-accepted interpretation of the results of this experiment by referring to another theory, namely, that objects contract at high speeds. These scientists claimed that during the Michelson-Morley experiment, the apparatus measuring the speed of light had shrunk in proportion to an actual change in the apparent velocity of light, thus making the instrument insensitive to real differences in light's relative velocity. Consequently, they said, the Michelson-Morley experiment was not critical. It did not prove that the speed of light is invariant.

Some might say that the attempt to disprove the existence of ether was not the central issue. The Michelson-Morley experiment may have been received enthusiastically because of the support it provided for Einstein's newly emerging theory of relativity. In any event, the scientists' decision to reject the theory of ether was based on much more than the results of a single investigation.

In the far less famous drug users study being examined here, the discussion section points out that the data partially supported both Eysenck's theory and common sense, but they supported neither theory completely. The investigators argue that both theories are probably wrong because another theory (theirs) is more consistent with both the data from this study and with findings from other investigations. Drug use in general, they argue, is associated with poorer overall psychological adjustment than is nonuse. They maintain that drug use of any kind does not increase extraversion but probably decreases it, if it has any effect on extraversion at all. These arguments are based mainly on the reported analyses that compared drug users, as a group, with the nonusers. Many would find the investigators' proposals more compelling had the actual outcome of the study been predicted before the data were collected or analyzed.

Passing note is then made in the article that the opiates users scored lowest among the user groups studied, although not significantly lower than the rest. The similarity of this outcome to outcomes reported by other investigators is noted. No interpretation of this finding is suggested, and a reader may wonder why it is even mentioned. One possible reason is that it establishes credibility by pointing out that the data of the research are not peculiar, at least in this one respect.

A review of relevant literature follows, in which it is noted that only one other research study seems similar to this one. That study is critically analyzed to demonstrate that the types of persons tested in it were not comparable to those examined in this research. The criticism clearly implies that, as a test of Eysenck's theory, this investigation is superior.

Finally, comments are made about the sizes of the groups in this research. The authors anticipate the claim that group sizes in this study are too small to support generalization. The article asserts that allowance must be made for the care with which persons were selected for participation in the study. In any case, the report says, obtained differences were statistically significant, and who can argue with success?

Anticipating the argument that the results might not hold up in other cultural areas, the article notes Eysenck's claim that extraversion is a biological phenomenon. Therefore, the data should not be affected by distinctive cultural factors. In the last sentence of the article, certain limitations of generalizability are acknowledged, specifically that the findings apply only to chronic drug users and not to others whose usage patterns are different.

A weakness of this section of the report is that it does not refer to the methodological problem mentioned earlier, namely, whether the data from the groups tested at the end of the 10-year project might have been affected by changes or events that occurred locally or nationally between the beginning of the research and its conclusion.

References

Readers should check the list of references not only at the very beginning, as a way of gaining information about the investigators' qualifications, but also while reading the research report, as citations of articles in the literature are made in the text itself. A survey of the list at the end of the first article shows that it contains 19 items, of which 6 are publications of one or more of the investigators who carried out this research. Two of these publications (by Shontz alone) are about methodology. The other four deal with drug abuse. Nevertheless, the reader may be left curious about what drug abuse has to do with dragon fights.

Three of the papers in the reference list include Eysenck as author or coauthor, which is not surprising, since Eysenck's theory is the one being tested. The other 10 papers seem to be mostly research reports from a variety of sources. Their titles are consistent with the statement made by the authors of this paper in the discussion section that little or no directly pertinent research has been published. Obviously, the research literature on a topic like drug use and personality must contain more than 10 investigations. Unless one is personally familiar with that literature, or wishes to become so, it is necessary to assume that the investigators' survey has been complete and their selection representative.

The Second Article

As noted earlier, the second article, "Correlates of Sensation Seeking by Heavy, Chronic Drug Users," will be analyzed differently from the first to avoid repetition and to highlight its distinctive features. The persons from whom test scores were obtained were the same ones who were used in the first research study.

Construct Validity

The abstract of this article contains the term *construct validity* (Cronbach 1970). This term was introduced in Chapter 1, but a brief review will help the reader understand why the study was conducted and how its outcome was interpreted. Some theoretical ideas (constructs) are simple enough in their implications that they can be measured almost directly. For example, reaction time, perceptual acuity, and rate of habit acquisition lend themselves to physical measurement in rather obvious ways.

Other theoretical ideas—such as intelligence, psychological adjustment, stress, and anxiety—are more abstract and cannot be converted so readily into specific procedures by which they can be measured. The particular theoretical idea, or construct, which is of interest in this second article is called *sensation seeking*, a hypothesized need for arousal, novelty, or change. Sensation seeking is presumed to account for, among other things, a person's tendency to use drugs (Zuckerman 1979). A questionnaire called the *Sensation Seeking Scales* (SSS) has been developed to measure the strength of this need.

Merely making up a questionnaire to measure the strength of a need is not enough to convince most psychologists that such a need exists. Evidence must be collected that confirms hypotheses derived from the theory that defines sensation seeking in the first place. If successfully acquired, such evidence would confirm the validity not only of the questionnaire but also of the construct the questionnaire is said to measure.

One derivation from the theory behind the sensation seeking questionnaire is that drug users with high levels of this need will try more different kinds of drugs than will users with low levels of the need. Moreover, drug users in general may be expected to show stronger needs for sensation than do nonusers. To the extent that data show these two expectations to be correct, the construct of a need for sensation seeking may be said to be confirmed, and the questionnaire may be said to have been validated.

In describing the rationale for their research, the authors note that several instruments, other than the SSS, seem to be measuring the same construct. The investigators therefore raise the question of whether these other instruments might produce data similar to those that are yielded by the five subscales and the General Score that comes from the SSS. They also note that none of these tests, including the SSS, has been used in research with carefully selected groups of chronic, heavy drug users. That raises the question of whether findings from such persons will be consistent with other findings reported in the literature.

With regard to the major research question, the most important indicator is the number of different drugs that had been tried by each man over the course of his life. As noted in the research report, these data were obtained from interviews covering each person's drug use history.

Effects of Group Differences on Correlation Values

Among the questionnaires used in this research are the three subtests of the *Eysenck Personality Inventory*, one of the questionnaires used in the first report. That research showed that the mean scores of the groups differed on the Extraversion Scale. Those same means, except for one slight variation due to rounding, can be seen in the fifth row of data in Table 3 of the research report (Appendix 12.B).

Statistically speaking, differences between groups on any test could affect correlation coefficients, if the coefficients are calculated without regard to persons' group membership. Notice in Table 3, for example, that cocaine users, who tend as a group to score low on extraversion, also appear to have tried relatively few drugs. The mean number of drugs they said they tried is only 13.7, a value that is clearly much lower than the mean for any other group. If the cocaine users as a group also scored low on sensation seeking, as appears to be the case, the overall correlation, based on paired scores of individuals one at a time, would tend to be high. The problem is that the correlation could be due to factors other than need for novelty, change, or excitement. What might some of these biasing factors be?

Recall that the cocaine users were the first ones to be examined in the study series. Perhaps the interviewer who obtained their drug histories was not as careful or as skilled about obtaining detailed information at that time as he later became. Another possibility is that reports of use of fewer drugs may be due to the long-term effects of cocaine itself (perhaps it affects users' long-term memory, so they recall less drug use than they should). Then the results would not be due to correlation between sensation seeking and drug use but to other factors.

In research of this type, it is never possible to eliminate all possible biasing factors. Nevertheless, certain allowances can sometimes be made. One way to handle the particular problem of differences among group means that arises in this research is to adjust all scores so that differences between groups are eliminated before correlation values are calculated.

These investigators took a rather direct approach to the task. Each person's score on every indicator was considered to consist of two components besides error. One component is due to group membership. The value of this component is assumed to be the same for all persons in a group. It can be estimated for any group on any instrument by calculating the difference between the mean of the group and the grand mean for all groups combined.

Because this component is unwanted, each individual's score on the instrument was then adjusted by adding to it, or subtracting from it, an amount that compensates for the difference. So, for example every cocaine user's score on Extraversion was increased to make up for the fact that the cocaine users as a group scored below the grand mean. Similar adjustments were made for all scores and all groups used in the analysis. The sizes of the adjustments that were made can be appreciated by examining the differences among group means that appear along the rows of Tables 2 and 3 in Appendix 12.B. The scores that remained were considered to consist of a combination of *true individual differences* (within groups) plus error.

If the assumptions that lie behind these adjustments are correct (and who is to know whether they really are?), the adjustments effectively eliminate differences between groups, leaving only variations within groups to be correlated with each other. More sophisticated ways exist for accomplishing similar adjustments in data. For example, in analysis of variance, the possible influence of an extraneous variable may be removed before tests of differences between means are carried out on the dependent variable. In that case, the procedure is called *analysis of covariance* (or ANCOVA). The approach taken in this research is probably easier to understand, and it is suitable for present purposes.

Results: Reading a Table

Calculating correlation coefficients on the adjusted scores produced the values shown in Table 4 of the article. Although on casual examination the table may look like a correlation matrix, it is not one. It does not contain correlations between all possible pairs of scores but includes only those that are of major research interest.

The five scores obtained from the SSS, along with the indicator of number of drugs tried, are listed across the top of the table. The rest of the questionnaires that were used are listed down the left side, along with a repeat of number of drugs tried. As is often done in research reports, values that are significant at the .05 level are marked with a single asterisk. Had any been significant at the .01 level, they might have been marked with a double asterisk. Had any been significant at the .001 level, they might have been marked with a triple asterisk.

Table 4 is so arranged that the answer to the primary research question is to be found along the bottom row (horizontal) of numbers. This is the question of whether the number of drugs a person tried correlates with scores on the SSS. The relevant values are all positive, and three of five are significantly different from zero, so it appears that the answer, in general, is yes. Notice, however, that the magnitudes of these values are not large.

The last column (vertical) on the right in Table 4 contains the answer to the question of whether number of drugs correlates with other tests that may be measuring the same construct as the SSS. The correlations for the four subtests of the *Novelty Experiencing Scale* are all close to zero. The correlations for the Extraversion Scale of the *Eysenck Personality Inventory* and for the *Change Seeker Index* are significantly different from zero. Other values are low but positive, except for those of the *Lie* Scale.

The rest of the table shows how the SSS scores correlated with those of the other instruments used. Most striking is the string of 6 out of 6 significant values for the *Change Seeker Index* (row 8) and of 6 out of 11 significant values for the General score of the SSS (data column 1).

Investigators' Conclusions

The authors of the article concluded that, for the most part, their results resembled those reported from other research. However, they also noted that other instruments appear to be measuring the same construct as the SSS. The data therefore suggest that while the construct called sensation seeking seems useful, it may not be very different from what others are measuring with other instruments under different names. If that is the case, little need is seen for having so many different questionnaires and scores cluttering up the research stage.

On theoretical grounds, the report cautions that any attempt to explain drug use by associating it with a single personality variable is probably an oversimplification. Other personality factors, such as a person's desire for status, probably enter the picture as well. Furthermore, the expression of internal traits, such as extraversion or need for change or stimulation, depends on environmental opportunities. Psychological states can influence number of drugs tried only if the environment makes it possible for a person to try a number of drugs should he or she wish to do so.

Some Final Notes

Neither of the studies that were presented and analyzed here is likely to make scientific history. However, both investigations make respectable contributions to the scientific literature on personality and drug abuse. For teaching purposes, they are especially useful because one is primarily an analysis of group differences, and the other examines correlations among test scores. One is therefore in the tradition of experimental or quasi-experimental methodology. The other is more in the tradition of the study of individual differences or psychometrics. The two research studies are also useful because, as such things go, they are fairly simple, straightforward, and easy to subject to critical analysis.

A word of caution is now in order. Do not expect all research reports to be as amenable to close examination as these. Reading and understanding research can be a demanding and time-consuming occupation. Nevertheless, it is also a challenge to the intellect.

Popular conceptions to the contrary notwithstanding, a piece of research is almost as much a creative work of art or craft as it is a contribution to knowledge. This is especially true in the behavior and social sciences and of research that is carried out in service settings. A meticulously planned, carefully conducted, and clearly described investigation can be appreciated for its aesthetic properties as well as criticized for its logical flaws and weaknesses, a few of which every study is bound to contain.

Some investigations, and the reports that result from them, are as ponderous as a Wagner opera or a symphony by Mahler. Others are as crystalline as a Mozart sonata or as complex, yet economical, as a Bach fugue. Admittedly, none is likely to have quite the same appeal as Beethoven's Ninth Symphony or Michelangelo's painting of the ceiling of the Sistine Chapel. But good research arouses its own type of excitement, especially for those who are directly involved in carrying it out or who are directly affected by its findings. In fact, understanding research does not really become possible until one becomes actively involved in carrying it out step by step.

This book does not open wide the doorway to direct research experience for everyone who reads it. The serious student still has a long road to travel and certainly requires advanced training before qualifying as an expert. Nevertheless, this book does unlock the latch on the door, and for the student who reads the book carefully, it even turns the knob. Some readers may merely push the door ajar, peek through the crack, close the door again, and go no further. They have still gained something. At least they have viewed a landscape they would not otherwise have seen. Others who plan a longer journey will open the door wide, cross the threshold, and begin down the path that lies before them. They should find that they are off to a good start.

Appendix 12.A

DRUGS AND PERSONALITY: EXTRAVERSION-INTROVERSION

James V. Spotts, Ph.D.
Assistant Director,
Greater Kansas City
Mental Health Foundation

Franklin C. Shontz, Ph.D.
Professor of Psychology,
University of Kansas

Abstract

Eysenck theorizes that stimulants induce introversion and that depressants induce extraversion; common sense leads to opposite expectations. Scores on the extraversion scale of the Eysenck Personality Inventory yielded statistically significant differences among carefully matched series of heavy, chronic users of cocaine, amphetamine, opiates, barbiturate/sedative-hypnotics, and a comparable series of nonusers. Cocaine users and opiates users were found to be more introverted; amphetamine users, barbiturates users, and nonusers were more extraverted. These findings did not fully support either set of hypotheses. The data also implied that, if drugs influence extraversion, they do so only by suppressing it. Data from two other measures of extraversion were consistent with this hypothesis.

INTRODUCTION

Only a few studies of drug users have employed the *Eysenck Personality Inventory* (Beaubrum, 1975; Buikhuisen & Timmerman, 1972; Gasser, Langrod, Valdes & Lowinson, 1974; Hemminki, Rissman & Mattila, 1973; Khavari, Mabry & Humes, 1977; Rosenberg, 1969; Kilpatrick, Sutker & Smith, 1976). This is remarkable because Eysenck is one of the few theorists to

This research program has been supported by contracts and grants from the National Institute on Drug Abuse. The authors wish to thank Dr. Daniel J. Lettieri for his encouragement and helpful suggestions.

Reprinted with permission from *Journal of Clinical Psychology* 40:624–628, 1984.

Editor's Note: This sample article has been reproduced exactly as provided by the author; no attempt has been made to edit it for content or style.

present not only an explicit formulation about how drug use influences personality, but a trait-specific test to measure the influence.

According to Eysenck (1965) the typical *extravert* is a gregarious person who likes parties, has many friends, needs to have people to talk to, craves excitement, likes change, and is generally impulsive, carefree, and optimistic. He prefers to keep moving, tends to be aggressive, and is not always reliable. The typical *introvert* is quiet, retiring and introspective, fond of books rather than people, and distant and reserved except with intimate friends. He is distrustful of impulses of the moment, keeps his feelings under close control, takes life seriously, and seeks a well-ordered mode of life. The typical introvert is reliable, somewhat pessimistic and places great value on ethical standards (pp. 59–60). Extraverts generate inhibition more quickly than introverts and therefore lose interest in tasks more quickly, but bear pain better and acquire conditional responses less readily than introverts (pp. 81–85).

Although Eysenck (1965) postulates that one's position on the introversion-extraversion continuum is hereditarily determined he also asserts that it can be changed by use of drugs. *CNS stimulants* such as amphetamine, caffeine, and presumably cocaine decrease inhibition and increase excitation. *CNS depressants*, such as alcohol, barbiturates, and presumably opiates, increase inhibitory potential and decrease excitatory potential (pp. 90–91). Stimulant drugs therefore push the user toward introversion, while depressant drugs push the user toward extraversion (p. 284). If this theory is correct, differences between chronic heavy users of these substances should be apparent in appropriate test scores.

Eysenck's own personality inventory (Eysenck & Eysenck, 1964) was administered, as part of a larger battery of tests, to persons committed to the heavy, long-term use of CNS stimulants and persons committed to the heavy long-term use of CNS depressants. Other relevant data were obtained from the *Si* scale of the *MMPI* and the second-order extraversion factor of the *Sixteen Personality Factors Questionnaire*. The study addressed three major questions.

1. Do EPI scores of heavy, chronic users of cocaine, amphetamine, opiates, barbiturate/sedative-hypnotics, and nonusers of drugs differ significantly?
2. Do EPI scores of heavy, chronic users of stimulant and depressant drugs and nonusers of drugs differ significantly?
3. Do EPI scores of heavy, chronic users of drugs (irrespective of type) and nonusers of drugs differ significantly?

Research Context

The men tested were participants in a program of research on four carefully matched series of long-term drug users and a comparable series of men committed to the nonuse of drugs. The research employs the Representative Case Method (Shontz, 1965, 1977) and is based upon intensive studies of carefully selected persons who epitomize people who engage in heavy, chronic drug use.

METHOD

Persons Tested

The first series consisted of adult males who preferred cocaine over all other drugs and had used it long enough to be expert as to its effects. A widespread network of intermediaries identified several hundred such persons in the Kansas City area. From these, nine were selected whose life styles represented those generally said to be associated with cocaine use (Spotts & Shontz, 1980a): a musician, a blue collar worker, a professional thief, a pimp, an ambitious, achievement-oriented individual, a scion of an exceptionally wealthy family, a drug dealer, a social misfit, and a two-worlder (who maintained full-time employment to mask illegal activities).

In later studies, the recruitment network was expanded to obtain four additional series. Persons in each series were selected to match the cocaine users in age, sex, IQ, socioeconomic background, and life style. Each was committed to the chronic use of a single drug or class of drugs. One or two low-level users were included in each series to insure coverage of the complete dosage continuum. The second series consisted of men committed to amphetamine and its substitutes; the third consisted of men committed to opiates; and the fourth consisted of men committed to barbiturates or sedative-hypnotics. The fifth series contained men who were matched with the other groups but who were committed not to use hard drugs. All series of drug users were matched on level of educational achievement. However, educational achievement of nonusers was unavoidably higher than that of all series of drug users, than combined users of stimulants, combined users of depressants or combined users of all drugs (Spotts & Shontz, 1983).

The median ages of the men were 27 to 29, with lower limits ranging from 21 to 22 and upper limits ranging from 42 to 52. The mean IQs (Revised Betas) ranged from 104.0 to 109.2, with standard deviations ranging from 5.06 to 11.22. The median chronicities of drug use were: cocaine users, 11 years; amphetamine users, 8 years; opiate users, 12 years; and barbiturate/sedative-hypnotic users, 11 years. Additional details are presented in Spotts and Shontz (1982, 1983).

Measures.   Each participant was examined individually for 14 or more full days over a period of 4–6 months. The MMPI and Sixteen PF Questionnaire were administered to all participants. The Eysenck Personality Inventory was administered to 43 men. One member of the cocaine series was killed, and one member of the opiates series absconded before taking this test.

RESULTS

One way analyses of variance of raw scores produced a significant F ratio on the Extraversion Scale of the Eysenck Personality Inventory, $F = 6.172$, df $= 4,38$, $p<.01$, but not on the Neuroticism Scale, $F = 1.527$, df $= 4,38$, $p>.05$ or the L Scale, $F = 1.00$, df $= 4,38$, $p>.05$. Analyses of standard scores, derived from percentiles based on industrial norms (Eysenck & Eysenck, 1968), yielded the same outcome. Nonusers obtained the highest scores on extraversion ($Mn = 14.8$; $SD = 3.42$) followed by amphetamine users ($Mn = 14.0$; $SD = 3.46$), barbiturate/sedative-hypnotic users ($Mn = 13.3$; $SD = 2.96$), opiate users ($Mn = 9.2$; $SD = 4.27$), and cocaine users ($Mn = 8.0$; $SD = 3.59$). Duncan's Multiple Range Test indicated that the means for the cocaine users and opiates users were not significantly different, but that both differed significantly from the means of the amphetamine users, barbiturate/sedative-hypnotic users, and nonusers. The last three did not differ from each other. The combined raw score mean for the cocaine and opiates users (8.6) places them at about the 35th percentile on Extraversion. The combined raw score mean for the other three series (14.0) places them at about the 84th percentile.

One way analysis of variance of raw scores for combined *CNS stimulant* (cocaine and amphetamine) users, *CNS depressant* (combined opiates and barbiturate/sedative-hypnotic) users and nonusers revealed no significant differences among groups on the Extraversion, Neuroticism or Lie Scales. Similar analyses, comparing a group, made up of all drug users regardless of substance preference, with nonusers also revealed no significant differences. The grand mean of 12.0 ($SD = 4.33$) on the Extraversion Scale places the entire group of 43 men at about the 68th percentile. The grand mean of 10.9 ($SD = 5.12$) on the Neuroticism Scale places the entire group at the 68th percentile. The grand mean of 1.8 ($SD = 1.49$) on the L Scale places the entire group at about the 40th percentile.

The *Si* scale of the MMPI did not yield significant differences among specific groups but did show that the combined group of all drug users ($Mn = 55.7$; $SD = 9.84$) scored significantly higher than the nonusers ($Mn = 44.6$; $SD = 5.9$), $F = 10.504$, df 1,43, $p<.01$. The second order extraversion scale of the Sixteen PF yielded no significant differences, but the combined group of drug users did score lower ($Mn = 5.303$; $SD = 2.52$) than the nonusers ($Mn = 6.38$; $SD = 1.09$).

DISCUSSION AND CONCLUSIONS

"Common sense" leads one to expect heavy, long-term users of stimulants to be extraverts, and heavy, long-term users of depressants to be introverts. Eysenck's theory is counter-intuitive, because it leads to opposite expectations. However, the data fully support neither set of expectations. Users of one stimulant (cocaine) and one type of depressant (barbiturates and sedative-hypnotics) scored consistently with Eysenck's theory. Users of another stimulant (amphetamine) and another depressant (opiates) scored consistently with common sense expectations.

Nonusers obtained the lowest scores of all on neuroticism and the highest on extraversion. The former is consistent with the theory that drug use in general is associated with personal maladjustment (Spotts & Shontz, 1980b; 1982). The latter suggests that, if drugs have any effect on extraversion, they depress it (especially the opiates and cocaine). The nonusers were characterized by greater extraversion on both the *Si* scale of the *MMPI* and the second-order extraversion scale of the *Sixteen PF* as well as by Eysenck's scale. If any drug increases extraversion, at least one of the series of users in this study should have appeared to be more extraverted than the nonusers, but none did.

Eysenck asserts that high Neuroticism scores indicate emotional lability and overreactivity, and occur in persons who are predisposed to develop neurotic disorders (1968, p. 6). In this study, opiate users obtained substantially (though not significantly) lower Neuroticism Scores than the other user groups. Similar findings have been reported by McLellan, Woody, and O'Brien (1979) in a 6 year follow up of narcotics users, stimulant users and depressants users.

No other published research tests the hypotheses that were tested in this investigation. Other studies using the Eysenck Personality Inventory focused upon addicts and methadone maintenance patients (Gasser, et al., 1974; Stewart & Waddell, 1972); marihuana or hallucinogen users (Beaubrum, 1975; Khavari, et al., 1977; Robinson, 1970); polydrug users (Kilpatrick, et al., 1976; Rosenberg, 1969) or student drug users (Buikhuisen & Timmerman, 1972; Hemminki, et al., 1973).

The study by Kilpatrick et al. (1976) which compared regular drug users with problem drinkers, occasional users of drugs or alcohol, and nonusers, most closely approximates the present research. Regular drug users obtained significantly higher extraversion scores (Mean 14.12) than did occasional users or nonusers. Regular drug users and problem drinkers also scored significantly higher on neuroticism (Mean 14.36) than the other groups.

The results reported by Kilpatrick et al. appear not to agree with the present investigation. However, these two studies cannot be compared, because of differences in populations studied and methodologies. For example, a majority of the regular drug users in the Kilpatrick et al. study were polydrug users, a group not studied here. All men studied by Kilpatrick et al. were hospitalized veterans and presumably were not using drugs or alcohol at the time of the research. None of the men in the present study was hospitalized; all were living independently in the community and virtually all were still actively using drugs. The nonuser comparison group employed by Kilpatrick et al. was drawn from the hospital's medical and surgical wards. Their backgrounds and life styles were undoubtedly different from those of the men being treated for drug abuse. In the present study the nonuser comparison series contained men specifically selected because their backgrounds and life styles were similar to those of the drug users. These men were at approximately equal risk to the drug users but had deliberately chosen *not* to use hard drugs.

Groups may appear to be relatively small in this research. However, each subject was "hand-picked" to represent as clearly as possible heavy, chronic use of his drug of choice. Though subjects were drawn from a common geographic area, research results should be unaffected because Eysenck maintains that introversion and extraversion are not cultural but biological phenomena. Finally, the study series were obviously not too small to produce statistically significant differences, a fact the investigators ascribe to the clear-cut differences between them in drug-use patterns. The findings of this report apply only to heavy, chronic users and do not depict the pattern of relationships one would expect to find with occasional or social recreational drug users whose usage patterns are determined by separate dynamics.

REFERENCES

Beaubrum, M. Cannabis or alcohol: The Jamaican experience. In V. Rubin (Ed.), *Cannabis and culture*. The Hague, Holland: Mouton Publishers, 1975.

Buikhuisen, W., & Timmerman, H. The development of drug-taking among secondary school children in the Netherlands. *Bulletin on Narcotics*, 1972, *24*, 7–16.

Eysenck, H.J. *Fact and fiction in psychology*. Baltimore, MD: Penguin Books, Inc., 1965.

Eysenck, H.J., & Eysenck, S.B.G. *Manual for the Eysenck Personality Inventory*. San Diego, CA: Educational and Industrial Testing Service, 1968.

Eysenck, H.J., & Eysenck, S.B.G. *Eysenck personality inventory*. San Diego, CA: Educational and Industrial Testing Service, 1964.

Gasser, E., Langrod, J., Valdes, K., & Lowinson, J. The Eysenck Personality Inventory with methadone maintenance patients. *British Journal of Addiction*, 1974, *69*, 85–88.

Hemminki, E., Rissman, A., & Mattila, A. Drug use among school children in Helsinki. *British Journal of Addiction*, 1973, *68*, 159–165.

Khavari, K., Mabry, E., & Humes, M. Personality correlates of hallucinogen use. *Journal of Abnormal Psychology*, 1977, *86*, 172–178.

Kilpatrick, D.G., Sutker, P.B., & Smith, A.D. Deviant behavior and alcohol use: The role of anxiety, sensation seeking, and other personality variables. In M. Zuckerman & C.D. Spielberger (Eds.), *Emotions and anxiety: New concepts, methods, and applications*. Hillsdale, NJ: Lawrence Erlbaum, 1976.

McLellan, A.T., Woody, G.E., & O'Brien, C.P. Development of psychiatric disorders in drug abusers: Relation between primary drug and type of disorder. In L.S. Harris (Ed.), *Problems of drug dependence, 1979. Proceedings of the 41st Annual Scientific Meeting, the Committee on Problems of Drug Dependence, Inc.* (NIDA Research Monograph 27, DHEW Publication No. (ADM) 80-901). Washington, DC: U.S. Government Printing Office, 1980, pp. 149–155.

Robinson, L. Marihuana use in high school girls: A psychosocial study [University of Maryland dissertation]. Ann Arbor, MI: University Microfilms No. 70-12, 1970.

Rosenberg, C. Young drug addicts: Background and personality. *Journal of Nervous and Mental Disease*, 1969, *148*, 65–73.

Shontz, F.C. *Research methods in personality*. New York: Appelton-Century-Crofts, 1965.

Shontz, F.C. Single-organism designs. In P.M. Bentler, D.J. Lettieri & G.A. Austin (Eds.), *Data analysis strategies and designs for substance abuse research*. (NIDA Research Issues No. 113, DHEW Publication No. (ADM) 77-389). Washington, DC: U.S. Government Printing Office, 1977.

Spotts, J.V., & Shontz, F.C. *Cocaine users: A representative case approach.* New York: Free Press, 1980a.

Spotts, J.V., & Shontz, F.C. A life theme theory of chronic drug abuse. In D.J. Lettieri, M. Sayers & H.W. Pearson (Eds.), *Theories of drug abuse: Selected contemporary perspectives*. (NIDA Research Monograph No.

30, DHEW Publication No. (ADM) 80-976). Washington, DC: U.S. Government Printing Office, 1980b, pp. 59–70.

Spotts, J.V., & Shontz, F.C. Ego development, dragon fights, and chronic drug abusers. *International Journal of the Addictions*, 1982, *17*, 945–976.

Spotts, J.V., & Shontz, F.C. Psychopathology and chronic drug use: A methodological paradigm. *International Journal of the Addictions*, 1983, *18*, 633–680.

Stewart, G., & Waddell, K., Attitudes and behavior of heroin addicts and patients on methadone. In National Institute for Prevention of Addiction to Narcotics, *Proceedings of the Fourth National Conference on Methadone Treatment*, San Francisco, January 8–10. New York: The Association, 141–144, 1972.

CORRELATES OF SENSATION SEEKING BY HEAVY, CHRONIC DRUG USERS

James V. Spotts
Greater Kansas City
Mental Health Foundation

Franklin C. Shontz
University of Kansas

Abstract

Product-moment correlations among number of drugs used and several measures of constructs related to sensation seeking were examined for four matched groups of chronic drug users and two supplementary groups of nine persons each. Number of drugs used correlated positively with all scores on the Sensation Seeking Scales, the Extraversion and Neuroticism Scales of Eysenck's Personality Inventory, and the Change Seeker Index. The pattern is consistent with the proposition that a need for stimulation or change underlies experimentation with a large number of chemical substances. The general pattern of correlations among tests resembled that reported by other investigators. The construct validity of the General Score from the Sensation Seeking Scales is enhanced by these findings. The data suggest that this score measures much the same construct as the Change Seeker Index.

INTRODUCTION

In recent years a number of scales designed to measure specific personality traits have appeared in the research literature. Three such scales, the Zuckerman Sensation Seeking Scales (Zuckerman, 1972, 1979), the Pearson Novelty Experiencing Scales (Pearson, 1970), and the Garlington and Shimota Change Seeker Index (Garlington & Shimota, 1964) apparently measure similar constructs and processes, and investigators have reported the scores on at least two of these scales to be associated with drug use/abuse (Brown,

Reprinted with permission from *Perceptual and Motor Skills* 58:427–435, 1984.
Editor's Note: This sample article has been reproduced exactly as provided by the author; no attempt has been made to edit it for content or style.

Ruder, Ruder, & Young, 1974; Carrol & Zuckerman, 1977; Hobfoll & Segal, 1983; Sutker, Archer, & Allain, 1978). For example, correlations of .34 to .47 have been reported between number of drugs used by male subjects and four of the five scores yielded by the Sensation Seeking Scales (Zuckerman, 1979, pp. 278–294). Significant correlations between scores on these measures and other tests that measure constructs similar to sensation seeking have been reported for American and British college students, Navy men, felons, preflight trainees, British apprentices, and psychiatric patients (Acker & McReynolds, 1967; Bone & Montgomery, 1970; Daitzman & Tumilty, 1974; Farley & Farley, 1970; Kilpatrick, Sutker, & Smith, 1976; Meyers, 1972; Thorne, 1971; Waters, 1974; Waters, Ambler, & Waters, 1976). To our knowledge, however, no one has tested the relationships among these variables with heavy, chronic drug users/abusers.

The analysis described in this report posed three questions. First, can the correlation reported between number of drugs used and scores on the Sensation Seeking Scales be replicated for groups of heavy, chronic drug users? Second, does the number of drugs used correlate significantly with tests measuring constructs that are similar to sensation seeking, as well as with the Sensation Seeking Scales? Third, is the pattern of correlations among such tests for heavy, chronic drug users similar to that found among other groups of non-users?

METHOD

Subjects

Although 54 adult males were tested, basic data for these analyses came from four matched cohorts of nine heavy, chronic drug users each. One cohort's drug of choice was cocaine; another's was amphetamine and its congeners; the third's was opiates; the fourth's was barbiturates or sedative-hypnotics. All were adult males, and all cohorts were matched with regard to age, IQ, level of educational achievement, lifestyle, and socio-economic background or status (Table 1 [deleted]). More detailed descriptions of the personal and drug use characteristics of these persons are presented in Spotts and Shontz (1983). For analytical purposes, the cohorts were combined into a single group of 36 heavy, chronic drug users.

A fifth matched cohort of nine non-drug users was also available, but their data were not of primary concern. A sixth cohort of nine heavy, chronic users of phencyclidine (PCP) had also been tested, but it was not possible to match these persons with others on important demographic and life style characteristics. Data from these two cohorts were examined separately and used in supplementary fashion.

Measures

The tests to which all other measures were related in this study are the five subscales of Zuckerman's *Sensation Seeking Scale* (Zuckerman, 1979). The instrument produces a General score in addition to scores on subscales called Thrill and Adventure, Experience Seeking, Disinhibition, and Boredom Susceptibility. The other measures were scores on the four subscales (External Sensation, Internal Sensation, External Cognition, and Internal Cognition) of the *Novelty Experiencing Scales* (Pearson, 1970), the three scales (Extraversion, Neuroticism, and Lie) on the *Eysenck Personality Inventory* (Eysenck & Eyskenck, 1964), the *Change Seeker Index* (Garlington & Shimota, 1964), and Scales 9(Ma) and 4(Pd) of the *Minnesota Multiphasic Personality Inventory*. Most of these tests measure constructs that are conceptually similar and that have been reported to be correlated with each other by previous investigators. The two exceptions are the Neuroticism and Lie scales of the Eysenck Personality Inventory. The Lie scale was designed to be a measure of dissimulation.

In addition, each person's drug-use history produced a count of the number of different drugs he had tried during the course of his life. This index was not confounded with age, since all subjects were adults (Table 1 [omitted here]) and had done the majority of their drug experimentation during adolescence.

This study concerned only relations among measures, not mean differences among cohorts. The latter might be attributed to drug effects rather than underlying personality differences. Therefore, scores were adjusted to eliminate cohort differences before product-moment correlation values were calculated. Each person's score on each instrument was adjusted by adding to it an amount equal to the difference between the grand mean for that instrument and the mean of his cohort. This adjustment made all group means equal on each test. Consequently, all resulting correlation coefficients are due to covariance among persons *within* groups and are not confounded by *between*-group (and therefore possibly drug-related) differences. An idea of how extensive the adjustments were may be obtained by examining the means and standard deviations of the groups in Tables 2 and 3.

In all instances where published findings permitted anticipation of directional outcomes, one-tailed probability tests were used. The only scores for which we felt positive correlations could not be expected, on this basis, were

Table 2. Raw Score Means and Standard Deviations of All Groups on the Sensation Seeking Scales

		Cocaine Users	Amphetamine Users	Opiates Users	Barbiturates Users	Non Users	PCP Users
General	Mean	10.2	14.1	11.9	13.1	12.8	10.4
	SD	4.47	2.98	4.91	3.02	2.49	3.43
Thrill and Adventure	Mean	7.7	11.7	9.7	10.0	9.7	8.0
	SD	3.50	1.66	3.28	1.32	3.46	3.39
Experience Seeking	Mean	9.8	13.1	9.8	11.0	11.4	9.0
	SD	2.95	2.89	3.73	2.40	3.00	2.40
Disinhibition	Mean	6.8	9.4	7.2	7.3	7.8	9.0
	SD	3.07	2.30	3.63	3.16	2.73	3.04
Boredom Susceptibility	Mean	4.9	8.0	7.6	7.2	7.0	5.9
	SD	2.09	2.87	3.91	4.32	2.29	2.85

Table 3. Raw Score Means and Standard Deviations of All Groups on Tests Correlated with the Sensation Seeking Scales

	Cocaine Users		Amphetamine Users		Opiates Users		Barbiturates Users		Nonusers		PCP Users	
	MN	SD	MN	SD	MN	SD	MN	SD	MN	SD	MN	SD
Novelty Experiencing Scale												
External Sensation	10.0	4.58	13.2	3.83	12.0	4.39	11.3	1.87	11.9	5.25	10.1	3.30
Internal Sensation	9.3	4.03	12.8	4.24	12.1	4.26	10.1	3.26	12.3	4.66	11.7	3.24
External Cognition	11.9	4.76	11.2	5.07	14.0	5.17	11.4	4.69	13.6	5.62	14.0	3.75
Internal Cognition	16.0	2.55	14.8	3.93	17.2	2.54	15.3	3.46	17.1	3.86	14.0	5.85
Eysenck Personality Inventory												
Extra- version	8.0	3.59	14.0	3.46	9.3	4.27	13.3	2.96	14.8	3.42	12.2	4.09

Table 3. *Continued*

	Cocaine Users		Amphetamine Users		Opiates Users		Barbiturates Users		Nonusers		PCP Users	
	MN	SD	MN	SD	MN	SD	MN	SD	MN	SD	MN	SD
Neuroticism	11.6	2.92	13.2	4.44	9.3	5.23	12.1	6.21	8.2	5.34	13.9	5.23
Lie	2.0	1.85	1.9	1.54	1.4	1.41	1.7	1.58	1.9	1.36	1.7	1.22
Change Seeker Index	54.7	13.56	60.7	8.68	54.0	11.98	60.4	9.04	59.7	10.99	54.2	10.63
Minnesota Multiphasic Personality Inventory												
Scale 4	72.7	11.25	71.2	9.95	75.3	13.48	79.1	12.55	63.8	10.75	73.3	7.19
Scale 9	70.8	8.38	70.6	11.89	76.2	12.36	77.6	12.07	73.8	11.98	75.9	10.03
No. of Drugs Used	13.7	4.53	33.3	4.77	29.9	17.5	37.9	12.84				

the Neuroticism and Lie Scale scores of the Eysenck Personality Inventory. (As it happened, these did not correlate significantly with any other scores.)

RESULTS

Number of drugs ever used correlated positively, and in three cases significantly, with scores on the Sensation Seeking Scales (see bottom row of Table 4). Unlike previous research, these data showed a significant positive correlation between number of drugs used and scores on the Disinhibition Scale. Number of drugs used also correlated significantly with the Extraversion Scale of the Eysenck Personality Inventory, and with the Change Seeker Index (see rightmost column of Table 4). Positive but not significant correlations were noted with the *Ma* and *Pd* scales of the MMPI, but not with scores on the Novelty Experiencing Scales, although the correlation with the scores on Internal Cognition tended to be negative.

The nearest thing to an over-all index offered by the Sensation Seeking Scales (Form IV) is the score on the General scale, which shares items with three of the other four scales. The pattern of correlations of the General score with scores on other tests was examined first. Consistent with previous findings (Zuckerman, 1979, p. 141), general scores of heavy, chronic drug users correlated significantly with External and Internal Sensation scores, but not with the External and Internal Cognition scores of the Novelty Experiencing Scales. On the Eysenck Personality Inventory, the significant correlation of the General score with Extraversion scores and the nonsignificant correlation with Neuroticism scores are also consistent with previous findings (Zuckerman, pp. 143–146). Our data showed a slightly negative correlation between the General Score on the Sensation Seeking Scales and the Lie Scale score on the Eyesenck inventory. The significant correlations between the General Score and scores on the Change Seeker Index and on the *Ma* Scale of the MMPI, and the non-significant correlation of the General Score with the *Pd* scale of the MMPI also agree with previous reports (Zuckerman, pp. 139 and 158).

Data from the cohort of nonusers of drugs and the cohort of PCP users were consistent with this over-all pattern, except that for these groups the correlation of the General score with the *Ma* Scale of the MMPI was slightly negative (r = −.24, for nonusers, −.24 for PCP users). Neither value was statistically significant.

None of the subscales of the Sensation Seeking Scale yielded the complete pattern of correlations shown by the General score, although each produced some of its features. The Disinhibition scale was least successful, perhaps because it is the only subscale that shares no items with the General Scale.

The Change Seeker Index correlated significantly with all scores derived

Table 4. Product-moment Correlations of Sensation Seeking Scale (IV) Scores with Other Measures Among Heavy, Chronic Drug Users

	General	Thrill and Adventure	Experience Seeking	Disinhibition	Boredom Susceptibility	No. of Drugs
Novelty Experiencing Scale						
External Sensation	31*	06	30*	14	12	02
Internal Sensation	31*	21	36*	10	46*	12
External Cognition	15	−06	−18	05	−07	−07
Internal Cognition	16	10	−02	−26	13	−29
Eysenck Personality Inventory						
Extraversion	50*	30*	23	26	36*	35*
Neuroticism	−25	−01	12	13	10	30
Lie	−31	−25	−22	−22	−15	−25
Change Seeker Index	70*	32*	50*	38*	68*	56*
Minnesota Multiphasic Personality Inventory						
Scale 9 (Ma)	37*	42*	22	11	15	27
Scale 4 (Pd)	01	07	19	−06	10	22
No. of Drugs	30*	22	36*	41*	25	

Note. $N = 36$ except for the *Eysenck Personality Inventory* where $N = 34$. Decimals omitted.
*$p < .05$ (one-tailed).

from the Sensation Seeking Scale and with number of drugs used. Its correlation with the Extraversion Score of the Eysenck Personality Inventory was .43 ($p<.01$) and with the *Ma* scale of the MMPI .29 ($p<.05$, one-tailed test). It appears that this index and the General Score of the Sensation Seeking Scale assess essentially the same underlying variable.

Conclusions

Number of drugs used correlated positively with all scores on the Sensation Seeking Scale and also positively and significantly with the Extraversion and Neuroticism scores of the Eysenck Personality Inventory and the Change Seeker Index. These findings are consistent with the proposition that a need for stimulation or change underlies the tendency to experiment with a variety of chemical substances.

The basic pattern of correlations among scores on the rest of the tests was much the same as that reported in other studies. Need for stimulation or change therefore seems to be a unitary trait, for it has now been shown in data from a variety of types of persons. However, the relationship between need for stimulation or change and number of drugs used is not a simple causal one. It probably affects number of drugs used only in persons who have the opportunity and desire to try a variety of substances. The need to satisfy a high need for stimulation or change specifically by trying drugs, rather than by engaging in other forms of activity, may stem from sources that were not measured in this study. For example, in adolescents, it might stem from needs for status in the sight of peers or the desire to feel like an adult or to rebel against authority. Nevertheless, the data are consistent with the theory that, once conditions are set for engaging in experimentation with drugs, the need for stimulation or change affects how many are tried.

Perhaps need for stimulation or change will be found in future studies to be a useful predictor of drug involvement, if it is considered along with other factors related to personal vulnerability to and environmental accessibility of dangerous substances. In this context, the General Score from the Sensation Seeking Scale appears to be the most useful of the several indexes this test produces. This score apparently has considerable construct validity and measures much the same trait as does the Change-Seeker Index.

REFERENCES

Acker, M., & McReynolds, P. M. The need for novelty: A comparison of six instruments. *Psychological Record*, 1967, 17, 177–182.

Bone, R. N., & Montgomery, D. D. Extroversion, neuroticism, and sensation seeking. *Psychological Reports*, 1970, 26, 974.

Brown, L. T., Ruder, V. G., Ruder, J. H., & Young, S.D. Stimulation seeking and the change seeker index. *Journal of Consulting and Clinical Psychology*, 1974, 42, 311.

Carrol, E. N., & Zuckerman, M. Psychopathology and sensation seeking in "downers," "speeders," and "trippers": a study of the relationships between personality and drug choice. *International Journal of the Addictions*, 1977, 12, 591–601.

Daitzman, R. J., & Tumilty, T. N. Support for an activation-regulation deficit in schizophrenia: Implications for treatment. *Newsletter for Research in Mental Health and Behavioral Science*, 1974, 16, 31–35.

Eysenck, H. J., & Eysenck, S. B. G. *Eysenck personality inventory*. San Diego, CA: Educational and Industrial Testing Service, 1964.

Farley, F. H., & Farley, S. V. Impulsiveness, sociability, and the preference for varied experience. *Perceptual and Motor Skills*, 1970, 31, 47–50.

Garlington, W., & Shimota, H. The change-seeker index: A measure of the need for variable stimulus input. *Psychological Reports*, 1964, 14, 919–924.

Hobfoll, S. E., & Segal, B. A. A factor analytic study of the relationship of experience seeking and trait anxiety to drug use and reason for drug use. *International Journal of the Addictions*, 1983, 18, 539–549.

Kilpatrick, D. G., Sutker, P. B., & Smith, A. D. Deviant drug and alcohol use: The role of anxiety, sensation seeking and other personality variables. In M. Zuckerman & C.D. Spielberger (Eds.), *Emotions and anxiety: New concepts, methods, and applications*. Hillsdale, NJ: Erlbaum, 1976, pp. 247–278.

Myers, T. I. *Psychobiological factors associated with monotony tolerance*. (Report No. 197-015) Washington, DC: American Institutes for Research, Institute for Research in Psychobiology, 1972.

Pearson, P. Relationships between global and specific measures of novelty seeking. *Journal of Consulting and Clinical Psychology*, 1970, 34, 199–204.

Spotts, J. V., & Shontz, F. C. Psychopathology and chronic drug use: A methodological paradigm. *International Journal of the Addictions*, 1983, 18, 633–680.

Sutker, P. B., Archer, R. P., & Allain, A. N. Drug abuse patterns, personality characteristics, and relationship with sex, race, and sensation seeking. *Journal of Consulting and Clinical Psychology*, 1978, 46, 1374–1378.

Thorne, G. L. The sensation seeking scale with deviant populations. *Journal of Consulting and Clinical Psychology*, 1971, 37, 106–110.

Waters, C. W. Multi-dimensional measures of novelty experience, sensation seeking, and ability: correlational analysis for male and female college samples. *Psychological Reports*, 1974, 34, 43–46.

Waters, C. W., Ambler, R., & Waters, L. K. Novelty and sensation seeking in two academic training settings. *Education and Psychological Measurement*, 1976, 36, 453–457.

Zuckerman, M. Drug abuse as a manifestation of a "sensation-seeking" trait. In W. Krup (Ed.), *Drug abuse: current concepts and research*. Springfield, IL: Thomas, 1972, pp. 154–163.

Zuckerman, M. *Sensation seeking: Beyond the optimal level of arousal*. Hillsdale, NJ: Erlbaum, 1979.

References

American Psychiatric Association: Diagnostic and Statistical Manual of Mental Disorders, 3rd ed. Washington, DC, American Psychiatric Association, 1980

American Psychological Association: Standards for Educational and Psychological Tests. Washington, DC, American Psychological Association, 1974

Campbell DT, Stanley JC: Experimental and quasi-experimental designs for research and teaching, in Handbook of Research on Teaching. Edited by Gage NL. Chicago, Rand McNally, 1963

Cattell RB, Eber HW, Tatsuoka MM: Handbook for the Sixteen Personality Questionnaire (16PF). Champaign, Ill, Institute for Personality and Ability Testing, 1970

Chassan JB: Research Design in Clinical Psychology, 2nd ed. New York, Halsted Press, 1979

Cohen J: A coefficient of agreement for nominal scales. Educational and Psychological Measurement 20:37–46, 1960

Colton T: Statistics in Medicine. Boston, Little, Brown, 1974

307

Cronbach LJ: Essentials of Psychological Testing, 3rd ed. New York, Harper Row, 1970

Greene RL: The MMPI: An Interpretive Manual. New York, Grune & Stratton, 1980

Grove WM, Andreason NC: Simultaneous tests of many hypotheses in exploratory research. Journal of Nervous and Mental Disease 170:3–8, 1982

Harris DB: Children's Drawings as Measures of Intellectual Maturity. New York, Harcourt, Brace World, 1963

Hays WL: Statistics for the Social Sciences. New York, Holt, Rinehart and Winston, 1973

Hendin H, Pollinger A, Ulman R, Carr AC: Adolescent marijuana users and their families [NIDA Research Monograph 40]. DHHS Publication no. (ADM) 81–1168. Washington, DC, US Government Printing Office, 1981

Kazdin AE: Research Design in Clinical Psychology. New York, Harper Row, 1980

Kneller GF: Science as a Human Endeavor. New York, Columbia University Press, 1978

Kuhn TS: The Structure of Scientific Revolutions, 2nd ed. Chicago, University of Chicago Press, 1970

Kuhn TS: The Essential Tension. Chicago, University of Chicago Press, 1977

Polanyi MP: Personal Knowledge: Toward a Post Critical Philosophy. Chicago, University of Chicago Press, 1962

Rhine JB: A new case of experimenter unreliability. Journal of Parapsychology 38:215–225, 1974

Rhine JB: Comments: second report on a case of experimenter fraud. Journal of Parapsychology 39:306–325, 1975

Rychlak JF: A Philosophy of Science for Personality Theory. Malabar, Fla, Robert E. Krieger, 1981

Scarr S: Constructing psychology: making facts and fables for our times. American Psychologist 40:499–512, 1985

Shontz FC: The problems and promises of psychological research in rehabilitation, in Readings on the Exceptional Child: Research and Theory, 2nd ed. Edited by Trapp EP, Himmelstein P. New York, Appleton-Century-Crofts, 1972

Shontz FC: A personologic approach for health psychology research. American Behavioral Scientist 28:510–524, 1985

Siegel S: Nonparametric Statistics for the Behavioral Sciences. New York, McGraw-Hill, 1956

Spotts JV, Shontz FC: Psychopathology and chronic drug use: a methodological paradigm. International Journal of the Addictions 18:633–680, 1983

Spotts JV, Shontz FC: Correlates of sensation seeking by heavy, chronic drug users. Perceptual and Motor Skills 58:427–435, 1984a

Spotts JV, Shontz FC: Drugs and personality: extraversion-introversion. Journal of Clinical Psychology 40:624–628, 1984b

Spotts JV, Shontz FC: The phenomenological structure of drug-induced ego states, I: cocaine. International Journal of the Addictions 19:119–151, 1984c

Spotts JV, Shontz FC: The phenomenological structure of drug-induced ego states, II: barbiturates and sedative-hypnotics: phenomenology and implications. International Journal of the Addictions 19:295–326, 1984d

Wainer H, Thissen D: Graphical data analysis. Annual Review of Psychology 32:191–241, 1981

Weimer WB: Notes on the Methodology of Scientific Research. Hillsdale, NJ, Lawrence Erlbaum, 1979

Wike E: Data Analysis: A Statistical Primer for Psychology Students. Chicago, Aldine-Atherton, 1971

Winer BJ: Statistical Principles in Experimental Design, 2nd ed. New York, McGraw-Hill, 1971

Zuckerman M: Sensation Seeking: Beyond the Optimal Level of Arousal. Hillsdale, NJ, Lawrence Erlbaum, 1979

INDEX

Abscissa, 62–65, 68, 97, 99, 107–
    109, 111, 232, 242
Acker, M, 296, 303
Adjustment term, 178, 186, 191,
    236, 239, 264
    see also Mean, adjustment for
        alpha
    coefficient, 9
    error, 33
    level, 33–34, 61, 183
Allain, AN, 296
Ambler, R, 296, 305
American Psychiatric
    Association, 20, 307
American Psychological
    Association, 10, 307
Analysis of covariance
    (ANCOVA), 228, 284
Analysis of variance (ANOVA),
    73, 179, 184–189, 195, 200,
    237, 245, 251, 264, 283
    complex designs, 203–221, 268
    factorial design, 203–221
    as information processing, 220–
        221
    mixed model designs, 215–221
    multivariate, 2
    one-way, 201–220, 268, 290
    one-way for more than two
        independent groups, 190–
        193, 194–195, 275
    purpose, 201–203
    for ranks, 156–157
    repeated measures, 193–194
    and t-test, 182
    2 by 2 factorial design, 204–210
    unbalanced designs, 210, 211
Anonymity, 45–46
Archer, RP, 296, 305
Association, concept of, 42, 151,
    251–253

strength of, 252–253, 265, 268
Austin, GW, 293
Average, 12, 20–22, 81, 101–104,
    173
    arithmetic, 101–102, 104, 111,
        114
    of ranks, 150, 161
    x-bar, 101
    see also Central tendency;
        Mean; Median; Mode
Average deviation, 112

Base rate, 129
Base line, 184
Beaubrum, M, 287, 291, 292
Behavior therapist, 3
Bentler, PM, 293
Best-fit line, 244
beta error, 33
Bias, 16, 92–93, 123, 125, 127,
    129, 132, 142, 194, 282–283
    in a comparison, 211
    in estimate of sd, 113
Binomial expansion, 97–99
    coefficients, 98
    binary situation, 97
Bone, RN, 296, 304
Bonferroni inequality, 183–184
Box-Jenkins analysis, 194
Brown, LT, 295, 304
Buikhuisen, W, 287, 291, 292

C, see contingency coefficient
Campbell, DT, 5, 307
Capitalizing on chance, 13, 33,
    123, 193, 221, 276
Carr, AC, 30, 308
Carrol, EN, 296, 304
Categorization, 148
Cattell, RB, 307
Causal model, 88–89

Causal modeling, 6, 228,
    analysis, 200
Cause, 5, 6, 16–17, 37, 41, 87–88,
    265, 272, 303
    and correlation, 38–42
Celsius, A, 172
Central limit theorem, 110,
    118, 156, 259–260
Central tendency, 102–104,
    111, 118
    see also Mean; Median; and
    Mode
Chance, 13, 21, 30, 31, 32, 33, 35,
    123, 153, 183
    see also Random
Change-seeker Index, 284–305
Chasson, JB, 16, 307
Chi-square, 2, 121–144, 156, 157,
    161, 253–256, 257, 259, 260
    calculations, 126–127
    correction for discontinuity,
        132, 134, 137, 139. 254
    degrees of freedom, 127, 131,
        139, 140
    discrete multivariate analysis,
        141
    marginal totals, 130–131, 139,
        254
    statistical significance, 126–
        127, 143
Class interval, 100, 103–104
Classification, 9, 72–73, 76, 77,
    79, 82, 83, 84–86, 121, 122
Clinical trials, 5
Cluster analysis, 82, 83
Coding, 19–20, 61, 75–76
    of subjects, 45–46
Coefficient of concordance, 161,
    162
Cohen, J, 10, 307
Colton, T, 16, 307
Combinations, 99–101
Communality, 225
Computers, 2–3, 21, 23, 56, 57,
    59, 61, 72, 80, 82, 84, 86, 87,
    148, 203, 209, 210

Concordance, coefficient of, 161,
    162
Confidence
    level, 35, 61, 132, 181
    interval, 119
    limits, 119
Confidentiality, 45–46
Contingency coefficient, 135, 223,
    257–258, 267
    formula, 257
Controls, 1, 4, 6–7, 31, 47, 51, 201
    waiting list, 44–45
    see also Groups, control
Correlation, 8–13, 14, 48–49, 59,
    62–65, 78–83, 132–135, 151,
    223–270, 282–284
    bivariate, 228, 230, 247, 268
    canonical, 228
    and causation, 38–42
    coefficient, 2, 8, 49, 82, 88–89,
        132–135, 223–230, 252–
        258, 262–263, 269, 302
    curvilinear, 229
    intraclass, 10, 269
    matrices, 62, 164–165, 224–226,
        247, 284
    multiple, 247–248
    multivariate, 228
    negative, 64
    positive, 64
    ranks, 161–167
    see also Coefficient of
        concordance; Contingency
        coefficient; kappa;
        Kendall's tau; Pearson
        product moment correlation
        coefficient; Phi coefficient;
        Product moment
        correlation coefficient; r;
        Spearman's rho
Counting, 2, 20, 76–79, 87, 109,
    121, 158, 162, 232, 257, 260
Covariation, 223, 224
Covariance, 297
    see also Analysis of covariance
Criterion, 11, 13–14, 61, 79, 226,

247
concurrent, 11, 128
predictive, 11
Cronbach, LJ, 9, 281, 308
Cross-classification, 78–79, 210–211
Crossover procedure, 28, 29, 136
Cross products, 234–237, 239, 240, 256, 260–262
formula for, 236
Cross validation, 14, 81
Curvilinear relationships, 229
Correlates of drug use, 295–305

Daitzman, RJ, 296, 304
Data, 2–4, 8–14, 18, 21, 30, 40, 48–49, 55, 61–70, 88–90, 274–275, 277, 278, 279, 285, 295, 310
anonymity, 45–46
bases, 56, 57
categorical, 62, 65
coding, 19–20
confidentiality, 45–46
continuous, 174
dependencies, 157, 193–195
describing, 104–108, 114–119
discontinuous, 62, 64–67, 95–96, 150
discrete, 64
frequency, 95–97, 121–122, 253–259
independence, 194
inspection, 77–79
loss, 46
non-independent, 157
objectivity, 75
qualitative, 65–66, 71
quality, 47, 93
quantitative, 71, 73
ranked, 122
raw, 154, 188, 260
redundancies in, 83–84
reliability, 93
similarities, 83–84

tables of, 78, 126, 128, 133, 136, 137, 139, 140, 147, 152, 175, 184, 206, 217, 235, 254, 266
transformation, 202
validity, 93
see also Scores
Deciles, 105
Definitions 36–38, 76, 84–87, 123, 273
operational, 37
class interval, 100
Degrees of freedom (df), 113–114, 127, 131–132, 135, 139–140, 178, 179–183, 192–194, 201, 206–210, 213–219, 241, 249, 252–253, 255, 258, 264, 275
between groups, 192
unequal ns, 209–210
within groups, 192
Depression, 11, 18
Description, 71–72, 83–86, 90, 105
formal, 72
Deviation, 93, 101–103, 111, 234
scores, 111–113
see also Variation
Diagnosis, 14, 19, 20, 23–24, 72, 80, 85, 109, 125–141
Diagnostic and Statistical Manual of Mental Disorders, Third Edition (DSM-III), 20, 23, 307
Difference
absolute, 158–159
among classes or types, 84–86
between groups, 68, 77–79, 123, 179–184, 190–195, 202, 203–221, 226–227, 253, 263–270, 275, 276, 282–285, 297
see also Differences, between means (or averages)
between individuals, 7, 15
between means (or averages), 20–22, 103, 179–184, 202,

203–221, 226–227, 253,
263–270, 275–276, 282–285
between scores, 7, 109
in chi square, 124–126, 132–
138, 146–161
rank, 260–262
scores, 189
second order, 206–208
standard deviation of, 156
standard error of, between
means, 119, 189
true, 32–35, 188, 283
unit of, 172, 173
and variation, 101
and z scores, 117
see also Variation
Dimensions, 74, 82, 100, 104, 106,
109, 121, 145, 205, 229, 233
see also Scale, Score, Variable
Discrete multivariate analysis,
141
Discriminant function analysis, 2,
80–82, 228
Discrimination, 23–24, 145–148,
150, 160, 161–162
Distribution-free statistics, see
Statistics, nonparametric
Double-blind procedure, 28
Duncan's Multiple Range Test,
193, 275–276, 290
Dunnett's test, 193

Eber, HW, 307
Empirical, 4, 7
Error, 31, 102, 161, 180, 202,
207–210, 269–270, 283
between means, 119
experimental, 105, 137, 176,
185, 217
see also Error, term
of the first kind, 33
human, 37–38
of means, 103
of measurment, 10, 100–101,
111, 229, 246–247
of the second kind, 33–34, 184
standard, 118

standard, of difference between
means, 119
standard, of mean, 118, 119;
formula, 189
standard, of mean of
differences, 189
term, 202, 207–210, 217–221
Type I, 33–35, 183
Type II, 33–35, 159, 214, 219
variance, 31, 195, 203
Ethics, 24, 45, 254
eta^2, 246, 269
Expected (expectancy;
expectation), 93, 114, 118,
124, 189
frequencies, 65–66, 109, 114–
115, 124, 129–133, 139–
140, 254
rational, in chi square, 124–127
Experiments and
experimentation, xvii, 14–17,
30–32, 36, 45, 55, 60, 61, 137,
201–203, 216, 285
control groups in, 17, 18, 44–45
critical, 277–279
crucial, 277–279
error in, 1, 6, 105, 137
experimental group, 17
as ideals, 17
laboratory, 1, 5, 6–7, 11, 15, 17,
29, 39, 47, 125
Michelson-Morley, 278–279
power, 15, 34, 35
treatment groups in, 17
Eyeball test, 79, 152, 161, 174,
186, 219, 254
Eysenck, HJ, 273, 279, 280, 287,
288, 290, 291, 292, 297, 304
Eysenck Personality Inventory,
275, 282, 283, 284, 287–305
Eysenck, SBG, 288, 290, 292, 297,
304

F-test, 187, 190–192, 201, 202,
208, 209, 214, 218, 221, 245–
247, 251, 258, 263–264, 275,

290
and product-moment
  correlation, 267
for repeated measures, 184–188
significance, 181–182, 196
summary table, 178–179
for two groups, 174–182, 183
formula, 181
Factor analysis, 18, 21, 50, 61,
  82–83, 225, 226, 228, 247
Factor loading, 83
False negatives, 128–129, 132
False positives, 128–129, 132
Farley, FH, 296, 304,
Farley, SV, 296, 304
Flow chart, 87, 88
Fourfold point coefficient, 253–
  258
Frequencies, 65–68, 77–79, 109,
  121–122, 150, 171–172
expected in chi-square, 124,
  126, 129–133, 139–140, 254
observed in chi-square, 124,
  126
Frequency distributions, 95–97,
  105, 153–154, 231, 260
goodness of fit, 123
obtained, 111
probability distribution, 96
rectangular, 259
skewed, 106
Friedman test, 161, 162
Functional relationship, 81

Gambler's fallacy, 234
Garlington, W, 295, 297, 304
Gasser, E, 287, 291, 293
Generalizability, 58–59, 219, 270,
  280
coefficient of, 9
GIGO, 3, 21
Graphs, 62–69, 73, 100, 105–106,
  309
bar graphs, 65–68, 100
histogram, 100
pie charts, 68–69
scattergram, 64–65

simple line, 62–63
Greene, RL, 14, 108, 308
Groups, 74, 140, 141–142, 151–
  161, 174–185, 190–195, 201–
  221, 226–227, 245–246, 253–
  254, 268, 269, 282–284, 298–
  301
comparison, 18, 94–95
control, 17, 18, 44–45, 46, 58,
  95
describing, 102–119
differences between, see
  Difference, between groups;
  Difference, between means
discrimination among, 80–83
equivalence, 79
matching, 58
random assignment, 141–142
treatment, 17, 46, 58, 94, 141
see also Sum of squares (betwen
  and within groups)
Grove, WM, 308

Halo effect, 166–167
Harris, DB, 75, 308
Harris, LS, 293
Hays, WL, 98, 221, 268, 308
Hemminki, E, 287, 291, 293
Hendin, H, 30, 308
Histogram, 100
Hobfoll, SE, 296, 304
Humes, M, 287, 293
Hypothesis, 201, 271, 278, 281
null, 22, 32–35, 37, 61, 77–79,
  109–110, 125, 127, 133,
  137–138, 140, 153–161,
  165–166, 174–175, 181–
  190, 195, 202, 214, 275,
  277, 287
testing, 5, 32–42, 50, 61, 69, 95,
  123, 142, 200, 202, 287–294
and theory, 11, 13, 16, 35–42

Individual,
assignment of, 253–256
in case studies, 48
classification of, 79–83

complexity of, 73–74, 86, 87
differences, 72, 283–285
and norms, 12
ranks, 157–167
score, 64–65, 105, 157–159,
180, 188–190, 231
see also Subjects
Informed consent, 45
Inspection, comparison by, 77–79,
140, 186
Intelligence quotient (IQ), 22,
100–101, 110, 118, 121–123,
172–174, 289, 296
Interaction, 185–188, 190, 194,
206–220, 268
higher order, 214, 217
Interviews, 6, 19, 30, 41–42, 72,
75–76, 282

Journal of Parapsychology, 57,
308
Judges, 8, 9, 19, 75, 77, 121, 146,
151–153, 156, 160–167
see also Ratings
Judgment, human, in research
37, 49, 89, 150, 154

kappa statistic, 9–10
Kazdin, AE, 16, 308
Kendall, MG, 161
Kendall's *tau,* 161–166, 169, 225,
260, 261
formula, 163
Kilpatrick, DG, 287, 291, 292,
293, 296, 304
Khavari, K, 287, 291, 293
Kneller, GF, 51, 278, 308
Kruskal-Wallis one-way analysis
of variance for ranks, 156–
157
Kuder-Richardson-20 formula for
reliability, 9
Kuhn, TS, 51, 308

Langrod, J, 287, 293
Laws, 36, 37

Law of averages, 234
Lettieri, DJ, 293
Likelihood ratio, 124
Lowinson, J, 287, 293

Mabry, E, 287, 293
Main effect, 185, 188, 194, 195,
205–206, 207, 208–220, 268
Mann-Whitney *U* test, 153–156,
168, 184, 259
formula, 154
Matched-pairs signed ranks test,
184, 188
Mathematics, xvii, 36, 115, 150,
174, 251
law of, 36
probability, 91–99
probability model, 95, 106, 124
treatment of data, 2, 20, 64, 88,
200, 226–228
Mattila, A, 287, 293
McLellan, AT, 291, 293
McReynolds, PM, 296, 303
Mean, 101–103, 173–179, 182–
195, 201–208, 212–213, 226–
227, 234–239, 242–245, 275–
276, 282–283, 298–300
adjustment for, 177
as central tendency, 102–103
formula, 102, 104, 105
grand, 175–176, 177, 179, 180,
205, 297
of ranks, 152–156, 160–162
regression to, 231
see also Average
Mean square (MS), 105, 113–114,
180–182, 185–188, 192, 201,
208, 213, 214
Measurement, 4, 22–24, 74, 109,
111, 171–174
appropriate, 17–22
definition, 2
repeated, 46, 157–161, 188,
190, 193–195, 207, 216–
219, 228, 231
tests as, 7–12

units of, 242
Median, 103–104, 105, 110, 118, 289
   split, 122, 204
Meyers, TI, 296, 304
Minnesota Multiphasic Personality Inventory (MMPI), 14, 108, 273, 277, 287–305, 308
Mixed-model design, 50
Mode, 103–104, 105, 110, 118
Montgomery, DD, 296, 304
Morgan, CR, xvii
mu (true mean), 102, 103
Multidimensionality, 82
Multiple regression, 2, 50, 226, 228, 231
Multivariate analysis of variance, 2, 216, 228

Neuman-Kuel's test, 193
Nonstatistical inferences, 29–30, 39
Normal curve, 95, 106–111, 114–119, 124, 146, 155–156, 173, 231, 259–260, 262
   area under, 110–111
   properties, 120
Norms, 7, 12, 108, 290
Novelty Experiencing Scales, 284–305
Null hypothesis, 22 32–35, 37, 61, 77–79, 109–110, 125, 127, 133, 137–138, 140, 153–166 174–175, 181–195,
Null standard, 31–32
Numbers, 2, 6, 67, 71–72, 74, 85–90, 102, 112, 148, 162–163
   meaning of, 20–22
   nominal, 19–20, 21
   random, 21, 141–143
Numerical data, 8, 22
   see also Data
Numerical values, 31, 95, 103, 256–257
   see also Data

O'Brien, CP, 291, 293
Observation, 2, 4–7, 35, 94–95, 100, 124, 127, 130, 253
Ohm's law, 36–37
Omega², 268, 269
Ordinate, 62–68, 108, 232
Organizational chart, 86
Orthogonal comparisons, 193
Orthogonality, 233
   definition of, 259

Parameter, 201, 202, 259
Parapsychology, 24, 57
Path analysis, 87, 228
Pearson, HW, 293
Pearson, K, 227
Pearson, P, 295, 297, 304
Pearson product-moment correlation coefficient (Pearson *r*), 64, 134–135, 161, 223, 227, 252
   see also Correlation; Product moment correlation
Percentages, 68–69, 76, 92, 129, 134, 225
Permutations, 99–101
Phi coefficient, 132–135, 223, 253–258
   formula for, 134, 255
Pie charts, 68–69
Placebo, 28, 59, 211
Planned comparisons, 193
Point-biserial correlation coefficient, 267
Polanyi, MP, 51, 308
Pollinger, A, 30, 308
Popper, Karl, 38, 278
Population,
   normative, 12, 110
   sampling from, 74, 76, 118–119, 254, 289
   see also Samples
   as statistical universe, 201
Pragmatics, 40–42
Precision, 6, 8, 10, 22, 36, 85, 89, 104, 119, 122–124, 146, 148,

171–173, 228
Prediction, 11, 13–14, 40–41, 48–
50, 61, 63, 65, 80–81, 88, 93,
226, 230–234, 243–245, 246,
279
Predictors, 36, 61, 224, 247, 303
Probability, 22, 30–35, 36, 81,
106, 113, 159, 182, 184, 202,
253
empirical, 93–94, 95
estimating, 91–120, 108–109
mathematical, 93–94
normal-curve model, 108–110,
114
one-directional (one-tailed), 96,
138, 154–155
theoretical, 93
two-directional (two-tailed), 97,
137–138, 154–155
see also Significance, statistical
(one-tailed); Significance,
statistical (two-tailed);
Values, critical
Product-moment correlation, 223–
249, 257–262, 265–268, 295,
302
coefficient, 8, 82, 227–230, 270
denominator, 237, 240, 241
deviation score formula, 238,
and F test, 267
numerator, 234–237, 239, 241
and point biserial r, 267
ratio, 238–239, 251
raw score formula, 238, 239,
241, 242, 266
significance, 246, 249
and t-test, 262–265
Proof, 29, 36, 38, 79, 93
Proportions, 68–69, 78–79, 92, 95,
109, 129, 138, 246, 252, 254,
267
see also Ratio
Psychometrics, 285

Quadrant, 62
Qualities, 22–24, 84

Quantification, 20, 23, 74–77
Quantity, 2, 65, 71
Quartile, 105
Quasi-experiment, 5, 17, 50, 271,
285, 307
Questionnaire, 6, 14, 17, 59, 60,
82–83, 99, 274, 281–282

r, 64, 134–135, 227, 228, 256–257,
258
see also Correlation; Pearson
product-moment correlation
coefficient; Product-
moment correlation
r², 246
R (multiple correlation
coefficient), 247
Random
assignment, 20–22, 28, 141–
142, 152, 155–156, 160,
166, 195, 204, 209, 220,
224, 254, 256
error term, 208
factors, 30, 103, 124, 161, 180,
269
numbers, 21, 141–143
sample, 118, 260
selection, 45, 95, 151, 156, 190
trials, 127
variations, 181, 188, 203, 205,
214, 269, 270
Randomness, 9, 234
Range, 104–105, 115, 119, 145,
155, 160, 172, 229, 289
Ranks, 122–123, 171–172, 259–
262
analyses of, 145–169, 175
composites, 148, 149
correlation of, 161–166, 223
natural order, 162, 164
ties, 146, 148–151, 154, 259
Rates, 8, 19, 75, 160, 166–167
Ratings, 24, 82, 136, 139, 263
see also Judges
Ratio, 32, 76, 92, 124, 181, 183,
202, 234, 243, 264, 269

likelihood, 124
Rectangular distribution, 259
Redundancy, 83–84, 226
Regression, 230–234, 242, 244,
    245
  analysis, 231
  equations, 231, 244–245
  formula, 243, 244
  least squares, 233
  lines, 65, 231, 232, 233, 241,
    242
  to mean, 231
  multiple, 2, 50, 226, 228, 233,
    247–248, 251
  scores, 102–103
  surface, 233
  weight, 243
  Y intercept, 244
Reinforcement, 15, 37–38
Reliability, 3, 7–10, 12, 19, 59,
    77, 160, 208
  alpha coefficient, 9
  alternate forms, 8–9
  coefficient of generalizability, 9
  of data, 93, 121
  equivalent forms 8–9
  interjudge, 9, 19, 75, 121, 166–
    167
  internal consistency, 9, 10, 12
  inter-rater, 19, 75, 166–167
  kappa coefficient, 9–10
  Kuder-Richardson-20, 9
  objectivity, 75
  split-half, 9
  test-retest, 8
Representative case method, 289,
    293
Research
  actuarial, 13–14, 224
  analytical, 5
  apparatus, 58
  applied, 1
  case studies, 48
  causal, 5
  clinical trials, 5
  conclusions, 61

control groups in 44–45
correlational, 271
decision making, 27
descriptive, 5, 6, 48, 61–62, 68,
    69, 71–72, 200
design, 3, 27, 34–35, 41, 47,
    136, 156, 174, 194–221,
    226, 307, 308, 310
empirical, 4, 7, 11
epidemiological, 6
evaluation research, 24, 73
expense, 43
experimental, 1, 5, 6–7, 11, 14–
    17, 29, 30–32, 39
  see also Experiments
exploratory, 5, 123, 183
field, 4–5, 6, 61
formal, 5, 6–7
grants, 43–44
hypothesis generating, 5
hypothesis testing, see
    Hypothesis, testing;
    Hypothesis, null
in clinical settings, 42–50, 124,
    128
informal, 5, 6
interpreting outcomes, 28–29
laboratory, 1, 6–7, 11, 15, 17,
    29, 39, 47, 60, 125
library, 4
methodology, xvii, 309
monitoring function, 49–50
multivariate, 74, 80–84, 200
naturalistic, 5, 6, 11, 30
objective component, 4
predictive, 13–14, 48–50
  see also Prediction; Predictors
preliminary, 5
prestige value, 42
procedures, 58–61, 199
qualitative, 30, 89, 90
quantitative, 21, 30, 73–74, 79,
    83, 85, 89, 90
subjective component, 4
survey, 5–6, 12, 13, 42, 48, 55,
    59, 60, 61, 68, 69, 104

tests, use of in, 7–12, 13
time series, 193, 194
see also Time series analysis
topics, 24–25, 37
Research reports, 3, 8, 12, 50–51,
    53–70, 72, 89–90, 106, 119,
    199, 271–305
  abstract, 57, 58, 70, 273, 295
  apparatus, 58, 59, 60
  author identification, 56–57
  conclusions, 61, 69–70, 277–
    280, 285, 303
  discussion, 69–70, 277–280
  introduction, 57–58, 273–274
  method, 58–61
  procedure, 58, 59
  references, 70, 272, 280–281
  results, 61–69, 275–277, 281
  review of literature, 57, 58
  statement of purpose, 58
  tables in, 61, 62, 78, 100
  title, 55–56
Researchability, 24–25, 77
Rhine, JB, 57, 308
rho, Spearman's, 161, 251, 260–
    262
  formula for, 261
  significance, 262
Rissman, A, 287, 293
Robinson, L, 291, 293
Root mean square, 113
Rorschach Inkblot Technique, 75
Rosenberg, C, 287, 291, 293
Rychlak, JF, 29, 309

s, see Standard deviation
s², see Variance
S statistic, see Kendall's tau
Samples
  number of, 259–260
  of items, 11
  of persons (or subjects) 12, 28,
    58, 74, 76, 78, 82
  random, 118, 260
  variations among, 22
  see also Groups; Subjects

Sampling, 48
  single-sample t-test, 188–190
  size, 155–156, 228
Sayers, M, 293
Scale, 24, 108, 121–124, 242–243
  continuous, 106, 171–174, 253
  equal interval, 21, 172, 173
  interval, 21, 171–174
  Kelvin, 172
  rating, 24, 263
Scarr, S, 88
Scattergram, 64–65, 231–234,
    239, 245
Scheffe's test, 193
Science, 2, 17, 24–25, 29, 35–42,
    57, 227–228, 308–309
  communication in, 53–55
  criticism in 51, 54, 55
Scores, 79–83, 99–100, 104–
    118, 173–174, 231–234,
    271–272, 281–284
  change, 135–137
  coding, 76
  consistency of, 8–9
  cut-off, 49, 132–133
  deviation, 111–113, 176–180,
    235–239, 241, 245
  difference, 157, 188–189
  dummy variable, 266
  meaning of, 134–135, 229
  and norms, 12
  raw, 108, 111–119, 176–179,
    234, 236, 238, 242–244,
    276, 298–300
  reliability of, 8–10
  standard, 107–119, 124, 155,
    156, 174, 242, 259
  calculating, 116–118
  sum of squared, 239
  T, 116–118
  transformation, 122, 243
  "true," 10, 102–103, 176
  validity of, 12
  z, 107, 110, 116–117, 155
  see also Data
sd, see Standard deviation

Segal, BA, 296, 304
Semantic differential, 24
Sensation seeking Scales (SSS),
    281, 284–285, 295–305
Service delivery, 16, 50, 73, 89,
    94, 124, 199, 253, 285–286
Shontz, FC, 48, 50, 73, 280, 287,
    289, 291, 293, 294, 285, 296,
    304, 309
Siegel, S, 151, 309
Significance, statistical, 21, 29,
    32–35, 110, 124, 125, 137–
    138, 181–182, 201, 213–214,
    219, 241, 252–255, 259
  one-tailed (directional), 96–97,
    137–138, 154–155, 158,
    159, 166, 168, 169, 174,
    181, 182, 184, 186, 189,
    193, 197, 201, 302
  two-tailed (nondirectional), 96–
    97, 137–138, 154–155, 158,
    159, 166, 168, 182, 189,
    193, 197, 201, 241, 265
sigma, 105
*Sixteen Personality Factors
    Questionnaire (Sixteen PF;
    16PF),* 9, 83, 273, 277, 288,
    289, 291, 307
Skinner box, 15, 59–60, 195
Smith, AD, 287, 293, 296, 304
Spearman's *rho,* 161, 251, 260–
    262
  formula for, 261
  significance, 262
Spielberger, CD, 293, 304
Spotts, JV, xvii, 73, 287, 289,
    293, 294, 295, 296, 304, 309
Standard deviation, 73, 104, 105–
    106, 110–114, 118, 119, 156,
    173, 177, 189, 233, 242–243,
    245, 259, 275, 289, 290, 297,
    298, 299–300
  calculation, 112–114
Standard error
  of mean, 118
  of mean difference, 119

of measurement, 101, 174
Standard scores, *see* Scores,
    standard; Scores, *z*
Stanley, JC, 5, 307
Statistics, xvii, 74–75, 102, 104,
    111, 113, 118, 124, 125, 150,
    153, 165–166, 173–174, 199–
    203, 234, 270, 307, 308, 310
  descriptive, 22, 119, 251
  family of, 258
  inferential, 22, 30–35, 97, 119
  multivariate, 74
  nonparametric, 151, 153, 258–
    262, 309
  parametric, 258–259
  supplementary, 157, 193, 209,
    275
Stewart, G, 291–294
Straight-line relationships, 63,
    64, 65, 228–230, 233, 242,
    245
Structural equations, 228
Subjects, 28, 34, 44–46, 58–60,
    77, 79, 103, 138, 140, 199,
    201, 204, 214–219, 296–297
  follow-up of 46, 60, 81
  as own controls, 136, 157
  reactivity of, 16
  see also Groups; Samples
Sum, grand, 175, 176, 190
Sum of squares (SS), 201–203,
    209, 234, 237–240, 245, 261
  between groups, 176–181, 191–
    192, 203, 264
  formula, 177
  between persons, 186, 216
  test periods, 187
  total, 178–180, 186, 190, 264
  within cells, 208
  within groups, 177–178, 180,
    181, 203, 264
Summary table, 178–179, 186,
    187, 192, 205, 208–209, 218,
    220, 264
Supernatural, 24 .
Superstition, 38–39

Symmetry, 105–110, 125

T scores, *see* Scores, T
t-test, 2, 20–21, 22, 32, 119, 182–
    184, 201–202, 246–247, 251–
    252, 258, 262
  and product-moment
      correlation, 262–265
  critical values, 197
  formulas, 182, 189, 247
  repeated measures, 188–190
Tukey's tests (A & B), 193
Tatsuoka, MM, *307*
tau, Kendall's, 161–166, 169, 225,
    260, 261
  formula, 163
Tests (psychological), 7–14, 41–
    42, 59, 62–63, 75, 80–86, 99–
    100, 105, 111–112, 128, 132,
    224, 226, 227
  alternate forms, 8
  aptitude, 8
  equivalent forms, 8
  internal consistency, 9
  item analysis, 12
  norms, 7, 12, 276
  parallel forms, 8
  reliability, 7–10, 12, 59
  standardization, 7, 12
  test-retest procedure, 8
  validity, 7–8, 10–12, 59
  see specific test names; see also
    Scores
Theory, 1, 11–12, 13, 35–42, 48,
    58, 59, 75, 83, 84–89, 224,
    278–279, 281–282, 285, 287–
    288, 303
  as analog, 86, 88
  constructs in, 11
  counter-intuitive, 273–291
  falsification, 38, 278
  as metaphor, 86–87
  as model, 86–88
  of processes, 87–89
Testing, 35–42
Thissen, D, 62, 309

Thorne, GL, 296, 305
Time series analysis, 3, 50, 193–
    194
Timmerman, H, 287, 291, 292
Tumilty, TN, 296, 304
Types, 72–73, 85–86

Ulman, R, 30, *308*
Universe, statistical, 11, 190, 192,
    201, 259, 270

Validation, cross, 14, 81
Validity, 3, 7, 10–12, 19, 59, 81,
    281–282
  of agreements, 166–167
  construct, 11–12, 281, 295, 303
  content, 10–11
  convergent, 12
  criterion-related, 11, 128
  cross-validation, 14
  of data, 93
  discriminant, 12
  divergent, 12
  of interpretation, 193
  of reports, 17
  of research, 16, 34
Values,
  absolute, 126
  critical, 127, 131, 168–169, 181,
      185, 196, 197, 202, 241,
      249, 252, 258, 262, 265
  expected, 124–127, 129–133,
      189
  as meaning or ethics, 24–25,
      53–54
  observed, 124–127, 131–133,
      138
  true (numerical), 102, 105, 113
Variable, 73–79, 104, 109, 215,
    223–229, 246–247
  continuous, 62, 100, 106
  dependent, 7, 17, 36, 61, 76–78,
      81, 195, 231, 272, 283
  dichotomous, 76, 267
  discontinuous, 62, 65
  dummy, 265–266

fixed (in analysis of variance), 270
independent, 7, 15, 31, 36, 61, 76–78, 81, 203, 210, 231, 247, 271–272
trichotomous, 77
underlying, 100, 106–107, 171, 227
unidimensional, 22–25
Variability, 100, 101, 104–106, 160–162, 205, 245
see also Variance; Variation
Variance, 61, 105, 113–114, 180–181, 201–202
accounted for, 245, 253, 267–270
analysis of, see Analysis of variance
common, 225, 245–246, 253, 265–267
error, 31, 195, 203
see also Error
homogeneity of, 202–203, 204
pooled, 220
remainder, 202
residual, 202
sources of, 179, 185, 213
see also Analysis of variance; Variables; Variation
Variation, 95–97, 223–227
among groups (means), 22, 189, 212, 220
among ranks, 161
around expected values, 133
around grand mean, 179

average, 102
controlled, 201–202
within groups, 180, 217–218
see also Variability; Variance

Waddel, K, 291, 294
Wainer, H, 62, 309
Waters, CW, 296, 305
Waters, LK, 296, 305
Wechsler Adult Intelligence Scale-Revised (WAIS-R), 7
Wechsler Intelligence Scale for Children-Revised (WISC-R), 7
Wechsler Pre-Primary Scales of Intelligence (WPPSI), 7
Weimer, WB, 29, 309
Wike, E, 203, 310
Wilcoxon matched-pairs signed-ranks test, 158–159, 168
Wilkinson, CB, xvii
Winer, BJ, 193, 216, 310
Woody, GE, 291, 293

X-axis, 62, 63, 64, 65, 108, 115, 232

Y-axis, 62, 63, 64, 67, 108, 232
Yates' correction, 132
Young, SD, 296–304

z scores, see Scores, z
Zuckerman, M, 281, 293, 295, 296, 297, 301, 305, 310